Tacfarinas:
An African Rebel Against Rome

By the same author

Publius Quinctilius Varus – The Man Who Lost Three Roman Legions in the Teutoburg Disaster (2023)

Tacfarinas: An African Rebel Against Rome

The Numidian Revolt Against the Emperor Tiberius (AD 17 to 24)

Joanne Ball

Pen & Sword
MILITARY

First published in Great Britain in 2025 by
Pen & Sword Military
An imprint of Pen & Sword Books Ltd
Yorkshire – Philadelphia

ISBN 978 1 39903 985 7

A CIP catalogue record for this book is available from the British Library.

Typeset by Simon and Sons ITES Services Private Limited
Printed and bound in the UK by CPI Group (UK) Ltd, Croydon, CR0 4YY.

The Publisher's authorised representative in the EU for product safety is Authorised Rep Compliance Ltd., Ground Floor, 71 Lower Baggot Street, Dublin D02 P593, Ireland.
www.arccompliance.com

For a complete list of Pen & Sword titles please contact

PEN & SWORD BOOKS LIMITED
47 Church Street, Barnsley, South Yorkshire, S70 2AS, England
E-mail: enquiries@pen-and-sword.co.uk
Website: www.pen-and-sword.co.uk
or
PEN AND SWORD BOOKS
1950 Lawrence Road, Havertown, PA 19083, USA
E-mail: uspen-and-sword@casematepublishers.com
Website: www.penandswordbooks.com

Contents

Illustrations

1a. A Numidian coin depicting either Masinissa or Micipsa, issued in the second century BC (© cngcoins.com)

1b. A Roman denarius minted *c.*56 BC depicting the Mauretanian king Bocchus I kneeling before Lucius Cornelius Sulla and offering an olive branch, with the Numidian king Jugurtha kneeling with his hands tied behind his back (© cngcoins.com)

2. The ruins of Roman Ammaedara, the base of the 3rd Legion Augusta during the war against Tacfarinas (© Astiosaurus via Wikimedia Commons, CC BY-SA 3.0)

3. Statue of Juba II in the guise of a Greek hero, found in the West Baths of Caesarea Mauretania (© Carole Raddato, CC BY-SA 2.0)

4a. A Roman sestertius issued during the reign of Augustus, found in Africa and countermarked APRON for Lucius Apronius during his proconsulship and his part in the war against Tacfarinas (© cngcoins.com)

4b. A denarius minted in Caesarea, featuring portraits of Juba II and his son Ptolemy of Mauretania (© cngcoins.com)

5. The Royal Mausoleum of Mauretania in Algeria, alleged burial site of Juba II and Cleopatra Selene (© Carole Raddato, CC BY-SA 2.0)

6. A fragment of an inscription from Leptis Magna, referencing a 'Scipio' – likely Lentulus Scipio, who commanded the 9th Legion Hispana in the region during the proconsulship of Junius Blaesus (© Marco Prins/ Livius, CC0 1.0 Universal)

7. A monument erected to Gaius Gavius Macer in Leptis Magna, probably for his role in the Roman victory against Tacfarinas (© Marco Prins/ Livius, CC0 1.0 Universal)

8. The so-called 'Mausoleum of Tacfarinas' (Mausolée de Tacfarinas) near Bouira, Algeria (© Hynox.qualaty via Wikimedia Commons, CC BY-*SA* 4.0 International)

9. The ruins of the Roman city of Ammaedara, at Haidra, Tunisia (Adobe Stock 1279524789)

10. Ammaedara, one-time base of the 3rd Legion Augusta (Adobe Stock 1279519353)

11. The ruins of the Roman city of Leptis Magna (Adobe Stock 151549144)

12. Leptis Magna, with the later Arch of Septimius Severus at the southwest entrance to the city (Adobe Stock 363626171)

Acknowledgements

If it takes a village to raise a child, it also seems to take one to support an author through writing a book! I am so grateful to everyone who has helped me along the journey – particularly those who reassured me that Tacfarinas is just as interesting an individual as Publius Quinctilius Varus.

Big thanks are owed to Phil Freeman, who once again read through the entire manuscript and offered some important insights, this is a much better book because of them. I am grateful also to those who read and commented on individual sections of the text while it was being written, and to my editor Jan Chamier at Pen & Sword for going through the final text. They all did an excellent job, and all errors which nevertheless made it into the final text are entirely my own.

Thanks again to Rachel Plummer for being a great friend, and an outlet for whenever I was frustrated with the book (or life generally) – we have moved on to pools, pizza, and Pedro Pascal, and are all the better for it!

I owe a lot to the wider archaeological community, so many of whom have helped me with this work and everything I have ever done before, and I am grateful to every single one of you. I hope our paths cross at conferences for many years to come! Especial thanks go to Andrew Kenrick for sharing his research about Juba II with me, and to David Mattingly for all his amazing archaeological work in northwest Africa – it has completely changed the way that we understand life and culture in the region and this book would be much poorer without it. Thanks also go to the Southport and Birkdale Classical Association, which has provided a wonderful new ancient history community in northwest England – Francesca Grilli, you have done an absolutely amazing job there!

The team at *Ancient Warfare* continue to be wonderful, and gave me the opportunity to discuss some of the Tacfarinas material with their audience while I was still writing this main work. Thanks to podcasters Neil Cozzi (*Ancient History Hound*), Matthew Harffy and Steven McKay (*Rock, Papers, Swords!*), and Tristan Hughes (*Ancient History Hit*) for their media support, you all make difficult things very easy on the guests! I am also grateful to the bookshop team – Gill, Jo, Julie, Kate, Louise, Marie, Mickey, Monica,

Sophie – for doing so much to support Varus, and I know Tacfarinas would have been welcomed just as warmly!

Finally, I would like to thank my family, who have taken on the burden of an archaeologist in the midst of deadline panic. My mother Christine has been amazing and makes sure I am kept full of wine and pasta (in that order). My father John deserves praise for using the Varus book to combat many mistruths online, and promoting my work at the same time! My sisters Judie and Vicky (Tors) continue to provide days of great happiness amidst the stress, while my nephew Thomas and niece Emily never fail to cheer me up even on difficult days (Mario Party and Bluey make all things better, it turns out). Lastly, thanks go to my partner Lee, for his support, editing, and discussion, and for coming with me to all manner of sites strewn with broken rocks – although we'll agree to disagree (for now) about Tacfarinas being an ancient Lawrence of Arabia…

List of Major Persons Mentioned in the Text

Where possible, dates of lifetimes and reigns have been given, otherwise the approximate time period is provided by reference to the general period and relevant events. The forms of the ancient names most familiar in the modern day have been used, so Mark Antony instead of Marcus Antonius, Cleopatra rather than Kleopatra.

Romans

Augustus (63 BC–AD 14) First emperor of Rome (reigned 30/27 BC–AD 14). Stepfather of Tiberius. Earlier in his life known as Octavian.

Caligula (AD 12–41) Third emperor of Rome (reigned AD 37–41). Second cousin of Ptolemy of Mauretania through Mark Antony. Also known as Gaius.

Gaius Marius (157–86 BC) A Roman general and politician who led the later stages of the Jugurthine War, and later fled to Africa due to conflict with Sulla.

Germanicus (15 BC–AD 19) A Roman politician and general most known for his wars in Germany. Nephew of Tiberius.

Gnaeus Domitius Ahenobarbus (died 81 BC) A Roman politician proscribed under Sulla, who fled to Africa and allied with Hiarbas of Numidia.

Gnaeus Pompey Magnus (106–48 BC) A Roman general and politician who campaigned against Hiarbas of Numidia. Also known as Pompey the Great.

Julius Caesar (100–44 BC) A Roman general and politician who campaigned in Africa during a civil war with Pompey Magnus.

Lucius Apronius Proconsul of Africa Proconsularis (AD 18–21), second to command in the war against Tacfarinas.

Lucius Cornelius Sulla Felix (138–78 BC) A Roman general and politician who served under Gaius Marius in the Jugurthine War. Later became Dictator of Rome. Usually known as Sulla.

Marcus Furius Camillus Proconsul of Africa Proconsularis (AD 17–18), the first to command in the war against Tacfarinas.

Octavian: *see* Augustus.

Publius Cornelius Dolabella (died AD 28?) Proconsul of Africa Proconsularis (AD 23–24), fourth to command in the war against Tacfarinas, and ended the conflict.

Publius Cornelius Scipio Aemilianus (185–129 BC) A Roman commander during the Third Punic War. The executor of Masinissa's will.

Publius Cornelius Scipio Africanus (236/5–183 BC) A Roman general and politician most notable for his victory over Carthage in the Second Punic War.

Publius Quinctilius Varus (*c.*44 BC–AD 9) A Roman politician and general best known for the loss of three legions in the Teutoburg Forest (Germany). Uncle of Publius Cornelius Dolabella.

Quintus Junius Blaesus (died AD 31) Proconsul of Africa Proconsularis (AD 21–23), third to command in the war against Tacfarinas. Uncle of Sejanus.

Sejanus (*c.*30 BC–AD 31) Prefect of the Praetorian Guard (AD 14–31) and confidant of the emperor Tiberius. Nephew of Quintus Junius Blaesus.

Tiberius (42 BC–AD 37) Second emperor of Rome (reigned AD 14–37). Stepson of Augustus. In power during the war against Tacfarinas.

In Northwest Africa

Adherbal (died 112 BC) King of Mauretania (reigned 118–112 BC). Son of Micipsa, grandson of Masinissa, brother of Hiempsal I, cousin and adopted brother of Jugurtha.

Arabio (died 40 BC) The last independent King of western Numidia (reigned 44–40 BC). Son of Masinissa II, grandson of Gauda.

Bocchus I King of Mauretania (reigned *c.*110–80 BC). Ally of Jugurtha, probably also his father-in-law.

Cleopatra Selene (40–5 BC) Queen of Numidia (reigned 25 BC) and Mauretania (reigned 25–5 BC). Wife of Juba II. Daughter of Mark Antony and Cleopatra, mother of Ptolemy of Mauretania.

Gaia (died 207/6 BC) King of the Massyli in eastern Numidia during the Second Punic War. Father of Masinissa. Also known as Gala.

Gauda King of Numidia (reigned 105–88 BC). Son of Mastanabal and half-brother to Jugurtha.

Gulussa (died *c.*145 BC) King of Numidia (reigned 148–*c.*145 BC). The second son of Masinissa, brother of Micipsa and Mastanabal.

Hiarbas (died *c.*82/81 BC) Usurper-king of Numidia (reigned 88–82/81 BC). Ally of Gnaeus Domitius Ahenobarbus during the Sulla–Marius civil war.

Hiempsal I (died *c.*117 BC) King of Numidia (reigned 118–117 BC). Son of Micipsa, grandson of Masinissa, brother of Adherbal, cousin and adopted brother of Jugurtha.

Hiempsal II (died *c.*60 BC) King of eastern Numidia (reigned 88/81–60 BC). Son of Gauda, brother of Masteabar, half-brother of Jugurtha, father of Juba I.

Juba I (*c.*85–46 BC) King of eastern Numidia (reigned 60–46 BC). Son of Hiempsal II. Fought against Julius Caesar in the Caesar–Pompey civil war.

Juba II (48 BC–AD 23) King of Numidia (reigned 30–25 BC) and Mauretania (reigned 25 BC–AD 23). Son of Juba I, husband of Cleopatra Selene, father of Ptolemy of Mauretania.

Jugurtha (*c.*160–104 BC) King of Numidia (reigned 118–105 BC). Illegitimate son of Mastanabal, grandson of Masinissa, cousin and adopted brother of Adherbal and Hiempsal I. Main protagonist of the Jugurthine War.

Masinissa (*c.*238–148 BC) First King of Numidia (reigned 202–148 BC). Son of Gaia, husband of Sophonisba, father of Micipsa, Gulussa, and Mastanabal.

Masinissa II Minor king of western Numidia (*c.*81–46 BC). Son of Masteabar, nephew of Hiempsal II.

Massiva Son of Gulussa, cousin of Jugurtha. A rival for the Numidian kingship murdered on the order of Jugurtha.

Mastanabal (died *c.*148 BC) King of Numidia (reigned 148–140 BC). The youngest son of Masinissa, brother of Micipsa and Gulussa, father of Gauda and Jugurtha.

Masteabar King of western Numidia in the early/mid-first century BC. Son of Gauda, brother of Hiempsal II.

Mazippa A Mauri commander who served under Tacfarinas in the early stages of the war.

Micipsa (died 118 BC) King of Numidia (reigned 148–118 BC). Eldest son of Masinissa, brother of Gulussa and Mastanabal, father of Adherbal and Hiempsal I, uncle and adoptive father of Jugurtha.

Ptolemy of Mauretania (died AD 40) Last King of Mauretania (reigned AD 17/23–40). Son of Juba II and Cleopatra Selene, second cousin of Caligula.

Sophonisba (died 203 BC) A Carthaginian noblewoman, wife of Syphax and subsequently of Masinissa.

Syphax (died 203/2 BC) King of the Masaesyli in western Numidia (reigned *c.*225–203 BC), and Roman ally who betrayed them for Carthage during the Second Punic War. Husband of Sophonisba.

Introduction

In the late summer or early autumn of AD 24, Roman troops in northwestern Africa ended a rebellion that had raged in the region for more than seven years. The rebellion had been led by a man named Tacfarinas, an indigenous Roman soldier-turned-rebel. The military and economic costs of the war had been high. Ripples from the disruption caused by the conflict had even reached Rome itself through its impact on the African grain supply, which had led to serious riots breaking out in the city during AD 19. The ending of the rebellion should have been a cause for celebration in Rome; instead, the entire incident has become one of the more obscure insurrections of the early Imperial period – and seemingly little more famous now than it was in antiquity. Further, no one is entirely sure who or what Tacfarinas actually was, or what he represented to the people who fought for him. For some, Tacfarinas was a legitimate rebel against Rome, one of the major enemy military figures of the first century AD, who led a sustained campaign that seriously threatened Roman interests in northwest Africa. For others, he was little more than a minor brigand whose activities escaped Roman control for a while, but who was eventually suppressed once Rome was able to dedicate a few more resources to the region.

Rebellions and revolts were fairly common events in the Roman world, as provincial peoples became increasingly discontented, often taking violent action against the ruling regime in an attempt to change their circumstances. Although any province could become discontented with Roman rule, rebellion was more common in the provinces which lay on the edges of the Empire – and indeed, often on their own borders. These revolts usually occurred some time after the initial period of conquest, particularly as the realities of Roman rule began to impact the indigenous population – and when Rome was perhaps no longer extending privileges to the allied elites as they had done previously. Often rebellion coincided with periods of increasing administrative and military action, particularly the introduction of taxation, land seizure, and interference with pre-existing cultural norms. Many anti-Roman leaders had formerly been associated with Rome on a positive basis, either as an allied ruler or (more commonly) having served in the Roman army as an auxiliary soldier. Both revolt and rebellion could break out when tensions reached such a level that parts of the provincial population were willing to risk their lives to try to win their independence from Roman rule – and these moments often seem to have taken the authorities, at least those located in Rome, by surprise. Thus there was an inherent political element to provincial rebellion, as it sought wholesale regime change rather than the acquisition of personal wealth through attacks on civilians, or even advancement within the Roman regime. Unfortunately, it is often difficult to determine why particular groups rebelled, as all the surviving evidence about the conflicts comes from a Roman perspective – though these sources can be a useful indication of the contentions and concerns the governing elites perceived the people of the provinces might feel towards imperial rule.[1]

The early Imperial period had more than its fair share of anti-Roman rebellion, with conflict breaking out in multiple parts of the Empire on a regular basis.[2] At the forefront of each rebellion was an indigenous leader who was able to channel provincial discontent with Rome into violent resistance. But not all of the rebel leaders were created equal. Some have become almost household names, particularly in their modern nations of origin – individuals such as Arminius/Hermann in Germany, or Boudica in Britain claim a level of notoriety and historical fame that has seen them feature as the subjects of novels, non-fiction, documentaries, operas, plays, TV series, and films. Others are less well remembered, known mainly to those who study the Roman world. Tacfarinas is a notable example of this latter group; outside of northwestern Africa, more specifically Tunisia, Algeria, and Morocco, he has become an unfairly obscure figure from early Imperial Roman history. This book reflects a longstanding interest in those who rebelled against Rome, and seeks to contribute to our understanding of the ones who are (often unfairly) misrepresented, maligned, or simply forgotten by history.

Roman Northwestern Africa

The events covered in this book took place in Roman northwestern Africa, an area encompassing parts of modern Libya, Tunisia, and Algeria; the region is sometimes referred to in the modern day as the Maghreb. Rome first established a direct territorial presence in the region in the second century BC. Eventually, Rome would control the entire Mediterranean coast of Africa, but at the time Tacfarinas operated, the territories of Mauretania (modern Morocco) had not yet been added to the Empire.

The war with Tacfarinas came at a time when Rome was significantly extending its activity and direct oversight in northwest Africa. The first province had been established in this region at least a century earlier, following the defeat of Carthage in the Third Punic War (149–146 BC). Rome had incorporated Carthaginian territory into her Empire, creating a province simply known as 'Africa', which was ruled with a relatively light touch in this period. To the east of the province lay Numidia, a powerful kingdom which was at different times both a loyal ally and an enemy to Rome, depending on who sat on the throne at the time. Roman Africa was demarcated from Numidia by a ditch known as the *Fossa Regia* (or *Fosse Scipio*), a boundary running between Thabraca (modern Tabarka) on the north coast of Tunisia to Thaenae (near modern Sfax) on the east coast. Roman sources suggest the boundary resulted from an agreement made between Scipio and the Numidian king(s) in the second century BC to divide the Roman province from the kingdom.[3] However, it appears to actually pre-date the Roman period and was probably established during the reign of the Numidian king Masinissa to mark the border between his land and that of Carthage.[4] Although Rome did not directly rule Numidia, its influence in the region was such that it could be drawn into dynastic disputes within the kingdom, most notably the Jugurthine War (112–106 BC). In the Late Republic period, provincial Africa was used as a battleground during the numerous Roman civil wars, leading to greater direct oversight and organization of the region. In 46 BC, Julius Caesar annexed Numidia and turned it into the province of *Africa Nova* ('New Africa'), with the previous territory correspondingly renamed *Africa Vetus* ('Old Africa'). In the 20s BC, the emperor Augustus had further reorganized the Roman territories in Africa, combining Africa Vetus and Africa Nova to create the single province of *Africa Proconsularis*.

Africa Proconsularis was bordered on the east by the province of Cyrenaica, and beyond that, Egypt. To the west lay the client kingdom of Mauretania, the only part of the north African coastal region not to be under direct Roman rule by the reign of Augustus. Mauretania was ruled by Juba II, an African client king raised in Rome and hand-picked by Augustus, to whom he remained loyal for his entire reign. But although Rome had a significant level of territorial dominance in northern Africa as a whole by the early first century AD, there were large elements of both the region's territory and indigenous population that remained beyond their direct control. Rome's influence, power, and interest were largely focused on the Mediterranean African coast, where opportunities for trade and agriculture were richest. Northwest Africa came to supply a significant amount of grain to Rome, supporting the city itself for up to eight months a year, and was rich in resources from salt and minerals to exotic animals.[5] According to the geographer Strabo, Carthage's imperial ambitions only extended to those territories that 'men can live in without living a nomadic life',[6] setting a pattern that was largely followed by Rome, particularly in the Republican period.

The Romans in northwestern Africa lived alongside the indigenous population of the region, a mixture of nomadic/transhumant and sedentary peoples who lived largely in the territory between the Roman provinces, Mauretania, and the Sahara. While the fertile coastal regions were heavily occupied by subsequent Phoenician, Punic, and Roman populations, the density and frequency of centres of settlement reduced inland towards the Atlas Mountains and Sahara, areas which remained occupied by a substantial number of indigenous peoples. The writer Pliny the Elder claimed that there were 516 different tribes/peoples in northwestern Africa, living between the Ampsaga river, which ran along what had been the border between Mauretania and Numidia, and the Greater Syrtes (now the Gulf of Sidra/Sirte in Libya) – and these were just the tribes Rome counted as allies in this region.[7] Only 63 of them were named in his text, leaving more than 450 peoples referred to but unnamed living in the region, although fewer than 200 can be identified archaeologically (mainly through inscriptions mentioning their names). Nevertheless, it is clear that there was a substantial non-Roman population living in northwestern Africa during the early Imperial period. Much of the time, the two groups would not necessarily interact on a regular basis as they inhabited different areas – the Romans on the coast, the tribes in the mountains and pre-desert fringe. Roman writers do not appear to have had particularly positive views of these nomadic populations and their fear of – even disgust at – the nomadic lifestyle comes through clearly in most of their descriptions of the people of northwestern Africa, commenting on aspects such as the frugality of their lifestyles, particularly the lack of meat and prevalence of dairy in their diet.[8]

In truth Roman writers likely exaggerated the prevalence of nomadism in the region, certainly by the last few centuries BC. They did acknowledge that agriculture had been introduced there by the later third century BC at the latest, with the Numidian king Masinissa being given much of the credit for this development.[9] In reality, farming had likely been introduced at a much earlier date. Archaeological research in recent decades demonstrates that the indigenous population of northwestern Africa was a mixture of nomadic and sedentary by the Roman period. By this time many of the tribes living within the desert fringe had become predominantly settled populations based around oases, growing a range of cereals, fruits, dates, and vines, some of which they traded within the region.[10] They developed an underground irrigation system of conduits (*foggaras*) to water the crops in arid soil.[11] Some of the tribes in the region had developed into proto-states by the later centuries BC, particularly the Garamantes in the southern Libyan desert.[12] Rome traded with the peoples living to the south of the province, and came into contact with nomadic groups as they moved their flocks through the traditional transhumant routeways which passed alongside and through Roman territory; the nomads could even provide them with valuable seasonal labour at harvest time.[13] But relations between the two groups grew increasingly strained as Roman activity began to intensify in the regions south of the province, bringing them into closer contact; unsurprisingly, conflict became more common as a result. However, it is important to recognize that these conflicts were not between an advanced settlement-based imperial power (Rome) and 'barbaric' nomadic peoples (the tribes), as the Roman sources often imply, but between two developed groups with conflicting priorities.

Setting the Scene

The rebellion of Tacfarinas was the last major episode in a series of conflicts between Rome and the indigenous population of northwestern Africa during the reign of Augustus and into that of Tiberius. What began as a campaign of banditry and raiding directed towards (Roman) settlements developed into a full-scale irregular conflict that was only ended after seven or eight years by the efforts of four proconsuls, two legions, and numerous auxiliary units – and by the death of Tacfarinas in battle. The war impacted much of the region, potentially extending from the Atlantic coast of modern Morocco as far east as Leptis Magna in Libya. Yet it was a conflict that, once over, Rome seems keen to have drawn a line under and their victory was evidently little celebrated outside Africa. The conflict is poorly documented in the Romans' historical record and Tacfarinas himself was never recognized by them as a legitimate rebel leader. Yet his war with Rome was one of the major conflicts of Tiberius' reign, and significantly destabilized Roman interests in that region of Africa.

From AD 17 northwest Africa became a warzone, as Tacfarinas led an escalating series of irregular actions, transitioning from small-scale raiding to attacks on Roman military installations and sieges of large towns, and from banditry to full-blown rebellion against Rome. Tacfarinas was a capable leader, who devised an effective field strategy which capitalized on the strengths of his troops while simultaneously exploiting Roman military weaknesses, particularly those associated with heavy infantry operating in semi-desert conditions. The level of wider tribal support appears to have varied over the course of the conflict, with levels seemingly highest in the first and final years of the war, but he does not seem to have had any significant problems with manpower levels. Among his recruits were likely some ex-auxiliaries, either those who had served out their time in the Roman army or who had deserted to join Tacfarinas. Some of these recruits were trained by Tacfarinas in the 'Roman style', passing on the skills he had acquired during his service in the military. His operations initially focused on the interior regions but advanced over time to the wealthy coastal areas, impacting communities from Mauretania to potentially as far east as Leptis Magna (Libya) and beyond. When the Roman army entered the field to try to stop him, the marching columns found themselves the victim of ambushes and other surprise hit-and-run attacks, to which the heavily-armed infantry of the legions could put up little effective defence. The uncertainties of the conflict took a psychological toll on the Romans, to the degree that even seasoned troops might flee in fear from Tacfarinas' army.[14] Tacfarinas avoided pitched battle wherever possible, only really fighting in one, at the very start of the war; he also made some attacks on military installations but abandoned this strategy when the Romans began to withstand them better. The rest of the time he stuck to irregular tactics and banditry and/or raiding, exploiting the weaknesses of the enemy and the effectiveness of his own men in such situations.

Three times Tacfarinas was thought to have been defeated – twice so confident were the Romans that the respective commanders were granted victory honours, only to find that he regrouped over the winter and returned to fight again. The campaign ultimately required a complete revision of Roman field tactics, which in the interests of maximum effectiveness were eventually adapted to closely resemble those of their enemy. Tacfarinas was finally defeated in a surprise attack at dawn, fought by light-armed cavalry and infantry, in what amounted to a very un-Roman victory. The relief that must have been felt on both sides of the Mediterranean to hear that after seven years the North African insurrection was finally over – and that Tacfarinas was dead – must have been enormous.

Tacfarinas in the Roman sources

Unfortunately, Tacfarinas' war against Rome is not well documented by the ancient historical record. The only source to provide even a basic narrative of the conflict is Tacitus' *Annals*, a work which gives us a year-by-year record of events during the reigns of Tiberius, Caligula, Claudius, and Nero. Tacitus (*c.* AD 56–120) was a Roman senator who, in the later decades of his life, dedicated himself to literary pursuits alongside his political activities. He wrote several major historical works, including the *Annals* and the *Histories*, which covered events from the accession of Galba to the death of Domitian, a period he had lived through, as well as the *Germania*, an ethnographic work on the German peoples, and the *Agricola*, a laudatory biography of his father-in-law, Gnaeus Julius Agricola. It is also alluded to twice by Velleius Paterculus, who provides no narrative of the conflict as his work only covers the period up to the death of Augustus in AD 14. Paterculus does not name Tacfarinas at any point, but does briefly refer to the war between him and Rome on two occasions. In a laudatory summing-up of the reign of Tiberius he notes, 'The African war also, which caused great consternation and grew more formidable every day, was soon extinguished under his auspices and in accordance with his plans'; he also refers to the honours won by a proconsul during the conflict.[15]

Perhaps surprisingly, the war against Tacfarinas is not mentioned by Cassius Dio, one of the major historians for this period of Roman history. Dio's 80-volume *Roman History*, written in the late second and early third century AD, completely omits any reference to conflict in northwestern Africa in this period – at best, it provides additional context about the prior and subsequent careers of some of the Roman commanders involved. This omission is difficult to understand. The sections do not seem to have been lost in transmission.

Chronologically, the war would fall into books 57 and 58 of the *Roman History*, which deal with the reign of Tiberius, but both appear to be complete as they are. Dio did not shy away from documenting other insurgencies against Rome – he is the main source for the rebellion of Arminius in AD 9, and provides a full account of Boudica's revolt in AD 60/61, among many other provincial conflicts. He surely would have been aware of the war, not least because he had served as proconsul of Africa in the AD 220s. Perhaps the conflict was already well documented by a source later lost and Dio felt there was no need to repeat the narrative in his own work. Or perhaps it was simply judged as being of no interest to his readers. There may even have been political elements involved. In the period where Dio was collecting his information and beginning to write, the Severan dynasty took the Imperial throne, spearheaded by Septimius Severus. The family had its roots in northwestern Africa, Leptis Magna more specifically, a city which had been directly impacted by Tacfarinas. Further, the region had become somewhat tumultuous during the reign of Septimius Severus, who was evidently not popular in Africa despite his regional connections.[16]

In AD 193, the territory of the former kingdom of Numidia, long-since absorbed into Africa Proconsularis, was separated off and made into a province in its own right, a significant change. Perhaps dwelling on a rebellion from the past was considered unwise at the time. There is also an incredibly brief reference to the conflict in the writings of the fourth-century historian Aurelius Victor, who simply notes that 'He [Tiberius] suppressed the banditries of the Gaetulii'.[17] This sentence appears to refer to Tacfarinas, in the absence of any other African conflict during the reign of Tiberius. There are no accounts of the conflict written from the African perspective.

The only overview of the war with Tacfarinas is in fact given by Tacitus, in the *Annals*, a narrative history which covered the period between the death of Augustus to the reign of Nero (AD 14–68) and is a key resource for understanding events in the early decades of the post-Augustan Roman world. Tacitus was born *c.*AD 56/7, so would not have lived through most of the decades covered by the *Annals* and was not a contemporary of the war with Tacfarinas. The temporal distance makes it highly unlikely that he could have spoken directly to anyone who had even fought in the conflict. Instead, it is likely that he relied on the *Acta Senatus* – the official record of minutes for the Roman Senate – which, as a senator, he had access to. The records would have contained details of all the issues discussed by the Senate in reference to the conflict, providing much information for his account.[18] He wrote the *Annals* in the early decades of the second century, so constructing his account of the Tacfarinas conflict approximately a century after the events had taken place.

Furthermore, Tacitus' account is far less detailed than would be desirable. As he wrote in the annalistic style, year-by-year, the war is referred to in multiple separate passages rather than in one single description. Tacitus spreads the events involving Tacfarinas over five discrete sections, raised as they occurred chronologically, although there are further references to Roman individuals connected with the war elsewhere in his text.[19] The narrative information revealed overall is limited. The names of the four proconsuls who commanded the army against Tacfarinas are all given, as are those of a few Roman soldiers who distinguished themselves during the conflict. Tacitus notes when major engagements between the two forces took place, although generally lacking any detail beyond who won. The only two combat incidents given any real narrative are one occasion where a Roman cohort fled the field in fear of Tacfarinas, for which they were severely disciplined, and the final battle of the war – although even then, neither are described in detail. The incident which Tacitus gives most attention concerns a message sent by Tacfarinas to Tiberius, asking for a land grant for himself and his men to live free of Roman control, threatening unending war if it was not given. The emperor, unsurprisingly, was furious at this audacity. The long, irregular campaign that Rome was forced to fight, repeatedly trying and failing to respond to Tacfarinas' raids, is largely skimmed over, while the repeated attacks that Tacfarinas made on their marching columns are referred to more to highlight the ineffectiveness of Roman operations than the skill of the rebels. Few place names are provided and even the geographic extent of the war as a whole is not clear. Nor does Tacitus attempt to provide any reason for Tacfarinas' actions, and the outbreak of war is simply ascribed to his initial banditry having escalated to the point where Rome had no choice but to take countermeasures.

Unfortunately, even these limited narrative details provided by Tacitus about Tacfarinas and the war in Africa cannot be taken at face value. The content of the text was shaped by numerous factors, including literary convention in historical writing, Roman cultural attitudes towards both Africans and bandits, politics in Rome, and Tacitus' own personal biases. Tacitus had a complex and often antagonistic attitude to the reputation of Tiberius, despite being born more than a decade after the emperor's death. As a result, the reliability and purpose of everything that Tacitus writes about Tiberius and his actions during his reign has to be evaluated extra carefully. More generally, Tacitus had a particular way of writing about provincial rebellion, which included a disproportionate focus on both the rebel leader and the Roman commander(s) who ended the conflict.[20]

Roman historical writing often contains subtle allusions to the similarities and differences between two different but connected events, leading to the deliberate shaping or even distortion of what happened to strengthen the comparison. Tacitus in particular also had a tendency to compare incidents in the Imperial period with similar ones from the Republican period to illustrate the growing degeneracy of his 'modern day'. At the time Tacitus was writing, around the turn of the second century AD, Rome was recovering politically from the problematic reign of Domitian, a ruthless ruler who ended up being assassinated by his own court officials. Tacitus had lived through this era as a career politician, and as a result developed a negative view of Imperial-era Rome, often in his writing harking back to past glories of the Republic. In the case of Tacfarinas, Tacitus was evidently trying to draw a parallel between this conflict and an earlier one in the same region, the Jugurthine War.[21] Both conflicts were fought in northwestern Africa, with the rebels led by an indigenous commander, a former-ally-turned-enemy who had abused his position of trust with Rome in his own interests – the earlier event thus a particularly relevant counterpart to the Tacfarinas war. They were also fought as largely irregular conflicts, with an enemy who avoided pitched battle where possible and each had caused significant damage to Roman interests in the region. Tacitus could use the narrative of the two conflicts to emphasize the excellence of the Roman Republican response to Jugurtha, contrasted with the problematic Imperial actions against Tacfarinas. The official response to the latter, particularly the length of time taken to get it under control, could be used to highlight the ineffective rule of both Tiberius and the Roman Senate under his stewardship.[22]

Nostalgia for the Republic is further highlighted by Tacitus' focus on several occasions on the revival of long-disused military practices (from triumphal honours for allies to decimation) during the conflict, emphasizing the traditions and customs which had been lost in the period between the two wars.[23] However, to make the comparison, the narratives of the two conflicts had to align in a way that made literary sense – or, more likely, be tweaked in order that these points could be made. How far Tacitus' account of the war against Tacfarinas was adapted to make it resemble that of Jugurtha is unknowable, but it cannot be in any doubt that an ancient reader was intended to come away having made a direct comparison between the two conflicts.

The war with Tacfarinas provided a way for Tacitus to criticize Tiberius as emperor. He may also have used the narrative to highlight the incompetence of Tiberius' regime overall, in that Roman officials in Africa, i) allowed bandit activity to escalate to the stage that it was a significant problem, and ii) having done so, were unable to get the situation back under control for at least seven years.[24] The severity of the conflict may also have been underplayed by Tacitus, as he likely did for other foreign wars during the reign of Tiberius, to avoid contradicting the carefully constructed impression of an emperor who was far inferior to his Republican predecessors.[25] But in contrast, others suggest that the scale of the rebellion was exaggerated because there were few other foreign wars in the early years of Tiberius' reign, and Tacitus needed a significant conflict through which to make narrative attacks on the emperor.[26]

Unfortunately, archaeological evidence of the conflict is also sparse. Few of the places mentioned by Tacitus can be identified today and none of those which can have been excavated, in part due to the political situation in the modern countries where it was fought. An inscription from Leptis Magna (Libya) makes direct reference to Tacfarinas, another from the same city was likely dedicated by or to a Roman commander named Scipio in the war, but does not make direct reference to it.[27] Inscriptions from elsewhere in the Empire help to reconstruct the careers of prominent Roman individuals connected with the conflict. Coins minted in northwestern Africa around that time provide another visual source of evidence, particularly those issued during the war by the kings of Mauretania, which make reference to their contributions to Roman victories in the campaign. From *c.*AD 15 Juba of Mauretania issued a series of coins celebrating an unspecified military victory, giving further indication of the scale of the conflict, if not its narrative.

A Rebel or a Bandit?

The presentation of Tacfarinas in Tacitus' account is not sympathetic. Unlike other rebel leaders (such as Boudica), Tacitus does not identify Tacfarinas as having any specific grievance against Rome which would justify him taking up arms against the state and thus he was not recognized as a legitimate belligerent. As a result he is generally described not as a rebel, or even an enemy, but as a 'bandit' (*latronus*). Towards the end of the conflict, Tacitus' terminology changes slightly, with Tacfarinas instead being referred to as a *dux* (commander) on two occasions, implying recognition of a more legitimate military role by that point.[28] This only comes in the context of the final year of the war, however, when the situation had undoubtedly changed from one of banditry to outright rebellion, with Tacfarinas commanding a large coalition army in which many of the peoples of the region took part.

Latronus was a highly pejorative term used with a specific social and political meaning, which drew focus to the irregular nature of the conflict and the methods used by Tacfarinas and his men. It also highlighted the lack of political motivation ascribed to their actions by Tacitus. In some ways, the terminology is justified. Tacfarinas' army consistently raided and looted settlements in Roman and Mauretanian territory, and – at least in the earlier years of the war – appear to have lacked any political motivation for their actions. The majority of Tacfarinas' attacks were directed towards civilians and only rarely did they take on the Roman army; even when they did, actual battle was avoided where possible. The impression he gives is of a local thug at the head of a powerful armed gang, with little interest in more than raiding and stealing from local communities and no wider political purpose. His operations were clearly directed towards Mauretania as well as Rome, which undermines the suggestion that it was a rebellion against Roman rule from the start.[29]

It can be difficult from such a temporal distance to distinguish the motivating factors in a particular conflict, particularly those which used irregular tactics as a matter of course. Political resistance using a raiding strategy can easily be identified as non-political banditry, and vice-versa.[30] Yet at the same time, even Tacitus gives hints that Tacfarinas was something more than just a common bandit – or perhaps that he *became* more than this. There are three points in the narrative where Tacfarinas' motives are alluded to: at the start of the conflict in AD 17, in the midst of events in 20/21, and in the later stages in 23/24. In AD 17, Tiberius suggests Tacfarinas was almost entirely concerned with acquiring as much booty as possible through settlement raids. By 20/21, this had changed to a desire for a land-grant and the right to live in peace there – a more political reason, albeit one which would not have benefited the population of northwest Africa as a whole, only Tacfarinas and his men. By the final years of the war, Tacfarinas' motives had evidently shifted again, perhaps in light of the refusal of his peace advances and Roman victories in the field against him: now he was apparently fighting to drive Rome out of the region. This evident evolution from soldier to deserter, bandit, and finally, freedom fighter, may have been a literary construct – it closely resembles the trajectories associated with figures like Spartacus – but if it even partially reflects reality it suggests that Tacfarinas eventually came to lead a serious regional rebellion with a political agenda, however he had started out. While the nature of the conflict in the early years is debatable, by *c.*AD 23 it had almost certainly developed into a legitimate rebellion, which Tacitus does imply.

So why would Tacitus consistently present Tacfarinas as a bandit rather than a rebel leader? His use of the term may partly reflect the fact that Tacitus felt that there was no need for Tacfarinas or the population of northwest Africa to rebel in this period, making their uprising against the Roman state automatically illegitimate. Rome itself recognized that sometimes rebellions were prompted by legitimate grievances, where provincial populations had genuinely been subjected to mistreatment, usually by corrupt Roman officials.[31] Tacitus himself did not necessarily shy away from admitting when the Romans had played a role in causing a rebellion, although he typically characterized the matter as the work of a few 'bad apples' rather than an inherent consequence of Imperial rule. But he does not seem to believe that any such mistreatment of the population had happened in northwest Africa. That said, Tacitus' definition of a genuine grievance may have differed significantly from that of the population itself. Roman actions such as encroachment on traditional nomadic pasture routes, and surveys which threatened to precede the introduction of land confiscations and taxation, were taking place around the same time as Tacfarinas became active in the region. While these things may not have seemed to add up to 'mistreatment' to Tacitus, it is easy to imagine that they might have been considered such by the people newly subjected to them. Grievance in this particular circumstance may have been entirely a matter of opinion.

There were other factors in the use of 'bandit' terminology, which may have been used to conjure certain impressions of Tacfarinas in the minds of readers. In the Roman world, a bandit was far more than a common thief or criminal – rather, it was someone who 'threatened the security of the social and moral order of the state by the use of private violence in pursuit of their aims.'[32] Their impact went well beyond just the economic losses associated with their activity and most Romans had strong negative views about bandits, who posed a risk in most areas of the Empire, including just a short distance from Rome itself. Travellers were vulnerable even on short journeys outside settlements and banditry could be viewed as a form of natural disaster, akin to a storm at sea. Many tombstones commemorate those lost in attacks on the road; *interfectus a latronibus* ('killed by bandits') was often inscribed to highlight their unfortunate manner of death, although recent research suggests that this phrase may also have been used when someone was killed in a raid or military expedition by anyone who came from outside the territorial boundaries of the Empire.[33] Leaders such as Pompey the Great and Octavian/Augustus had developed popular support among the Roman people by taking action against banditry.

Further, the description of an opponent as a 'bandit' may not always have reflected their actual behaviour, but might also be used to delegitimize them. Enemies, particularly political ones, could be branded *latrones* to cast doubt on the legitimacy of their actions, particularly at times when the Roman state was under pressure;[34] the accession of Tiberius in AD 14, just a few years before the war with Tacfarinas broke out, could certainly have satisfied this criteria. By labelling Tacfarinas and his men exclusively as bandits, Tacitus stripped them of any moral or political legitimacy[35] and enabled Rome not to recognize events in Africa as a grievance-fuelled rebellion against their regime. The term also signposted for Roman readers that this enemy was a dangerous one, whose actions had threatened the state itself – not necessarily on a military basis, but on a social and ethical level. It ensured that Tacitus' audience would not be tempted into sympathy for Tacfarinas and his cause. He was thus dismissed as little more than a deserter and a bandit and never presented in the text as a capable military commander or even a legitimate rebel. This impression is heightened by the lack of detail given to his successes in the field;[36] even his victories against Roman troops are presented as being the fault of the troops being cowardly and falling below expected military standards.

While Tacfarinas and his men were characterized as bandits, embodying the dangers and illegitimacy that term communicated, Tacitus changes the picture slightly in the language used to describe the conflict itself. He does not refer to it as a *latrocinium*, a campaign specifically against banditry, or even as putting down an uprising (*tumultuatum*),[37] but as a *bellum*, a full-scale war that would typically be fought between two recognized states or peoples.[38] Typically, banditry and warfare were mutually exclusive, the former term potentially being used to describe anything short of all-out war, but not appropriate once an actual war had been declared.[39] The use of *bellum* may reflect Tacitus' wider literary preoccupations, particularly if he wanted his readers to view the conflict as a particularly serious incident. But he is not alone in recognizing the conflict as a war. In his brief reference to the actual event, Velleius Paterculus also refers to it as a *bellum*. Later Roman legal texts suggest that Rome did not declare formal war against bandits, further evidence that the conflict with Tacfarinas was viewed as far more than just a campaign against problematic banditry: 'Those are enemies who declare war against us, or against whom we publicly declare war; others are robbers or brigands.'[40]

Not all enemy leaders were treated in the same way by Tacitus. In some cases, he was seen to show at least a modicum of respect to rebel commanders, most notably Arminius in Germany, about whom he wrote:

> Assuredly he was the deliverer of Germany, one too who had defied Rome, not in her early rise, as other kings and generals, but in the height of her empire's glory, had fought, indeed, indecisive battles, yet in war remained unconquered. He completed thirty-seven years of life, twelve years of power, and he is still a theme of song among barbarous nations, though to Greek historians, who admire only their own achievements, he is unknown, and to Romans not as famous as he should be, while we extol the past and are indifferent to our own times.[41]

Tacitus' almost sympathetic presentation of Arminius stands in complete contrast to his assessment of Tacfarinas, which instead focuses on the barbarity of his army and their actions, and Tacfarinas' desertion from the Roman army and his disrespect towards Rome. The positive attitude displayed towards Arminius demonstrates that turning from ally to enemy and then leading a rebellion or war against the Empire was in itself not enough to provoke universal hostility from Tacitus. Unlike Arminius, Tacfarinas had deserted the army before completing his term of service which may have counted against him in Tacitus' eyes; by contrast, although the German had seemingly not completed a full military career, he was asked by Rome to take up his tribal chieftainship *c.*AD 6, which legitimately released him.

Ultimately, based on current evidence there is no way to be certain whether Tacfarinas began his war with Rome as a bandit or a rebel leader, or to know for sure how his motivation evolved over time. In a postcolonial era, it is very tempting to counter Tacitus' open hostility towards Tacfarinas by reinterpreting him as a heroic freedom fighter, satisfying our own narrative desire to treat indigenous enemies of Rome with greater humanity than the Romans had.[42] But care must be taken not to recast Tacfarinas as an African Robin Hood figure just because his Roman portrayal as a barbaric bandit appears distasteful. The reality, no doubt, lies somewhere between these two extremes.

Aim and Structure of this Book

This book draws together the available evidence about Tacfarinas and his rebellion against Rome to create a narrative of the war, alongside discussion of its causes, and the consequences for the population of northwestern Africa. In providing a detailed account of this little-known but highly problematic conflict, this work will, I hope, help to introduce a fascinating episode of Roman history to a wider audience – and make the case for Tacfarinas being re-evaluated as a serious rebel against Rome. It will therefore also consider Roman views on the conflict, and why Tacfarinas was dismissed as a mere bandit in contrast to leaders such as Arminius and Boudica. To further this aim, the conflict in northwestern Africa is not considered in isolation, but contextualized against the broader politico-military situation in the Empire at the time. Discussion of other near-contemporary rebellions, particularly those in Illyricum (AD 6–9) and Germany (AD 9–17), is included at relevant points for additional context, particularly where it sheds light on Roman or rebel field strategy at certain points of the war.

The first three chapters explore the history of Rome in northwestern Africa, from its first direct involvement in the Middle Republic through to the early Principate. Chapter 1 details the earlier history of interactions against the backdrop of Rome's conflict with Carthage, up to the end of the Third Punic War. Chapter 2 moves on to explore the region during the Late Republican period, including the Jugurthine War and the civil wars of the first century BC. Chapter 3 discusses northwestern Africa under early Imperial rule, through the reign of Augustus to the imminent outbreak of rebellion under Tiberius. It explores in greater depth the indigenous population of the region and Rome's growing contact and tensions with these peoples, including several conflicts prior to that with Tacfarinas. Collectively, these three first chapters aim to provide a sociopolitical background for the outbreak of war under Tacfarinas, contextualized not just against events a few years or decades before the conflict, but in the wider structure of Roman rule. Chapter 4 introduces Tacfarinas, with a summary of what is known or can be inferred about his life prior to the outbreak of open hostilities with Rome in AD 17. Chapter 5 details potential reasons for the outbreak of conflict, considers whether it satisfies the criteria for a formal 'rebellion', and discusses how Tacfarinas found himself at the head of the army which would challenge Rome for the next seven years.

The following four chapters deal with the war itself, chronologically divided based on the tenure of each proconsul: Marcus Furius Camillus (Chapter 6), Lucius Apronius (Chapter 7), Quintus Junius Baesus (Chapter 8), and Publius Cornelius Dolabella (Chapter 9). Each provides a biographical summary of the proconsul's career to date, followed by a narrative summary of the war under their command. Analysis of the strategic approach of each individual commander is contextualized against their previous experience, with discussion where appropriate of wider political considerations. The book ends with a review of the aftermath of Tacfarinas' revolt and its impact on the region, and his treatment in subsequent history (Chapter 10).

A Note on Names and Terminology

In recent years it has been suggested by some scholars that 'Tacfarinas' is almost certainly a Roman name given to him, either as a Latinized version of his Numidian name, or (less likely) a completely different name he adopted when joining the Roman army.[43] As a result, the case has been made to refer to him instead as 'Tiqfarin', considered to be a more accurate rendition of his original name.[44] Although appreciating the motivations behind this suggested change, I have continued to use 'Tacfarinas', to avoid both confusion and difficulties identifying other sources discussing him. This editorial decision is also motivated by a desire for a standard approach to other rebels mentioned in the text, who are all referred to by the name given them in the Roman sources; more widely, other Latinized names such as Arminius have not been changed in modern historical discourse to better reflect their perceived ethnic background.

In most instances, the Roman terminology for the conflict as a war rather than a rebellion, revolt, or insurrection is preferred. Both rebellion and revolt contain the inherent suggestion that a conflict was being carried out for political reasons, with the specific intention of changing a government, something which is not necessarily the case for the Tacfarinas war (certainly not at the beginning). While the term 'insurrection' has a lot of crossover with rebellion and revolt, in that it is also a form of violent resistance against the state, it does not necessarily aim as far as regime change. Knowing which term to use in any Roman context is difficult, not least as the ancient historical record rarely communicates the intentions of the provincial resistance. In the case of Tacfarinas, the earlier stages of the conflict are probably best described as an insurrection against Rome – violent action without the explicit aim of regime change – eventually developing over the years into an active rebellion.

Identification of Tacfarinas and his men as 'bandits' has generally been avoided as potentially problematic terminology – the word imposes Roman judgements on them which are not necessarily justified. They are instead variously described as 'rebels' or simply 'Tacfarinas' army/force/men'. Tacfarinas himself is identified simply as the 'leader' or 'commander'. Although Tacfarinas is identified by Tacitus as Numidian, and many of his men are associated with particular indigenous peoples, ethnic terms are generally avoided due both to inherent problems with their accuracy as communicated by the Roman sources, and to avoid giving the impression that the men belonged to formal armies raised by a particular tribe. Ethnic or tribal identifiers will only be used in specific relevant situations. Likewise, Tacfarinas is not referred to as 'the Numidian commander / leader', but simply either by his name or as the 'rebel commander'.

Some choices on other names have been made in the interests of clarity. The emperor Augustus will consistently be referred to by that name even when considering events predating his assumption of that title in 27 BC, until which time he was named Octavian. King Juba II of Mauretania is generally referred to simply as 'Juba' (his father, Juba I of Numidia, occurs less frequently in the text and will remain Juba I). 'Roman Africa' refers specifically to the areas territorially claimed by the Empire between the first annexation of territory in the second century BC and the creation of Africa Proconsularis by Augustus; otherwise, all references to 'Africa' refer to the continent and not the province. The geographic setting of the war is purposefully identified as 'northwest(ern) Africa' rather than 'north(ern) Africa' in recognition of the fact that it was centred around the Roman province of Africa Proconsularis and the kingdom of Mauretania (modern Morocco, Algeria, Tunisia, and Libya), leaving the northeastern African provinces of Cyrenaica and Egypt largely unaffected.

Where ancient place names are mentioned, if they can be identified, they will be associated with their modern location on their first appearance in the text, with the most widely-used transliteration of Arabic names used wherever possible. Most places will then be referred to by their ancient names for the remainder of the text, and where possible, the ancient names for provinces and kingdoms are preferred over the names of the modern states. While recognizing the historiographical and accuracy issues associated with both the word and modern concept of 'tribes' this term has been used in the text, although 'people' is preferred where practical.[45] Although other authors may favour different editorial choices, these decisions have been made in the interests of clarity, consistency, and accuracy throughout.

Chapter 1

Rome in Northwest Africa: *The Punic Wars Era (264–146 BC)*

The story of northwestern Africa in antiquity is often told through the prism of those who came there as colonizing outsiders – first the Phoenicians, from whom Carthage and her empire developed, followed by the Greeks, and then the Romans. Political change could be rapid. In the early decades of the third century BC, the dominant imperial power in northwestern Africa was Carthage. By the mid-second century BC, Carthage had been supplanted by Rome, its power destroyed over the course of three wars between the two. The end of the conflict would see Rome establish its first province in Africa (known simply as 'Africa' at this stage, later distinguished as Africa Vetus and Africa Proconsularis). The three Punic Wars (264–146 BC) between Rome and Carthage affected large parts of northwestern Africa, as well as southern regions of Spain and Italy.[1] Carthage was finally defeated in 146 BC, from which point Rome would play a more direct role in the history of northwestern Africa, although the scale of its territorial presence in the first decades after this date is difficult to map with any certainty. The sociopolitical background of pre-Roman Africa had a significant impact on the development and expansion of the provincial territory. The wars also provided Rome with its first experience of warfare in the problematic terrain of northwestern Africa, and the irregular tactics used by the indigenous population against 'superior' Imperial armies.

The Punic Wars drew many of the peoples living in the region into choosing either alliance or conflict with Rome, positions which would be variously entrenched or abandoned over time. This period also saw the rise of the kingdom of Numidia, a state which would play a significant role in the Second and Third Punic Wars, and indeed in the subsequent history of the region through to the early Imperial period. During this time, Numidia established a particularly close relationship with Rome which would see the former gain favour in exchange for military assistance, most notably in the form of the ferocious Numidian cavalry. In return, they received the benefits that came from such alliance, including political and military support for their kings (when they kept faithful to Rome, at least) and minimal interference in their daily life. The significant changes in northwestern Africa during this period – Phoenician colonization, the development of the Carthaginian empire, and the wars with Rome – shaped the politics of the region in ways that would eventually lead to the war with Tacfarinas.

Phoenician Colonization

In the ninth century BC, northwestern Africa was colonized by the Phoenicians (the Greek name for the inhabitants of the cities of Aradus, Tripoli, Byblos, Berytus, Sidon, and Tyre, all in the Levant). It is not known why there was a wave of Phoenician emigration at this time, with suggestions ranging from overpopulation in the cities to the desire to establish new trade networks, or to gain direct access to raw materials elsewhere in the Mediterranean region. It was a widespread movement, with settlements also developing in Cyprus, Sicily, southern Spain, and Morocco. More than 300 Phoenician colonies were established in the Maghreb region, including Carthage, Hadrumentum, Leptis Magna, Sabratha, and Utica.[2] Most of these settlements were located along the coast, giving them easy access to the Mediterranean trade routes, and the Phoenician colonies remained important economic players in the centuries after their settlement. Over time, the migrants became increasingly politically, socially, and even linguistically distant from their native origins, developing into a separate culture usually referred to as Punic.

Before Rome, the principal power in northwestern Africa was Carthage (in modern Tunisia). Carthage began as a Phoenician settlement and became the centre for Punic power, lending its name to the large empire which developed from it. Carthage was originally founded in the ninth century BC, just one of the many trading colonies in the region.[3] The colony prospered and became wealthy from both trade and the agricultural and mineral wealth which lay within its territory. From the late sixth century BC onwards, Carthage began to occupy a more important role, particularly after Persian subjugation of the Phoenician cities in the Levant at that time led the Phoenician colonies to seek new leadership.[4] Carthage consequently developed an army and fleet, heavily manned by mercenaries, which enabled it to become one of the dominant military powers of the western Mediterranean by the fourth century BC. It subsequently took direct control of many other Phoenician colonies, establishing its rule over coastal Africa from Morocco to western Libya, and creating an empire which at its greatest extent also incorporated southeastern Iberia (in modern Spain), Sardinia, Corsica, Malta, the Balearic Islands, and parts of Sicily (the rest was under Greek control).[5] Although Carthage dominated the region politically, there was probably no systematic colonization of the region by Carthaginian settlers (nor had there been by the Phoenicians), and settlements likely remained a mixture of Punic and indigenous peoples.[6] Further, they appear to have taken limited interest in the indigenous peoples living in the mountains and desert fringes away from the coast, which may have allowed them to continue living in relative independence from Carthage for several centuries.

The Indigenous Population of the Maghreb

It is difficult to be certain about the history of the indigenous people who were already in northwest Africa when the first Phoenicians arrived in the ninth century BC. The first classical historical references to the period date to the fifth century BC, and describe ethnographic curiosities more than anything else. Roman sources provide slightly more detail about the indigenous population, but they are largely hostile and full of stereotypes, either underinformed about the complexities of societies in northwestern Africa or deliberately playing it down. These sources provide very little basis for reconstructing the history or understanding the peoples of the region prior to the third century BC and the era of the Punic Wars – and indeed, relatively little reliable observation afterwards either. The overall impression given is of a region still populated almost exclusively by nomadic peoples up until at least the late third–early second centuries BC, who did not make their own advances in agriculture or urbanism and relied on colonial powers for such developments. The arrival of the first Phoenician colonists in northwestern Africa at some point in the ninth century BC was consequently an event viewed in antiquity – and by many later historians – as a turning point in the region's history. The image presented of the population they came to live alongside is typically of backwards and largely nomadic people, struggling to survive in a hostile landscape which they did little to develop. They were thought not to have been introduced to agriculture or permanent settlement until the late third century BC and until recently, it was generally assumed that all developments in urbanization, agriculture, and even culture in northwest Africa had to postdate the arrival of the Phoenicians. However, this was clearly not the case.

In fact, the archaeological work done thus far strongly indicates that the people of northwestern Africa were already independently moving towards sedentarism and the creation of proto-urban settlements, either prior to or at the same time as the earliest Phoenician colonies, a process which continued through to the Roman period. Gaps in our knowledge of this period are increasingly being filled through the excavation of sites occupied by the indigenous populations in the earlier half of the first millennium BC, and the discovery of numerous settlements predating the third century BC. Excavations at the Numidian and Roman town of Althiburos (in modern Tunisia) reveal that substantial permanent stone buildings were being constructed as early as the tenth/ninth centuries BC, far earlier than would be expected based on the historical presentation of the local population at the time. The site has evidence of agricultural cultivation beginning around the same period and its overall archaeology suggests it was intended as a permanent settlement from the start.[7] What is perhaps more surprising is that it was not a particularly unique or exceptional place. At least two other Numidian sites (Mdidi and Bagat) have characteristics in common with Althiburos. While they all later became Roman towns, they were originally developed from an indigenous urban tradition which far pre-dated the rise of Carthage or the arrival of Rome.

However, outside of a small number of sites, relatively little is known about wider settlement patterns in pre-Roman northwestern Africa – partly because many may have been buried under later settlements and a lack of excavation makes it difficult to identify how many were originally indigenous settlements. Elsewhere in the region, excavation has demonstrated that the Garamantes people, based in southern Libya in the area now known as Fazzān, had also started to develop a settlement system as early as 1000 BC (the Garamantes are discussed in more detail in Chapter 3).[8] They had their own system of agriculture, supported by underground irrigation channels (*foggaras*), and were involved in trans-Saharan trade. Just like the Numidians, the Garamantes were not subsistence-level nomads trying to eke a living out in a harsh pre-desert terrain, but a largely sedentary society with some nomadic elements. That the population was developing its own urban settlements independent of colonial powers may explain why this later became one of the most densely urbanized areas in the Roman Empire.[9] The evidence suggests a region very different from what previous scholarship had imagined, with an indigenous population independently developing urbanism and agriculture: the period spanning the first millennium BC and into the first centuries AD is now referred to by some as the 'North African Iron Age' to reflect what seems to have been a unified period of social development.[10] It was against this backdrop that the Carthaginian empire grew up, alongside an increasingly socially complex and sedentary indigenous population.

Perhaps because of this growing level of development, even in its imperial phase Carthage does not appear to have expended much effort in trying to bring the indigenous population under direct territorial control. As a primarily coastal power, it likely had little interest in occupying the mountainous and semi-desert areas inland, particularly as they could already access those resources through trade with people like the Garamantes. The two societies did not live entirely separately, and tribal mercenaries served in the Carthaginian army, but evidently there was little need to subjugate the indigenous population. Indeed, some of the tribes began to develop into proto-states in the fourth and third centuries BC, particularly in the area of Numidia, to the west of Carthage; though this development may have been at least partly prompted by the rise of Carthage, as their neighbours banded together into groups better able to withstand outside pressure.[11] By the later third century BC, the peoples of Numidia had formed into two main tribal coalitions led by kings: the Massyli, based in the eastern region, and the Masaesyli in the west. By that date too, complex tomb structures were being constructed by the Numidian elite, demonstrating access to significant architectural, economic, and manpower resources.[12] Carthage made alliances with various Numidian kings and became increasingly reliant on Numidian troops, particularly cavalry, to serve in its army. These troops went on to play a particularly important role in the Second Punic War. Numidia itself would become one of the major powers in the region, after playing a key role in the Punic Wars between Carthage and Rome.

Carthage and Rome

For several centuries, Carthage and Rome had developed separately on opposite sides of the Mediterranean Sea, with no need for any armed rivalry between them. Carthage actually spent much of its time from *c.*580–265 BC at war with Greek city-states, trying to ensure economic dominance over the Mediterranean and the key maritime trade-routes; the presence of both Greeks and Carthaginians on Sicily was a particular conflict point. Diplomatic relations between Carthage and Rome developed from the later sixth century BC, when they agreed a treaty demarcating areas in which each was to exercise political and commercial control. At this time, Rome was not a particularly important power in the region, its territory limited to parts of central and southern Italy, and it was in the interests of both for their trade and expansion to continue unhindered by the other. Carthage had a powerful navy and an impressive army, the latter heavily reliant on mercenary recruitment both from areas under their direct control (Numidians, Iberians, Sicilians, Italians, and Balearics) and beyond (Greeks, Gauls/Celts). The Carthaginian military would be called on to fight in numerous conflicts in the sixth and fifth centuries BC, particularly against the Greeks, who wanted to expand their territorial holdings on Sicily.

For much of the fifth and fourth centuries BC, Carthage and Rome maintained non-conflicting interests. Roman attention was turned particularly towards expansion within Italy, establishing territorial dominance over much of the area by the early third century BC.[13] In this way Rome had established itself as a new power in the Mediterranean, and if it wanted its power to grow further it would eventually have to take on the other major players in the region, the Greek city-states – and Carthage. With hindsight, it was becoming increasingly inevitable that Rome and Carthage would come to blows sooner or later. However, even in the first decades of the third century BC, Rome and Carthage had not yet become direct enemies. They even fought together as allies in the Pyrrhic War (280–275 BC), when Pyrrhus of Epirus invaded Italy having apparently being asked to do so by the people of Tarentum. After mixed fortunes in combat against the Romans, in which he technically won battles but lost many of his troops (the origin of the 'Pyrrhic victory'), Pyrrhus moved on to Sicily, threatening Carthaginian interests on the island. He inflicted several defeats on Carthage, but refused to make peace unless the Carthaginians abandoned the island entirely, which they refused to do. However, after three years Pyrrhus was driven out of Sicily and back to the Italian mainland, in part due to his mistreatment of the local population which led to popular unrest. Rome was then able to inflict a decisive defeat on Pyrrhus at Beneventum (275 BC), finally ending the conflict. But by now another war, this one between Rome and Carthage, was on the horizon.

The First Punic War

When Pyrrhus left Sicily, he was said to have looked back at the island and remarked, 'My friends, what a wrestling ground for Carthaginians and Romans we are leaving behind us!'[14] The Pyrrhic War had illustrated to everyone concerned that Rome's power had developed far beyond its humble beginnings and Pyrrhus was correct to suggest that it would not be long before these two rivals would find themselves in direct conflict. There was a slight delay to the hostilities, but the First Punic War began in 264 BC, just over a decade after the Pyrrhic War. The war was a devastating one for the region and lasted for 23 years, one of the longest continuous conflicts of antiquity and one of the most prominent naval conflicts of this period.

The outbreak of hostilities was prompted by events in Sicily, a key strategic point for both Rome and Carthage. A group of Italian mercenaries, the Mamertines, had seized control of the city of Messana (modern Messina) in 288 BC when the death of their employer, Agathocles of Syracuse, had left them abandoned on the island. In 265 BC, Hiero II of Syracuse attempted to drive out the Mamertines from their stolen territory. The Mamertines agreed they needed allies, but disagreed about who would best suit their interests, Rome or Carthage; requests were sent to both by different groups. Carthage sent a fleet and garrison to Messana, but the population became concerned that this was a precursor to them coming under Carthaginian control, and they sent a further request to Rome for help, this time also to expel Carthage. Noting that their presence in Messana gave the Carthaginian fleet control of the Strait of Messana, the narrow channel between Sicily and mainland Italy, Rome decided that Carthage posed a clear and present danger to Roman interests and committed itself to act against them. It sent a small expeditionary force to help the Mamertines and eject Carthage from Messana. The consequent Roman attack on Carthaginian troops was the opening action of the First Punic War.[15]

This is not the place to provide a lengthy narrative of the First Punic War, so our discussion will be limited to a few key points.[16] Unlike in the later wars between Rome and Carthage, northwestern Africa was largely untroubled by the conflict. Much of the action took place on or in the waters around Sicily, with Carthage aiming to achieve victory through its impressive navy; however, Rome was able to develop its own fleet capable of challenging Carthaginian naval supremacy. Hoping to bring an end to the conflict, Rome sent an invasion force to North Africa in 256 BC, evidently thinking to weaken Carthaginian efforts by putting military pressure on their heartland.[17] A large fleet of 330 ships facilitated the invasion, carrying a force estimated in antiquity to number 140,000 men (although ancient manpower figures are notoriously unreliable).[18] Carthage readied 350 ships to counter the Roman force, preparing to intercept them along a route they would almost certainly have to use. The ensuing battle, at Cape Ecnomus (256 BC), was said to have been the largest naval battle of antiquity, if not history more generally, and ended in a comprehensive defeat for Carthage, who lost at least 94 ships (30 sunk, 64 captured).[19] Rome proceeded to rampage through Carthaginian territory, which also found itself under attack from Numidia; Carthage attempted to negotiate a peace, but found Roman terms too harsh. But Rome proved unable to capitalize on its naval victory through its land operations, particularly once Carthage recruited a Spartan mercenary named Xanthippus to train and command the troops. He inflicted a heavy defeat on the Roman army in pitched battle, leading to the evacuation of Roman survivors. The fleet was hit by a storm off the south coast of Sicily, resulting in heavy casualties and the loss of all but 80 ships, in what was considered one of the worst maritime disasters of antiquity.[20] Rome attempted another invasion of Carthage in 253 BC, but it is not clear that it achieved much, and the fleet was once again hit by a storm during its return to Italy, with the loss of more than 150 ships.[21]

The war dragged on for another decade, primarily along the coast of Sicily, with neither side able to gain a decisive advantage.[22] It finally ended in 241 BC when the Carthaginians negotiated peace after a heavy defeat at sea in the Battle of the Aegates Islands. As part of the settlement Sicily was ceded to Rome and Carthage agreed to pay significant monetary reparations. Although the Carthaginian losses were significant, the First Punic War did little to damage its interests in northwest Africa, and the region as a whole was minimally impacted. The indigenous population may have been largely unaffected throughout this war, and are unlikely to have suffered from the consequences of the peace either – this had been a Carthaginian affair, not an African one. But when hostilities between the two powers broke out again a few decades later the impact on northwestern Africa would be very different.

The Second Punic War

The First Punic War ended in a Roman victory, but Carthage was far from comprehensively defeated and remained a significant rival to Rome in the Mediterranean. A second conflict between the two was thus as inevitable as the first had been, and the Second Punic War broke out in 218 BC. Although not as lengthy as the first war, lasting for a mere 17 years until peace was again brokered in 201 BC, it was much larger in scale, resulting in significant losses on both sides.

During the interim peace, both sides had made preparations for a renewal of hostilities. Carthage had attempted to reinforce its economic power in the Mediterranean, most notably by significantly expanding its territorial control in southeastern Iberia. The new areas were rich in resources and manpower and would provide a solid economic foundation for a new assault against Rome. Meanwhile, Rome focused on expanding its possessions still further, particularly into the areas just north of Italy across the river Po, a continuation of its earlier power-building strategy.[23] There had been a spate of skirmishing between the Romans and the Gallic peoples who lived in the region up until *c.*238 BC – then they had actually provided protection to Roman territory in 230 BC when Transalpine Gauls had raided across the Alps into Italy.

Most notably, Roman troops had started to advance over the Po into the northern Italian regions south of the Alps, the area which would later become the province of Cisalpine Gaul, in an attempt to subjugate the Gallic peoples of the region who posed a security risk. In 225 BC the Boii and Insubres, both local tribes, paid Gaesatae mercenaries from the other side of the Alps to ally with them against Rome.[24] They subsequently invaded and overran Etruria and began to march on Rome. Catching the invading force in battle at Telamon (Tuscany) the Romans won a resounding victory, inflicting heavy casualties on the Gauls and ending what had been one of the major incursions into Italy at that time.[25] Over the next few years the Roman army undertook multiple military expeditions into Cisalpine Gaul and by 222 BC most of the tribes had surrendered. It was prudent for Rome to secure northern Italy before any hostilities with Carthage broke out again, not expecting that the Alpine region would be involved in the conflict; when Hannibal crossed the Alps in 218 BC, many of the peoples in this region supported him over Rome.

Although a renewal of war between Carthage and Rome was only a matter of time, some attempts were seemingly made to delay it to a more opportune moment. In 226 BC, Carthage signed a treaty with Rome stating that it would not expand its holdings in Spain north of the Ebro river; this came at a time when Rome was under pressure in northern Italy and willing to make a deal to avoid fighting on multiple fronts. For the most part, the Carthaginians did not violate this agreement, but either failed to note or did not care that a city south of the river, Saguntum, had an independent treaty with Rome which guaranteed their protection against Carthaginian aggression irrespective of the 226 agreement. In 219 BC, Carthage laid siege to Saguntum and after eight months was able to capture and sack it. Rome sent an embassy to Carthage to demand restitution for the siege, but found its demands rejected. This incident became the outward justification for war – the Romans liked to claim that they never went to war without a *casus belli* ('cause for war') – but it is likely that Rome was looking for a fight, at a moment which was most to their own advantage.[26] By attacking Saguntum, Carthage had provided them with just such an excuse, and may have been equally eager for conflict. Carthaginian command of the conflict was dominated, especially in the early stages, by the Barcid family, and in particular by the brothers Hannibal, Hasdrubal, and Mago Barca. They were sons of Hamilcar Barca, a Carthaginian commander in the First Punic War, whose hatred for Rome was so great he was said to have made Hannibal swear an oath to the gods to become an enemy of Rome, when he was just nine years old.[27]

Rome declared war on Carthage for the second time in the spring of 218 BC. What followed was an intensive struggle for supremacy, which led to mass destruction, suffering, and the death of hundreds of thousands of soldiers and civilians on both sides. Several of the worst military defeats Rome ever experienced took place in this conflict, most notably at Cannae (216 BC). The events of the Second Punic War are too extensive to go into in detail in this work.[28] However, this is the period in which the blueprint of Roman northwest Africa was first drawn, and a degree of narrative is necessary in order to contextualize both how Rome gained its first territory here and the rise of the kingdom of Numidia. Northwest Africa was far more directly impacted in this conflict than it had been by the First Punic War. While the early stages of the war were fought in mainland Europe, particularly Italy and Spain, the conflict would later spread to Carthaginian territory in Africa, where Roman field operations would prove far more effective than they had done previously. Troops raised in northwestern Africa were involved in the European operations from the start, including numerous cavalry drawn from a range of Numidian tribes – and some elephants.[29] Many of these troops gathered with Hannibal at Carthago Nova (modern Cartagena, Spain) in 218 BC, and were part of his army when it marched into Italy over the Alps a few months later. It took two weeks to cross the mountains, a gruelling journey which claimed many lives (including most of the elephants), but the surprise arrival in Italy was a strategic masterstroke. Rome had planned to divide her armies between Spain and Africa, hoping that a campaign in the Carthaginian heartlands would force them to recall their armies from abroad; on hearing that Hannibal had crossed the Alps, the plan was immediately abandoned as the troops were needed in Italy.[30] Not for the first or last time, Rome was thrown by an unexpected African deployment in the field.

The Second Punic War in Italy

The Carthaginian presence in Italy caused significant problems for Rome for many years.[31] Several severe and infamous defeats were inflicted on them, including in a battle at the river Ticinus, and an ambush at the Trebia (both late 218 BC), the latter proving a disastrous engagement for Rome in which 20–30,000 casualties were sustained.[32] This was quickly followed by another Carthaginian victory at Lake Trasimene (in spring 217), in which the Roman army was again ambushed with severe casualties. Many of the Roman allies captured in the battle were given amnesty and released, so they could spread the word at home of Carthaginian power and clemency, possibly inspiring defection from Rome.[33] The Romans responded by putting Quintus Fabius Maximus in charge of the war. He decided to avoid further pitched battles until Rome could replenish its manpower – the so-called 'Fabian strategy' – winning him the unflattering nickname of *Cunctator*, 'the Delayer'. While effective in some ways, the Fabian strategy was unpopular as it effectively gave Hannibal a free rein for destruction in Italy. In early 216 BC Fabius Maximus was replaced by Gaius Terentius Varro and Lucius Aemilius Paullus, who both felt a more offensive approach was needed. A few months later, Varro and Paullus led Rome to one of its most devastating military defeats of all time, near the town of Cannae on the banks of the river Aufidius. Rome fielded an army of up to 86,000 soldiers, of which 67,000 or more were said to have been either killed or captured.[34] African troops had played a key role in the earlier stages of the Second Punic War, especially the Numidian cavalry, who served as scouts in addition to fighting on the battlefield; they had proved particularly fearsome to the Romans when caught in open spaces, and in running down the Roman cavalry when their lines broke.[35] After Cannae, the Numidians were also used to attack various fortifications to which the defeated Romans had fled, further demonstrating their adaptability in the field. The war clearly demonstrated that Rome's cavalry was noticeably inferior to their African counterpart.

In the aftermath of Cannae, the Numidian commander Maharbal is said to have told Hannibal, 'You, Hannibal, know how to gain a victory; you do not know how to use it' when the Carthaginian general refused to march immediately on Rome.[36] The short delay in advancing was later said to have saved the city and allowed Rome to continue fighting the war and Hannibal was seemingly never able to gain such an advantage again. For the next eleven years, the war raged across southern Italy and Sicily in a situation of near-constant stalemate. Rome managed to keep replenishing its losses, even as its allies began defecting to Carthage. By continuous recruitment Rome was able to save itself from defeat and limit Hannibal's activities to certain areas, but was not able to risk taking Carthage on in a decisive pitched battle.

Numidia

To try to shift the focus of the war, the Romans began operations in Carthaginian-held territories in southwest Iberia, aiming to disrupt the supply of resources and manpower to Hannibal in Italy. They were able to record numerous victories over the Carthaginian troops there, winning the support of some new allies, and making significant progress. Their efforts in Spain were further assisted by the sudden defection of Syphax, ruler of the Masaesyli, to their side.[37] The Masaesyli were based in western Numidia, their territory probably extending from their capital, Cirta (modern Constantine, Algeria) to the area around modern Fez in Morocco.[38] In the early stages of the Second Punic War, the kingdom of the Masaesyli was more powerful than that of their neighbours to the east, the Massyli, who were staunch allies of Carthage. When war broke out Syphax, the indigenous chieftain or king of the Masaesyli, was evidently considered the most powerful of the Numidian rulers.[39] He was generally sympathetic to Rome, at least at the start of the conflict.

After Syphax had started independent military operations against Carthage *c.*214/213 BC, Rome sent him an embassy led by three centurions offering him an alliance in simple terms: if Syphax would continue to harass the Carthaginians in Africa, Rome would owe him a great debt of gratitude which it would repay after the war. This may have been the first such treaty made between Rome and Numidia, and marked the point at which the two powers started to build a direct relationship (albeit, at this stage, with only part of Numidia). Syphax began attacking the Carthaginians in Africa, but proved largely unsuccessful – likely because the best Numidian troops had already been recruited into Carthaginian service in Spain and Italy. He therefore asked Rome for help in training an effective field army with which he could campaign more effectively, to fulfill his part of the bargain, aware it would also provide him with better resources to defend his own kingdom. The Romans agreed and a centurion, the experienced Quintus Statorius, remained in Africa to train the Masaesylian army. Syphax noted that his army lacked discipline and organization, and were unsuited to infantry warfare, putting them at a severe disadvantage in the field against Carthage. Statorius set about imposing Roman military training on the Numidians, dividing them into cohort-esque units, teaching them to form and hold battle array, to obey commands on the battlefield, and even to create fieldworks. The result was an effective infantry force capable of taking on Carthage in pitched battle, although they were only to prove successful in doing so once. But Statorius' training had set the idea in the Roman mind that Numidian troops, cavalry or infantry, could be highly effective when properly trained and commanded. This would later influence their own recruitment of allied and auxiliary troops from the region – and indeed was something which Tacfarinas further demonstrated when he implemented Roman military training methods with his own men.

At this same time, Numidian representatives travelled to Iberia to try to convince their compatriots serving in Carthage's army to defect to Rome, which apparently did result in numerous desertions. This may have contributed to the Roman perception of Numidian soldiers as disloyal and prone to defection, though their actions had actually been of benefit to Rome in this instance. Carthage saw its armies in Italy and Iberia weakened by this turn of events, so even as they were finding it necessary to transfer some troops back to Africa to deal with Syphax's attacks there, their manpower resources had been noticeably depleted by the Numidian desertions. In an attempt to restore some military balance in northwest Africa while they redeployed troops, Carthage formed an alliance with the Massyli, the rulers of eastern Numidia. The Massyli were persuaded that it was in their interests to ally with Carthage against Syphax and to try to subjugate him and his growing power, before he was sent any additional Roman military resources.[40] The ruler of the Massyli, Gala (also referred to as Gaia) agreed, evidently mostly due to the urging of his 17-year-old son Masinissa, who also persuaded his father to put him in command of the war efforts.

Masinissa would go on to become an incredibly important figure in Numidian history, and is still commemorated today as one of the great rulers in North African history – to the degree that children in the modern region are still named after him. Based on references to his age in the historical record, he was born *c.*240–230 BC; the earlier date prompted by references to him being 89 in 150 BC, the later by his being recorded as aged 17 when Syphax allied with Rome *c.*213 BC. He certainly grew up amidst the growing tensions between Carthage and Rome. Assuming the younger date (as his youth is particularly focused on by the sources), he would have been aged about 12 when hostilities actually broke out. He was raised in Carthage, and treated as part of the aristocratic elite even though he was probably there as a hostage to ensure the good behaviour of his father[41] and was probably still there in the early stages of the war. He was clearly recognized by Carthage as an excellent prospect for the future and consequently had been betrothed to Sophonisba, the daughter of Hasdrubal (son of Gesco), a prominent Carthaginian commander. This apparently angered Syphax, who was keen to marry Sophonisba himself, and may have been one of the reasons that he entered into the alliance with Rome against Carthage. When Masinissa returned to Numidia he did so determined to support Carthaginian interests in the conflict, explaining his efforts to persuade his father to act against Syphax and Rome.

The Carthaginian command now aimed to destroy Syphax's army before it could either receive Roman reenforcements or link up with the Roman forces; plans for a joint Roman-Masaesylian attack on Carthage were already drawn up. A large combined Carthaginian-Massylian army marched against Syphax and inflicted a heavy defeat on him, a battle in which over 30,000 were said to have been killed.[42] Syphax and the remnants of his army fled to the Mauretanian coast, probably to an area around modern Tangiers, from where they intended to sail to Spain and link up with Roman forces there. But Masinissa and his army arrived before they could leave and inflicted a heavy defeat on them; though Syphax himself was left alive and was not deposed as ruler of the Massyli. Masinissa is credited by the Roman sources for this victory and it is noted positively that he had overseen the final stages at the coast without Carthaginian help. Masinissa then sailed to Spain himself to serve in the army of his (prospective) father-in-law Hasdrubal, commanding troops in multiple Carthaginian victories, including the double-engagement Battle of the Upper Baetis (211 BC). It is worth noting that at the time he was probably still not quite 20 years old.

Despite fierce Carthaginian resistance, Rome was able to make increasing headway in Iberia and captured the important strategic city of Carthago Nova in 209 BC. Over the following years, a series of defeats saw Carthaginian territorial possessions in Iberia severely reduced, culminating in a decisive Roman victory at Ilipa (in 206), one of the most significant Roman victories of the war to date. At this point, the focus of the war shifted to northwestern Africa – Rome was able to take the war to Carthage for the first time. Carthaginian power in the region had been further impacted by the death of Gala in 206 BC, as his sons Masinissa (who was still in Spain) and Oezalces disputed the succession. Syphax stepped into the consequent power-vacuum, annexing large parts of Masaesylian territory. In the interests of restoring their security, the Carthagians reassessed the political situation and decided that their interests now lay more in an alliance with Syphax rather than Masinissa, and looked for some way to make him defect from Rome. Without the knowledge of either Masinissa or Hasdrubal, both of whom were still in Spain, Syphax was promised marriage to Sophonisba[43] (as mentioned, his resentment over her betrothal to Masinissa was said to have been one of the reasons he allied with Rome in the first place). While realizing that the breaking of the betrothal would not be well-received by Masinissa, Carthage may have hoped that this alone would not be enough to break their alliance with the Massyli, given Masinissa's long-standing history with Carthage.

At about this time Masinissa agreed to become a Roman ally, possibly while he was still in Spain. His defection to Rome may have been prompted in part by the loss of Sophonisba – or the insult of it, at least. On a more practical level, it was probably also prompted by a growing realization that Carthage was likely to lose the war (it was already close to losing all its territory in Spain) and Masinissa wanted to be on the winning side. He met with Publius Scipio in person to settle the deal, one which would initiate a lifelong loyalty to Rome.[44] Perhaps sensing Masinissa's shift in loyalty, his commander Hasdrubal, son of Gesco, decided that the best thing would be to send him back to Africa and have him quietly executed soon after arrival.[45] Unfortunately for him, although Masinissa sailed for Africa as planned, he learned about the plot on his life during the journey and managed to escape after disembarking. His alliance with Carthage was now completely over, leaving him vulnerable in enemy territory with few men at his command. He proceeded to gather together a force of up to 20,000 hardy Numidian cavalrymen, described by one Roman historian as,

> a body of cavalry who were trained to hurl the javelin advancing and retreating and advancing again, either by day or by night; for their only method of fighting was flight and pursuit. The Numidians also know how to endure hunger. They often subsist on herbs in place of bread, and they drink nothing but water. Their horses never even taste grain; they feed on grass alone and drink but rarely.[46]

Masinissa's army launched raids against other tribes in the region. Both Syphax and the Carthaginians were concerned this army would be used against them, so launched a campaign against Masinissa in the hope of rapidly ending the threat. Unfortunately for them, Masinissa proved to be a highly effective commander and well able to withstand the offensive. He prioritized speed in the field, even going without a baggage-train of any kind, relying on his men being able to seize whatever they needed from the locality on a daily basis. His army did not have a fixed base, but took overnight refuge in whatever stronghold best suited their situation. The force was frequently split up in the field, reuniting at a pre-agreed position at an appointed time, allowing them to cover far more ground than a single force was able to. Masinissa employed a variety of irregular tactics against Carthage, focused on hit-and-run manoeuvres which made the most effective use of his very light-armed cavalry. Pitched battle was avoided in favour of constant harassing attacks on the Carthaginian army on the march, in which the Numidian cavalry would launch a volley of javelins and then retreat before they could be engaged in further fighting. His men were given a share of the raiding spoils, ensuring high levels of recruitment and retention – the material rewards were far better than the regular pay offered by any army. Masinissa's campaign against Carthage provided a blueprint for Tacfarinas in how to operate against a large Imperial army in this region, and there are many overlaps between the strategy and tactics of the two commanders. Notably, Masinissa was not criticized by any of the Roman sources for the way that he conducted the campaign against Carthage.

By 206 BC, Carthage had lost all its holdings in Spain, although it still had a large army in Italy under the command of Hannibal. In the last years of the war, the active front moved to northwest Africa, and Scipio arrived in the region with an army in 204. Syphax and Carthage attempted to negotiate a peace with Masinissa to avoid him joining forces with Scipio, with the full intention of betraying him once the Romans had been defeated.[47] Masinissa worked out their plan, but initially pretended to go along with it so he could gather intelligence about the strength and location of the Carthaginian forces – or perhaps he was initially tempted to betray Rome before changing his mind. Masinissa and the Carthaginians advanced towards Scipio, who was able to launch a counter-ambush after receiving intelligence in secret from Masinissa. Scipio and Masinissa then openly joined forces, raiding Carthaginian territory and freeing many Roman prisoners-of-war who had been enslaved after capture in Spain. Their army was formidable, and Carthage had only a limited ability to respond to it because much of their force was still in Italy, as were many of the best surviving commanders. In their absence, Rome inflicted defeats on Carthage in the Battle of the Great Plains, the Battle of Bagbrades, and the Battle of Cirta (all 203 BC). After the last Syphax was captured, and was abused for his earlier betrayal when he first entered the Roman camp as a prisoner– although his fallen state drew sympathy from some onlookers.[48]

Sophonisba was also captured, and Masinissa married her soon afterwards, evidently to save her from punishment by Rome, having believed her explanation that she had been forced into marriage with Syphax.[49] Nevertheless, Syphax warned him that her loyalties would never be turned from Carthage and that she would try to turn him against Rome, blaming her for his own defection several years earlier.[50] Fearing he might be right, Scipio ordered Masinissa to place Sophonisba into his custody, intending to send her to Rome to appear in the triumphal parade.[51] Unable to refuse, Masinissa accompanied a Roman detachment sent to collect her. However, he met her in secret and offered her an alternative to Roman captivity: a dose of poison. Willingly or not, she took it, and thus avoided falling into Roman hands.[52] A Roman fresco from Pompeii (in the Casa di Giuseppe II) showing an African woman about to consume a cup of liquid is thought to depict Sophonisba in the act of taking poison, although some suggest that was too obscure a historical reference for a Roman audience and that the figure is more likely Cleopatra of Egypt.[53] Masinissa arranged for her to have a royal funeral and found himself richly rewarded by Scipio as a consolation for his loss, the Roman general hoping to preserve their alliance.[54] Masinissa was permitted to take as much of Syphax's land as he could, leading him to hope that he would soon rule over a united Numidia.

Masinissa was also granted the highest military decorations a non-Roman ally could receive: the symbolic awards included a gold crown, a gold signet ring, an ivory chair, a purple robe, armour, and a horse with gold trappings. Syphax, meanwhile, was sent to Rome as a prisoner.[55] Within a year (203/202 BC) he had died of 'grief', while arguments still raged in the Senate about whether he should be forgiven or punished for his betrayal.

Following this series of events, Carthage opened peace talks with Rome in 202, while at the same time recalling Hannibal and the armies from Italy. The arrival of these troops in Africa led both sides to abandon the negotiations. Hannibal's troops brought much-needed reinforcement to Carthaginian forces, although his army was weak in cavalry; by contrast, Masinissa's cavalry meant that the Romans now had a large contingent of horsemen. Any hopes Carthage had for final victory in the war were dashed at the Battle of Zama (202 BC).[56] The Carthaginian losses were devastating, the majority of their 40–50,000 men either killed or captured. In the aftermath of the battle, they asked to reopen peace negotiations, which Scipio accepted rather than face the difficulties of capturing Carthage itself. Hannibal advised his Senate to accept whatever terms Rome offered, and the results were harsh.[57] All Carthaginian territories outside of Africa, and some of their domestic ones, were confiscated and given to Rome. Carthage was ordered to pay war reparations of 10,000 silver talents. Their military capabilities were also limited by the treaty, which prohibited them to train war elephants, to have more than 10 warships, to wage war outside Africa, or even inside Africa without Roman permission. Hostages from the Carthaginian elite were demanded and given to ensure that they adhered to the terms of the treaty. Scipio was rewarded for his actions in bringing the war to an end with a triumph in Rome, and the honorific nickname/agnomen 'Africanus'. Masinissa, meanwhile, would use the period following the conflict to build on the power he had gained during the conflict to make Numidia into a unified and powerful kingdom.

Masinissa and Numidia

Although the peace settlement had left Carthage with much of their domestic territory (if none of their non-African lands), their holdings after the Second Punic War suffered significantly at the hands of Roman allies, particularly Masinissa of Numidia. He had proved to be a competent military commander during the war and a reliable Roman ally who had worked closely with them during the African campaigns. Over the coming decades, he would use his favourable position to transform Numidia into one of the powers of ancient Africa, if not the Mediterranean more widely.[58] His territory extended over a far larger area than any previous Numidian ruler, after having been invited by Scipio to take as much Masaesylian territory as he could following the capture of Syphax. Masinissa became the king of both the Massyli and the Masaesyli, uniting eastern and western Numidia as a single kingdom for the first time. Rome did not take any direct territorial holdings in northwest Africa after their victory in the Second Punic War, no doubt because they felt that Masinissa could oversee security in the region and their alliance meant he could be trusted – or forced – to promote Roman interests where necessary. Numidians served in increasing numbers in the Roman army, particularly as light-armed cavalry, their abilities becoming famous throughout the ancient world (see Chapter 4). It was an ideal alliance on both sides.

Numidia blossomed under Masinissa's rule. Roman writers credited him with the introduction of agriculture and urbanism to the region – wrongly, as the archaeology demonstrates, but it shows the esteem in which he was held in by Rome. The Roman narrative about Masinissa is suggestive of a respected foreign ally who was more enlightened than most of his compatriots, but whose influence was such that he was able to 'develop' them. In his rule, Masinissa adopted the style of Hellenistic kingship (Rome being a Republic and not easy to pay tribute to through any style of monarchy). He may also have been inspired by the Hellenistic dynasty of the Ptolemies, who had ruled in Egypt for over a century following the death of Alexander the Great. Masinissa visually cultivated a Hellenistic image through his coinage, and culturally through interactions with the Greek world, such as his son competing in the Panathenaic games in Athens. He was evidently accepted at least partially into the fraternity of Hellenistic kings, and statues were dedicated to him on the island of Delos by Athens, Bithynia, and Rhodes, probably in recognition of the grain he supplied to the Greek world.

Greek architecture also began to influence monumental buildings in Numidia, most notably in the case of the Medracen (or Madghacen) in Batna province (Algeria), a large circular tomb which measures 18.5m tall and 59m in diameter. The oldest such tomb in the Maghreb, it was circled by 60 Doric columns and likely built either for Masinissa, or his father, Gala. Its form demonstrates that the Numidians were among the earliest in Africa to adopt aspects of Hellenistic architecture. Not all funerary architecture became Greek-style, however. Elsewhere, tower tombs proliferated by the later third century BC – three-storey structures topped with a pyramid. A tomb like this had been dedicated to Syphax at Sigam Micipsa at the Souma a el Kroub, and the type likely spread in the aftermath.[59] The resources needed to build such structures demonstrate that Numidia was fairly far along the process of state formation even before Masinissa's reign.[60]

As an ally of Rome, Masinissa was able to push the boundaries in the ongoing development and consolidation of his kingdom. Many of his policies were to Carthage's detriment. Numidian forces made repeated incursions into Carthaginian territory, meeting minimal opposition because the peace treaty with Rome had limited Carthage's military capabilities and forbidden them to campaign in Africa without Roman permission. Their requests to defend themselves against the attacks were consistently either denied or not acted on. On one occasion, pleading their case to the Senate in Rome, Carthaginian envoys stated that 'Masinissa would fix no limits [on expansion] other than what his greed and ambition might determine', and suggested that they would rather live under Roman rule than Numidian.[61] Gulussa, one of Masinissa's sons, was in Rome at the time, and when questioned about the Numidian attacks, replied that he could not answer on his father's behalf. The Senate ostensibly agreed with Carthage that they should not lose land in peacetime, but did nothing to help. On another occasion, Gulussa simply replied that the Carthaginians were lying.[62] Ignored by Rome, the campaigns significantly increased the size of the Numidian kingdom to the point where Roman authorities may just have started to worry that their victory in the Second Punic War had done little to change the political situation in the region beyond swapping Carthage for Numidia.

The Road to the Third Punic War

With the Second Punic War over and Masinissa securing northwest Africa, Rome was able to turn its political and military attention to expanding into other areas of the Mediterranean world. For nearly five decades after the Second Punic War the situation in Africa was sidelined, as Rome instead engaged in a number of campaigns of conquest predominantly in the Greek world, including the Aetolian War (192–188 BC), the First Celtiberian War (181–179 BC), and the Third Macedonian War (171–168 BC). Roman troops also had to suppress a major rebellion in Lusitania (modern Portugal, 155–139 BC) led by Viriathus, a member of the local elite warrior class who has been compared to Tacfarinas in some modern scholarship, not least as both were categorized as bandits by Rome rather than legitimate rebel leaders.[63] Although these campaigns took Roman attention away from Africa, they had not forgotten Carthage, merely postponed a further conflict while the peace treaty held and there were more pressing concerns elsewhere.

By the mid-second century BC, Carthage was growing tired of the constant attacks from Masinissa and the damage they caused – for almost 50 years Masinissa had picked away at Carthage while Rome constantly denied them permission to defend themselves. Most of the other terms of the peace treaty had been spent by this point, including the payment of 10,000 silver talents of war reparations, and Carthage may have felt ready to start getting back on its feet. In 151 BC the Carthaginians resolved to act against Masinissa with or without Roman permission. Perhaps they hoped that Rome would overlook the breaking of treaty terms in what was basically only a domestic dispute, or that Masinissa – aged nearly 90 by this point – would prove an easier enemy than he had in the past. Whatever the thinking, Carthage raised an army to launch a counter-attack against Numidia. Unfortunately for them, the campaign was a complete disaster and their forces suffered a heavy defeat at the Battle of Oroscopa (late 151 BC). Despite surrendering, many of the survivors were executed anyway. Carthage had gambled against Numidia and lost, a sign of how much the fortunes of each had changed since the early days of the Second Punic War. Numidia did not ask Rome for any help in dealing with the Carthaginian attack. Masinissa may have hoped to use it as an excuse to add yet more Carthaginian territory to his kingdom, a prospect which would not have pleased the Romans, who may already have been less than happy about the large kingdom Masinissa had slowly and quietly constructed. Were he to conquer all of Carthage, Numidia would extend from modern Morocco to Libya, a daunting prospect even for Rome.

Even though the Carthaginian army had been comprehensively defeated, the act of raising it had broken their treaty with Rome, so there would be repercussions.[64] The war between Carthage and Numidia was taken as a *casus belli* for a renewal of hostilities by Rome. There was no need for this; there was no threat to Rome and little sign that Carthage had anywhere near the resources to become a real rival for power in the Mediterranean again. Nevertheless, Rome used the excuse for a new war with Carthage, exactly why remains unclear.[65] Masinissa had not asked for any help – indeed, he may have resented it, as it curbed any opportunity to conquer the Carthaginian territory in its entirety and add it to his kingdom. It may have been that an ideological Roman hatred of Carthage, one which would ultimately require its destruction, had resurfaced. There had long been calls in Rome that Carthage must be destroyed, particularly by the censor Cato the Elder. The infamous *Carthago delenda est* ('Carthage must be destroyed') is attributed to him.[66] Although it was not yet a direct threat, it was beginning to prosper once more in trade, particularly having paid off the war reparations, perhaps fuelling concerns in Rome that it was only a matter of time before it became a military rival again.[67] Carthage's recent failures fighting Numidia, however, suggest that this was far from a pressing concern. Perhaps, then, it was not Carthage itself that was seen as the threat, but the risk it posed to the destabilization of Roman interests in northwestern Africa, through its refusal to submit to Roman authority and the challenge it posed to Numidia; in this case, its destruction would be the only real permanent solution.[68] There may have been another reason, however, which would not just explain why Rome went to war with Carthage again, but why it did so in 150/49 BC, when it was already fighting numerous wars elsewhere. The impetus may have come from northwest Africa – not Carthage, but Numidia.

By 150 BC, Masinissa was approaching 90 years old and his reign would soon be over, the throne open in what had become a large and powerful kingdom. With regime change looming, Rome may have decided that it was in its interest to establish a direct territorial presence in the region, in case the next king proved not to be such a reliable ally. Masinissa had slowly and relatively quietly constructed a large Numidian kingdom, to the degree that Rome may already have been wondering if their alliance had become more of a liability than an asset. They were doubtless not keen to hand such a powerful state over to an unknown heir. It was not clear who the next king would be as there was no single obvious heir to Masinissa, making it possible that civil war would break out.[69] Not only might the winner not be as friendly to Rome as his predecessor, but there was a risk that they could ally with a newly-resurgent Carthage – a turn of events which would present a serious challenge. Rome's increasing reliance on Numidia for cavalry made it an even more pressing issue. Although Rome becoming involved in the conflict might have annoyed Masinissa, there were many reasons for them to do so – and he would likely not be around to object for much longer.

The Third Punic War

The Third Punic War officially started in 149 BC. This time, the conflict would play out entirely in northwestern Africa instead of on Roman territory and was much shorter than either of its two predecessors, lasting just under three years. Before open hostilities even began, some of the Carthaginian allies decided their prospects were brighter with Rome and defected, most notably the wealthy harbour city of Utica, which allied with Rome in 150 BC. The tide was also turning for the Romans in northwest Africa – within five years they would have a direct territorial presence in the region.

A Roman army landed at Utica in 149 BC, under the command of both the consuls for the year. During the early stages of hostilities Carthage attempted to appease Rome, putting themselves 'in the faith of Rome' (*dedere se in fidem*).[70] This was a state of absolute surrender, putting their entire territory and everything in it into the trust of Rome.[71] The Carthaginians agreed (unhappily) to a number of conditions, including the surrender of all their weaponry, and the burning of all their warships.[72] But Rome evidently took it a step too far when they demanded that the people of Carthage abandon the city so that it could be destroyed. Faced with this prospect the Carthaginians abandoned the negotiations and prepared for the inevitable attack on their city. They raised an army from citizen volunteers and slaves freed for the purpose, which although much smaller than the Roman force still numbered around 20,000 soldiers. The main military target for the Romans was Carthage itself – in fact, their attempt to capture the city was the only major military operation of the entire conflict.

After unsuccessfully attempting to scale the city walls, the Romans besieged Carthage.[73] A large number of Numidian cavalry took part, commanded by Gulussa, who had also been involved in counterinsurgency operations and raids earlier in the conflict.[74] Several attacks on the city failed and the Romans suffered heavily with disease in their first camp; after moving to shake off the pestilence, the new camp was unfortunately found to be much more vulnerable to attack. Assaults on the main Carthaginian army at its base at Nepheris, a short distance from Carthage, proved unsuccessful, and the war dragged into 148 BC with little conclusive action. The second year saw the continuation of the siege and Roman attacks on other Carthaginian cities nearby, mostly unsuccessful. Masinissa of Numidia died in this year, still a Roman ally, though no doubt annoyed at the turn of events in the region. There was greater progress for Rome in 147, when sole command of military operations against Carthage was given to Scipio Aemilianus, who had distinguished himself during the earlier stages of the war; he also happened to be the grandson of Scipio Africanus. He oversaw the construction of extensive new earthworks around Carthage, including a brick structure which stood as high as the city walls, and succeeded in destroying a large part of the Carthaginian army at their winter camp at Nepheris. Apart from military strategies, he also called on the gods of Carthage to abandon the city and settle in Rome instead, where they would be much honoured – a process known as *evocatio*.[75]

Later that year, many Carthaginian cities which had previously resisted Rome surrendered, marking the beginning of the end of the war. Scipio Aemilianus remained in command into 146 BC. That spring he launched a massive assault on Carthage, finally breaching its walls and allowing the Romans into the city. They took their time, spending six days moving through it, killing any inhabitants they came across and setting fire to the buildings once they had passed;[76] and eventually the commander of the city surrendered. Some prisoners were allowed to live, but 900 Romans who had defected to Carthage are reported to have burned themselves to death in one of the city temples and the wife of the Carthaginian commander walked, with their children, into the fire to die, disgusted by her husband's surrender.[77] The city was razed to the ground, with men sent out to demolish those buildings not already levelled by fire, and the land itself was dedicated to the gods of the underworld, with a curse upon it for anyone who ever tried to settle there again.[78] There is no contemporary evidence for later claims that the fields were sown with salt.

With victory in the Third Punic War, Rome had finally defeated a major rival for power in the Mediterranean. In the aftermath of the conflict, it would go on to establish a province from the territories which Carthage had once ruled over, the first territory it would directly hold in Africa. From this point, northwest Africa became an integrated part of the Roman world and the people of the region had to live side-by-side with Rome rather than in a distant alliance, with all the consequences that would bring. Over the next 150 years, the region would adopt elements of Roman culture, receive numerous Roman settlers and colonies, and become a battleground for both internal conflicts and the civil wars of Rome itself. The Punic Wars may have been over, but in many ways, the battle for Africa had only just begun.

Chapter 2

Rome in Northwest Africa: *The First Province to the End of the Republic (146 BC–30 BC)*

Following the end of the Third Punic War, Rome had to decide what to do with the territory Carthage had previously controlled. At some point – likely in the immediate aftermath of the war, but possibly decades later – a Roman province was established, incorporating all the territory previously claimed by Carthage (at least that which had not already been lost to Masinissa). The existence of the province would permanently change the relationship between Rome and the peoples of northwestern Africa, whether local rulers or the ordinary population. But provincialization was only the first of many steps in the Romans' conquest of this part of Africa. It would be several centuries before their control was fully extended throughout the region, only really reaching its height during the reign of Hadrian in the early second century AD.

Although this slow progress might suggest that Africa was a difficult province to manage, it was not particularly unusual in Roman Imperialist expansion, particularly in areas of more limited indigenous urbanism and social development. In such places, Rome would attempt to manage resistance by only advancing a short distance into the area under conquest, heavily garrisoning it with military installations at key strategic points, overcoming any opposition, and then advancing a little further, and so on. This approach was used in provinces like Spain, where the conquest took almost two centuries to encompass the entire area, and in Britain, where they took more than forty years to reach Scotland and never succeeded in submitting some regions to Roman control.

The period between the end of the Third Punic War and the end of the Republican period was one in which Africa as a whole was transformed from being a marginal enemy on the southern edge of the Roman world to becoming an integral part of the Mediterranean. It was not a time without conflict, some of it internal (most notably the Jugurthine War 112–106 BC) and some external, as parts of several Roman civil wars were fought there, including the Sullan Civil War (83–81 BC), the Caesarian Civil War (49–46 BC), the Liberators Civil War (43–42 BC), and the War of Actium/the Final Republican War (32–30 BC). Throughout, Numidia played a key role in much of the political upheaval. A reliable alliance with Masinissa, which had kept stability in the region, developed into a much more volatile situation under his heirs.

The Province of Africa

The defeat of Carthage in 146 BC created a power vacuum in northwest Africa. The potential volatility of the situation was only exacerbated by the death of Masinissa of Numidia during the Third Punic War, and the ensuing succession. At some point Rome decided to take direct control of the former Carthaginian territories and make them into a Roman province, initially known just as 'Africa'. Doing so removed any debate about which extant African kingdom would take control of them instead and avoided any of them becoming an overpowerful state. The province was probably established in the immediate aftermath of the Third Punic War, but it may have happened a few decades later, following the Jugurthine War.[1] It encompassed most of modern Tunisia, and also incorporated territories now part of northeast Algeria and western Libya, establishing a firm control over the central section of the North African coastline. The acquisition of Carthaginian territories gave Rome access to the rich agricultural lands which lay within and immediate efforts were made to exploit them – the region would become a major supplier of grain to Rome. For the early period of the occupation the province of Africa was administered from the city of Utica, which lay on the northern coast of modern Tunisia near the outflow of the Medjerda River, *c.*40km (25 miles) from Carthage. This decision was partly made to reward Utica for its defection to Rome in 150 BC, but was also a recognition of its excellent location and harbour facilities. As it had been an ally before the war began, it had suffered no adverse effects. The impact of direct Roman administration appears to have been limited in the early decades of the province, with high levels of continuity from the Carthaginian period.

There does not appear to have been any great strategic aim behind Rome's creation of a province in northwestern Africa. The primary motivation may simply have been to ensure that no one could take advantage of the power vacuum created by the destruction of Carthage and the death of Masinissa – including the next Numidian king. With Masinissa gone, Rome no longer had a strong and reliable ally in the region and the issue of succession in the kingdom became slightly complicated. Even with a direct Roman presence (if it was established in 146 BC), the death of the king did destabilize the political balance of northwestern Africa. Throughout the rest of the second century BC Rome faced significant challenges from the kingdom, escalating at one point into a direct conflict, the Jugurthine War; it also played a significant part in many of the Roman civil wars of the first century BC. For better or worse, Rome was now a direct presence in northwestern Africa.

Roman Attitudes towards Africa and Africans

Despite Pliny noting the existence of over 500 known tribes in northwest Africa, Roman knowledge of the different peoples who lived in the region was fairly limited. Little enquiry seems to have been made to actually understand the identification and social structures of indigenous population groups and generic labels were employed to indicate with which overall group any particular person or people should be associated. The 'Libyans' tended to indicate the coastal population (particularly those who had lived under Carthaginian rule), while 'Numidians' and 'Mauri' (Moors) were terms applied to the (semi-)nomadic groups living further west. Those to the south were often described as simply 'Gaetulians', a term applied both to a specific group of people(s) and, more generally, to those living to the south of the coastal province and kingdoms. The Musulamii, for instance, were an independent tribe but were also identified as being Gaetulians. Given that many Roman readers of these ancient works would likely never have heard of many of these African peoples before, the use of generic ethnic umbrella terms allowed them to be broadly categorized both in terms of their perceived lifestyle, and – more importantly – Rome's relationship with them. If a people were identified as Libyan (whether they actually were or not) the reader would know to interpret them as a semi-civilized, partially-urbanized coastal population. 'Numidian' and 'Gaetulian' would similarly indicate how to treat other indigenous groups, again irrespective of whether they would have identified themselves in that way or not. There were evidently layers of political and ethnic identity – in the same way that someone from modern Munich could be simultaneously identified as a Münchner, Bavarian, German, and European – that impacted how Rome interacted and received the peoples of the region. A lot of the indigenous groups in northwestern Africa (and the wider empire) are defined by their physical distance from Rome, their position on the periphery of the Roman world. Due to the fact that most scholarship is based on the ancient written sources and thus the Roman perspective, that sense of marginalization is often carried into modern scholarship, without our realizing that of course all these peoples lived at the centre of their own world – and that indeed, to them the Romans were just a presence on the edges of that world, especially before the Imperial period.

Rome often had fairly negative attitudes towards the peoples who lived outside the territorial borders of the Empire. The sources employ a range of generic, often dehumanizing stereotypes to describe those living beyond their frontiers, demonstrating a significant level of cultural and ethnic prejudice. Typically, the further a people lived from Roman territory, the more negative the portrayal, a process which one modern historian has termed 'progressive barbarization'.[2] Those who lived within or on the margins of Roman territory would be represented relatively positively in the sources, with the portrait gradually becoming more critical the further away people were, eventually reaching the point where they were no longer recognized as fully human. This form of stereotyping particularly came into play with peoples who lived in and beyond the provinces on the very margins of the Roman world, particularly places like Britain and Africa. Such constructs were in many ways necessary to underpin Imperialist attitudes, and the 'othering' it facilitated allowed Rome to wage aggressive wars more effectively against populations already judged to be not quite as human as the Romans.[3]

The indigenous population of northwestern Africa was no exception. The process of progressive barbarization can be very clearly seen throughout Roman writing about the region. Those living in the coastal regions were accepted as at least semi-civilized, inhabiting towns, with a lifestyle superficially similar to that of the Romans themselves. Moving towards the African interior, these people gave way to pastoralists who lived in scattered hut and tent-based settlements rather than towns, and further on to lawless, warmongering, sexually-promiscuous nomads who did not even partially live in settlements; beyond that lay peoples portrayed as living almost like animals, naked, speaking in batlike languages and dwelling in caves or just the open air.[4] Differences in diet were often highlighted, such as the fact that the Numidians were said to live mainly on milk and game, and cooked without using salt, because they believed (so the Romans thought) that food and drink should just be treated as fuel rather than an indulgent luxury.[5] Although obviously inaccurate, the Roman descriptions of the peoples of northwestern Africa provide an insight into the ethnic prejudices which they brought to their interactions with them in the region.

It was the peoples who still incorporated a level of nomadism into their lifestyle who drew the most negative judgement from Rome. A generalized sense of fear and disgust runs through the accounts of nomadic populations, as describing something that was completely contrary to the Roman character – although, as discussed in the previous chapter, its prevalence even by the second century BC was completely exaggerated by underinformed Roman sources.[6] The Roman historian Sallust described nomads as,

> rude and uncivilized tribes, who subsisted on the flesh of wild animals, or, like cattle, on the herbage of the soil. They were controlled neither by customs, laws, nor the authority of any ruler; they wandered about, without fixed habitations, and slept in the abodes to which night drove them.[7]

The Roman perception of parts of the North African population being largely nomadic – and consequently, barbaric – were echoed by Strabo in the late first century BC/early first century AD. He noted that what settlements there were tended to be small and scattered, and that wild animals kept the population away from some areas which could otherwise have been settled.[8]

Nomadic peoples posed a particular problem to Roman sensibilities, representing a lifestyle completely outside their sphere of understanding and one which was difficult to control by conventional means; this would become a particular problem in the early Imperial period. Probably few among the indigenous population would have spoken any Latin, adding to their negative cultural baggage; in the mid-first century BC it was remarked as notable that a member of the Numidian royalty spoke Latin, suggesting that it was not part of an elite curriculum even after the Punic Wars.[9] In many ways, the presentation of some northwestern African peoples suggests that they were seen as an existential threat, a symbolic representation of the struggle between Rome and the barbarian 'other', which was always lurking on the margins waiting for its chance.[10]

In fact, negative Roman stereotypes extended to almost everyone whose ethnic origins lay in northwestern Africa. Africans were felt to be particularly prone to duplicity and a common phrase, *punica fides* – literally 'Carthaginian loyalty' – came to denote the treachery and disloyalty Rome associated with Carthaginians, and consequently Africans more widely.[11] Carthage thus became a widely-used shorthand for faithlessness in Rome, reinforced through allusions in wider culture and present even in works which ostensibly tried to present a positive view of a Carthaginian figure, as in the portrayal of Queen Dido in the *Aeneid*.[12] Even Numidia did not have a particularly glowing reputation in Roman eyes. One writer suggested that the Numidians had a propensity to 'grow disgusted with what pleased them' and observed 'how lightly they always break their faith to gods and men alike', suggesting they were seen as useful but not particularly reliable allies.[13] Another noted with evident disapproval that Numidian soldiers did not find any shame in abandoning a defeated commander, rather than fighting on in a potentially lost cause.[14] That said, Numidians were judged more than capable of service in the Roman *auxilia*, which came to rely on the area particularly for the supply of light-armed cavalry troops.

Numidia after Masinissa

The death of Masinissa during the Third Punic War threatened to destabilize the political situation not just in Numidia, but the region more widely. Masinissa had ruled for over half a century and the kingdom had flourished, making it a potential threat should power fall into the wrong hands. The situation may have been one of the factors that prompted Rome to establish its first province in Africa, and the coming decades would confirm that the security and friendship of the kingdom could not be taken for granted.

After Masinissa's death, the kingdom passed to his sons Micipsa, Gulussa, and Mastanabal, each taking a share; Scipio Aemilianus was to have charge over which of them would be assigned what part of the kingdom.[15] Their inheritance was not necessarily a major problem for Rome, at that time in a friendly relationship with all three heirs, Micipsa and Gulussa in particular. Gulussa had acted as Numidia's representative to the Senate on numerous occasions, answering questions about his father's attacks on Carthaginian land, and had campaigned alongside Scipio Aemilianus during the Third Punic War as a commander of the Numidian cavalry. Micipsa and Mastanabal were loyal to Rome, but had not been as supportive as they might have been during the war, and were apparently 'always promising arms and money to the Romans, but always delaying and waiting to see what would happen',[16] as though hedging their bets in case Carthage should somehow triumph – or simply avoiding expending resources they wished to keep for themselves. Still, all three were men that Rome could work with in the future. The only potential problem came from the fact that the kingdom was to be divided in three – albeit in a manner decided by Rome – which could have led to civil war within the kingdom. But offsetting that was the prospect that a Numidia divided three ways would be less of a threat than a kingdom united under one single, strong leader. Either way, it was not to be an issue for too long, as both Gulussa and Mastanbal had died of illness by *c.*140 BC, leaving Micipsa as the sole ruler in Numidia.[17]

In general Rome found Micipsa an acceptable and reliable ally and there were no problems during his reign. The Hellenistic nature of Numidia continued to be promoted and Greek colonists were invited to come and live in cities like Cirta, the capital.[18] Micipsa also proved better at following through with the troops promised to Rome, sending war elephants to Lusitania in 142 BC to help fight Viriathus, and both troops and elephants to Spain in 134 BC to aid in the siege of Numantia.[19] In fact, like his father, Micipsa proved a good friend to Rome and continued to maintain stability in the region until his death in 118 BC, at an advanced age and possibly suffering from dementia or another age-related mental incapacity.[20] The relationship between Numidia and Rome would change dramatically under his heirs.

Micipsa also divided his kingdom between three heirs – his biological sons, Hiempsal and Adherbal, and his nephew Jugurtha, the illegitimate son of his brother Mastanbal.[21] Jugurtha had been raised as part of the royal household and initially seemed to be a credit to them. He was strong, handsome, and intelligent, trained from his earliest years in traditional Numidian warfare (particularly javelin throwing). He seems to have been more popular with the people than either of his cousins, to the degree that Micipsa grew concerned about the safety of his sons. Jugurtha was consequently sent away from Numidia *c.*134 BC, travelling to Spain with a cavalry unit to assist Scipio Aemilianus in the Numantine War (144–133 BC). If Micipsa hoped to reduce Jugurtha's power by sending him to Spain the plan backfired significantly, as the posting allowed the young man to form a friendship with Scipio Aemilianus and to meet a number of prominent Romans, including Gaius Marius.[22] He also learned to speak Latin during the siege of Numantia (134–133), which may have ingratiated him to the Roman authorities when the question of his potential kingship later arose.[23]

Jugurtha distinguished himself in the war, with Scipio Aemilianus noting both his courage and wisdom, and writing to Micipsa that in him they had 'a hero worthy of yourself and of his grandfather Masinissa'.[24] Some prominent Roman political figures began to hope that when Micipsa died, Jugurtha would become the sole king of Numidia. In recognition of his growing status, it is believed Jugurtha was married to a daughter of Bocchus I, the king of Mauretania (modern Morocco) and one of Numidia's most powerful neighbours; this was an excellent marriage for the illegitimate son of a dead king, no matter how accomplished he was.[25]

Micipsa did later recognize how ineffective his actions had been in reducing Jugurtha's popularity with both the Numidian people and Rome. On his deathbed he urged the three heirs to respect his wishes to divide the kingdom between them after his death, but inevitably they began to argue almost as soon as the funeral was over. Jugurtha suggested that the late king's acts and decrees made in the last five years be annulled, arguing that his intellect had been compromised in that period. Hiempsal replied that this was an excellent idea, as Jugurtha had only been named a co-heir three years ago, leading Jugurtha to abandon the proposal. Shortly afterwards, Jugurtha had Hiempsal assassinated.[26] Despite Jugurtha's popularity, Numidian public opinion now largely sympathised with Adherbal, the surviving son of Micipsa – although Jugurtha drew more support from the kingdom's military. With them he gathered an army which defeated that of Adherbal in battle; Adherbal fled to the Roman province for protection and then headed to Rome to try to win their support against his rival. Envoys were also sent to Rome by Jugurtha, along with generous gifts to his friends in influential positions; the intention was obviously to win support through bribery rather than (or possibly as well as) because he was in the right.[27]

Rome was left in an awkward position by the dispute between the two surviving Numidian heirs. Both Jugurtha and Adherbal could legitimately call on Roman support: to help neither was to risk chaos in northwestern Africa, to help both would have been pointless, and to help one and not the other was to pick a side. Jugurtha was in control of the entire Numidian kingdom and had the support of the armed forces, while Adherbal had already fled to Rome. Trying to make the best of the situation, Rome decreed in 116 BC that the Numidian kingdom be divided in two, with the east (which bordered the Roman province) given to Adherbal, the west to Jugurtha – returning it more or less to the situation it had been in before Masinissa's unification. Rumours abounded that Jugurtha heavily bribed Roman officials to ensure he was allocated the better half of the kingdom, previously ruled by Syphax and the Masaesyli. The division won a short period of peace, but little more.

The Jugurthine War

The fragile peace between Jugurtha and Adherbal lasted until 113 BC, when Jugurtha launched a new attack on his cousin and co-ruler. Adherbal again appealed to Rome for support and Jugurtha was ordered to cease his attacks, a command which he ignored, launching a second wave. Rome did send envoys to try to stop the conflict, but they arrived too late to prevent Jugurtha trapping Adherbal in a siege at Cirta.[28] Jugurtha evidently did feel some concern about the consequences of defying Rome in this way, but his misgivings were easily overcome by his ambition. Despairing of real help from Rome, Adherbal surrendered to Jugurtha on the advice of others, who expected him to be treated with some mercy. He was promptly tortured to death, and the armed men who had defended Cirta on his behalf were executed, including some Italians and Roman citizens. The executions finally prompted Rome into more direct action, despite Jugurtha laying down bribes to try to stop it from being debated in the Senate until the initial shock and outrage had worn off. Slightly reluctantly, Rome declared war against Jugurtha in 111 BC.

Several African leaders very quickly declared their support for Rome in this conflict, which alarmed Jugurtha, especially when he discovered that Bocchus I in Mauretania – his own father-in-law – was among them. He lost his nerve and surrendered to Rome immediately. Under the agreement which followed, Jugurtha was allowed to remain as sole king of Numidia, in exchange for a small fine and the confiscation of his war elephants, most of which he was able to buy back anyway at cut-price. So generous were the terms of the peace in fact, that an enquiry was then launched in Rome, on the basis that Jugurtha must have bribed his way into such a settlement; quite fittingly, he then bribed two Roman tribunes to drop the investigation. In theory the matter could have been settled at this point, leaving Jugurtha as the friendly allied king of Numidia, as Micipsa and Masinissa had been before him, but in reality, the peace did not last. Jugurtha now became concerned about the kingship aspirations of his cousin Massiva, son of Gulussa. Massiva had sided against Jugurtha in the initial stages of the war and had fled to Rome after the murder of Adherbal.[29] He had been persuaded to ask the Senate to give him the throne of Numidia, apparently talked into it by one of the year's consuls, who was keen to go to war in Africa. Jugurtha, himself also present in Rome at the time, arranged for his cousin to be assassinated, an action for which he was initially put on trial – and denied all responsibility. Soon after, he was ordered to leave Italy and returned to Numidia, where he began to prepare for all-out war against Rome.

A Roman army was despatched to Africa in 110 BC to bring Jugurtha under control.[30] The war which followed was dominated by Jugurtha's highly effective use of irregular tactics and desert warfare. In the early stages the Romans tried to force Jugurtha into pitched battle, a situation he generally avoided. Towards the end of the campaigning season, unwilling to leave without at least one battle, the Romans were lured into a trap in the Sahara, probably partly facilitated by Jugurtha bribing some of the Roman officers. The Numidians attacked the field camp the Romans had constructed for the night, causing many of the soldiers to throw down their weapons and flee, seeking safety on a nearby hill. With the Romans trapped and surrounded, Jugurtha noted that he had them 'at the mercy of starvation or the sword', but offered to let the survivors go if they first passed 'under the yoke', a humiliating sign of defeat, and then left Numidia within ten days, which they did, returning to the Roman province.[31] When the news reached Rome, the Senate and people were horrified by the army's cowardice and demanded that the treaty be disregarded and hostilities renewed.

What followed was a conflict defined by a highly irregular nature; again, the engagements are too extensive to give more than an overview here.[32] It was not an easy war for Rome. It was the first time that they had fought Numidia itself (although they had faced Numidian troops against Carthage in the Punic Wars), and they had limited experience of how to operate against an enemy who could escape into the fringes of the Sahara when things were going badly. Jugurtha himself was a formidable enemy. Having learned Numidian-style warfare in his younger years, he had gone on to serve alongside the Roman army in Spain, giving him an insider view of how they manoeuvred in the field. He was able to shape his strategic and tactical approaches to take advantage of the weaknesses of the Roman troops, avoiding engaging in pitched battle whenever possible and instead relying on raiding, settlement attacks, and ambushes on the Roman marching column. The Romans were forced at times to adopt an irregular approach themselves: laying waste to the countryside and crops, burning towns, and killing civilians.[33] Jugurtha himself did much the same, also contaminating fodder and water supplies that his enemy would need in the field. The Roman troops were ordered to travel light, carrying far fewer provisions than they would usually on campaign, identifying speed and flexibility as vital factors in this conflict.

The war raged on for several years, with multiple episodes of Roman victory that were yet insufficient to actually end the conflict. Every time Jugurtha felt close to defeat he offered to negotiate with Rome, particularly if he feared he was about to fall into their hands, but every time he renewed the war before a peace could be negotiated. The Romans came to believe that there would only be an end when Jugurtha was either killed or captured, and intended to replace him with Gauda, another son of Mastanabal and Jugurtha's half-brother. Jugurtha effectively maintained the war by employing guerrilla tactics against Rome, using light-armed infantry and cavalry who could move swiftly across the terrain in a way the heavily-armed Romans struggled to do. He maintained high levels of manpower, facilitated by an evident popularity among the local peoples – at least, more so than Rome. He even managed to recruit some soldiers from the Gaetulians, who joined him despite apparently never having heard of Rome before and thus having no direct reason to fight them. Bocchus I of Mauretania, Jugurtha's father-in-law, was also persuaded to join his war effort by the promise of a third of the Numidian territory as a reward.

Frustrated at the lack of progress in Africa, in 107 BC the Senate put Gaius Marius in command of the war against Jugurtha; his military staff included Lucius Cornelius Sulla, at the very start of his public career. Marius had no interest in negotiation, and immediately set about trying to force Jugurtha to face him in pitched battle. The Roman army rampaged through Numidia anew, capturing and plundering settlements, including the capital, Cirta. Rome's tactics became increasingly brutal as the conflict progressed. At one town, Capsa, Marius executed all adult survivors simply to stop them giving their support to Jugurtha in the future.[34] Although there were several pitched battles between Rome and Jugurtha, none of them resulted in a decisive defeat, in part because the Numidians were fast enough to escape when the engagement started to go against them. The war grew increasingly unpredictable. One ambush threatened disaster for the Roman troops caught in it, but they were able to retreat to high ground and wait for Jugurtha's men to fall asleep after prematurely celebrating their victory; the Romans then attacked at dawn, completely unanticipated, and slaughtered many of the enemy who were unable to escape in time.[35]

As it became clearer that Rome would eventually prove victorious, one way or another, Bocchus appears to have questioned the wisdom of his decision – he preferred the alliance with Jugurtha, but was afraid of the consequences for himself of a Roman victory.[36] He therefore entered negotiations with Rome via Sulla, although at this stage he had not fully committed to the idea of betraying Jugurtha. A deal was struck however, in which Bocchus would lure Jugurtha into an ambush where he could be taken into Roman custody. Even to the last minute, Bocchus appears to have struggled with betraying his son-in-law, but eventually decided he had no choice. The two arranged to meet, unarmed and with only a few companions; when Jugurtha arrived, concealed soldiers burst out, slaughtered his companions and took him captive. He was delivered up to Sulla and then Marius. The capture of Jugurtha was evidently seen as a significant moment in Sulla's career and an indication of what Roman diplomacy (when backed up by arms) could achieve. It was later portrayed on a denarius issued in 56 BC by Sulla's son, Faustus Cornelius Sulla, which showed Bocchus kneeling to the seated figure of Sulla and presenting him with an olive branch, while the bound figure of Jugurtha knelt nearby.

Jugurtha was sent to Rome to be displayed as a captive in Marius' victory triumph in 105 BC. After being paraded, he was incarcerated in the Tullianum prison, now known as the Mamertine and to be found below the church of San Giuseppe dei Falegnami. When he was taken into prison his clothes were torn from him, as was a gold earring he wore, apparently with such force that it ripped away part of his earlobe.[37] Plutarch goes on to say that Jugurtha had begun to lose his reason by the time he ended up in the Tullianum and was bewildered by being thrown naked into the prison pit – but apparently still able to wisecrack 'Hercules! How cold this Roman bath is!' He died in the prison a short time later, either from starvation (according to Plutarch) or surreptitious execution, and was survived by at least two sons, Iampsas and Oxyntas, both of whom were paraded alongside him in the triumph. Nothing is known of what subsequently happened to Iampsas, but Oxyntas was sent to live in southern Italy, where he survived until at least 89 BC, after which he too disappears from the record.[38] In the aftermath of the conflict, most of western Numidia was given to Bocchus I and absorbed into the kingdom of Mauretania. This left a small area of the eastern regions to be ruled initially by Gauda, a legitimate son of Mastanabal and Jugurtha's half-brother. Gauda's rule ended with his death in 88 BC, a year which would see the beginning of a period of significant turmoil in the region.

The Sulla-Marius Civil War

The first century BC in Rome was a period of political turmoil, as the Republic slid gradually towards its end amidst a series of civil wars between prominent political figures, who saw their official military commands as essentially giving them private armies to seize power. The conflicts spilled out into Africa – in both the Roman provinces and independent (allied) kingdoms – and the region came to play a significant role as a place of refuge and a war zone. By the early first century BC, Rome had evidently decided that the time had come to increase its territorial holdings in Africa. In 96, the kingdom of Cyrenaica, which lay between Egypt and the Roman province of Africa (modern eastern Libya), was bequeathed to Rome by its king, Ptolemy Apion, who died without an heir. For the first few decades Rome left the administration of the kingdom to local officials who understood the sociopolitical situation in the region. However, by the 70s BC direct intervention became necessary when internal problems developed, particularly among the Jewish population, resulting in several small-scale uprisings. Consequently, in 74 BC Rome formally annexed Cyrenaica and faced no major resistance in doing so. The island of Crete was later added to the province in 67 BC. Rome now had direct territorial control over most of the central coastal region of North Africa, between Egypt in the east and Numidia/Mauretania in the west.

Numidia suffered further problems in the early decades of the first century BC. After Gauda's death, the already diminished kingdom was divided in two – a western region to be ruled by his son Masteabar, and a more powerful eastern kingdom, that went to another son, Hiempsal II.[39] Hiempsal II was deposed in 88 BC by a Numidian usurper named Hiarbas, as his brother Masteabar probably also was displaced in the western Numidian territories. That same year, Gaius Marius was exiled from Rome by Lucius Cornelius Sulla – the same man who had been his quaestor during the war against Jugurtha and who had been instrumental in the capture of their enemy. Marius sought refuge in Africa, landing near the ruins of Carthage and asking for sanctuary in the Roman province. He was turned away by the governor, who threatened to have Marius executed if he entered the provincial territory.[40] On hearing this, Marius compared his own downfall in fortune with that of Carthage, noting that he, a once-great man now brought to ruin, sat as a fugitive among the scattered remains of that once-great city.

Meanwhile his son, Gaius Marius the Younger, had journeyed to seek assistance from Hiarbas, the usurper-king of Numidia.[41] The king received him and his men and initially treated them well, leading to an alliance between the two. However, it became clear over time that Hiarbas intended to permanently detain Marius the Younger and his men in Numidia for his own purposes; eventually they managed to flee with the help of one of the court concubines who had apparently fallen in love with the young Marius. In 87 BC Marius himself, his son, and their men returned to Rome, having effectively established northwestern Africa as somewhere that the Roman elites could flee to in times of political crisis. Within a few years, civil war broke out between the factions of Gaius Marius and Sulla, the first of the major internecine conflicts in this period.[42] Sulla won, and Marius died during the hostilities. His defeated supporters fled for safety where they could, some joining those who had already fled Rome in northwest Africa. One of Marius' supporters, Gnaeus Domitius Ahenobarbus, began to gather an army in the region to challenge Sulla, with the support and assistance of Hiarbas, who was still reigning in Numidia. Sulla sent Gnaeus Pompey Magnus (Pompey the Great) to deal with the threat in Africa, which he did by winning a comprehensive victory in the Battle of Utica (81 BC). Recognizing that Hiarbas was not a friend to Sullan Rome, Pompey was then sent to depose him from the Numidian throne.[43] Hiempsal II was restored as king of the eastern kingdom, with the western part to be ruled by Masinissa II, a son of Masteabar. Hiempsal II in particular became a staunch ally of Pompey as a result.

The Pompey-Caesar Civil War

The conflict between the factions of Marius and Sulla was far from the last Roman civil war to impact northwestern Africa. The region would play an important role in the war between Pompey and Caesar (49–45 BC), becoming one of the major battlegrounds of the conflict. Numidia, as always, was to prove significant.

By the time the next civil war broke out, part of Numidia was under the rule of a new king. Hiempsal had died *c.*60 BC[44] and was succeeded by his son

Juba I, who evidently inherited his father's positive relationship with Pompey and was also fairly antagonistic towards Julius Caesar. During a visit to Rome made by Juba I in his youth, Caesar had pulled on his beard while presenting a court case, an insult which was evidently never forgotten.[45] Unsurprisingly, when conflict came between Caesar and Pompey, both Masinissa II and Juba I declared their support for Pompey and the *optimates* faction, uniting Numidia against Julius Caesar and the *populares*. Africa became a stronghold for the Pompeian cause in the early stages of this war and control of it was seized by Publius Attius Varus, who had previously held a propraetorship there and was consequently a well-known figure. But the resources and manpower there were too rich for Caesar to allow the Pompeians to hold unchallenged, so he sent two legions in 49 BC to try to wrest control of Africa from them.

The army was commanded by Gaius Scribonius Curio, Caesar's long-time ally and had initially been recruited to Pompey's cause. However, when Caesar spared their lives after they surrendered at the Siege of Corfinium in 49 BC, they switched their allegiance to him. Curio's army landed near Utica, where it prepared to fight the troops led by Publius Attius Varus, which included Numidian cavalry and infantry given to the cause by Juba I. An appeal was made before the battle by one of the Pompeian officers, a man named Sextus Quinctilius Varus (not related to Publius Attius Varus), for the legions to turn against Caesar once more. Despite knowing him from previous days, as he had also fought at Corfinium, the legions refused.[46] In the ensuing Battle of Utica, Curio's troops routed Varus' army. Curio then prepared to lay siege to Utica, the fear of which led its citizens to beg Attius Varus to surrender before the attack began. He refused, knowing that reinforcements were on the way with Juba; while Curio, hearing the same thing, abandoned the siege to confront the Numidians before they could combine with Attius Varus' army.

The two armies met in battle at the river Bagradas, Curio having been lured by reports that Juba's force was significantly under-strength – information which turned out to be false. The Roman troops were harassed to the point of exhaustion by the Numidian cavalry and further debilitated by the hot weather and a lack of water during the preliminary stages of the battle. The cavalry then started to attack the main Roman battle formation, dropping back periodically and trying to isolate small groups of troops away from the lines, then surrounding and killing them. Recognizing that his troops were reaching a point where they would no longer have the energy to fight, Curio attempted to withdraw them from the field, only to find the retreat cut off by the Numidian cavalry. The combat cohesion of the Roman lines disintegrated, with some soldiers fleeing the field in a disorganised mess, others simply giving up and lying down on the ground to wait for death. Curio fought to the death, claiming he could not face

Caesar after losing an army and preferring to die. Most of the two legions were destroyed, and only a handful of survivors made it back to their camp, where a small force had been left. Attius Varus and Juba began to approach the camp from two sides, leading to a mass panic in the Roman ranks that saw many of the transport galleys set sail without waiting for the soldiers to board, the desperate men swamping and sinking those ships which remained for them. Those who could not escape surrendered to Attius Varus, who promised them amnesty but soon after changed his mind and executed all but a few high-ranking senators – even these did not survive long, as they were subsequently transported to Numidia for public display and execution.

As the war progressed badly for the Pompeians elsewhere, Africa became an even more important stronghold for them and the alliance with Juba I ever more necessary. After a severe defeat in the Battle of Pharsalus (48 BC) in Greece, many of the major Pompeian figures fled to Africa. Attius Varus was asked to hand over command of the army to Metellus Scipio, a prominent commander against Caesar, although Varus remained a high-ranking *legatus*.[47] But the situation was soon turned around when Caesar arrived in Africa to command the campaign against the Pompeians. He initially led a large and experienced six-legion force, bolstered soon after by the arrival of more troops. As his army marched through Africa, the Numidian cavalry attempted to harass it on the move, but Caesar was able to keep his soldiers disciplined and moving quickly enough that little significant damage was sustained. After losing several small engagements to Caesar, the *optimates* asked Juba to return to help them, which he duly did, bringing a large Numidian army with him.

The two armies eventually met at Thapsus in 46 BC, where Caesar led an army of 12 legions against a combined *optimate* force of 8 Roman and 3 Numidian legions, supplemented by a large number of cavalry, light infantry and war elephants. In the ensuing battle Caesar's force proved victorious, beginning by provoking the enemy elephants to panic, which led to them trampling their own men.[48] As the battle progressed, Caesar's soldiers gradually won more of the field and eventually the Numidian troops broke and fled, making an *optimate* defeat inevitable. The aftermath was notable for an incident that showed a remarkable lack of discipline among Caesar's soldiers, who usually obeyed orders well. The *optimate* survivors were slaughtered despite Caesar ordering that they should be spared; he was known for his *clementia* (mercy) towards the enemy in civil war where possible.[49] It was suggested that he had suffered an epileptic seizure at the moment of giving orders, leading some to be confused about what he wanted and others to simply follow.[50] However, this slaughter may have been a recurrence of the same type of hatred once directed towards the Carthaginians, now aimed at their successors in the region. The Romans had fought a long, hard campaign in Africa and had to avenge the loss of two legions under Curio a few years earlier. Added to this, some of the worst instances of Roman violence took place during civil wars, so it is perhaps not surprising to find this scenario playing out on the fields of Thapsus.

After the battle, Pompeian resistance in Africa was effectively over. Attius Varus fled to Pompey in Iberia, as did several other commanders along with Arabio, the son of the western Numidian king Masinissa II. Juba retreated to Numidia alongside another surviving Roman commander, Marcus Petreius. Hearing that a Roman army was advancing on them, Juba and Petreius concluded that suicide was their best option, deciding to duel each other in the hope that this would provide an honourable death for both. Juba was killed by Petreius in the fight, who in turn made a slave kill him.[51] As news of Caesar's victories in Africa spread several other prominent Pompeians followed their example, including Cato the Elder, who had remained in relative safety in Utica. With the Battle of Thapsus, the civil war was effectively over in Africa. The conflict continued across the Mediterranean in Iberia, where Pompey fought on with his troops and those few who had fled to him from Africa, but there was no more direct fighting in Africa – and, after the disaster with the war elephants on the battlefield, their use in Roman warfare was also effectively ended.

With the death of Juba I, eastern Numidia had no king. Western Numidia was also in turmoil, as Juba's cousin and co-ruler, Masinissa II, had been deposed during the civil war by Bocchus II of Mauretania and he now disappears from the historical record, strongly suggesting that he died in this same period. Bocchus II had broadly supported Caesar during the civil war in Africa, probably as much due to his enmity for Juba I as any liking for Caesar. During the conflict in Africa, Bocchus II had sent expeditions against Numidia, splitting Juba's focus and forces between two fronts, to Caesar's benefit. Consequently, Caesar decided to split western Numidia between his two main allies in the region. Bocchus II received the western territories, while the east was given to Publius Sittius, a Roman mercenary commander who had led the Roman and Mauretanian troops against Juba. By splitting the kingdom of western Numidia between two allies, Caesar had effectively established control over an even larger part of northern Africa. The eastern kingdom of Numidia, until recently ruled by Juba I, was taken into direct control as a new Roman province, Africa Nova.

Africa Vetus and Africa Nova

The territory of Africa Nova (literally 'New Africa') pretty much directly corresponded with that of Juba I's former kingdom in Numidia. To distinguish them, the existing province of Africa was renamed Africa Vetus ('Old Africa'). The two were run as distinctive entities with their own administrations. Africa Nova offered a new source of food security to Rome, after Caesar announced that it would provide 8,000 tonnes of corn each year in tax.[52] New Roman settlers were drawn to the region, particularly to the area around Cirta, the former capital, but also to Africa Vetus, hoping to exploit Africa's agricultural wealth for their own benefit; some were no doubt military veterans resettled in a new area to try to make their fortune in civilian life. New colonies were founded, although it is difficult to know whether they date to the time of Caesar or slightly later; Augustus appears to have finished much of the work started by his adopted father on these African sites. Caesar may even have drawn up the plans for Carthage to replace Utica as the administrative centre of Roman Africa, but it was almost certainly Augustus who put them into practice, with the shift taking place by the end of his reign.

Caesar's new province in Africa did not last for long. In 44 BC, about the time of his assassination in Rome (it is not clear if it was just before or shortly after), Masinissa's son Arabio returned from the *optimates* in Iberia to claim his father's throne and the Numidian territories which had not become part of Africa Nova. The *optimates* helped him to gather and train troops, and he was able to claim western Numidia from Bocchus II with minimal effort. Soon afterwards he managed to get Publius Sittius assassinated and established control over the entire kingdom of Numidia.[53] For a few years there was relative peace, until another Roman civil war broke out – this time between the supporters of Caesar's assassins, commanded by Marcus Junius Brutus and Gaius Cassius Longinus, and the Second Triumvirate, composed of Caesar's heir Octavian, Mark Antony, and Marcus Aemilius Lepidus. Despite having earlier been associated with the anti-Caesar cause, Arabio now decided to support the Second Triumvirate.

The Last Civil War of the Roman Republic

Conflict erupted in Africa in 42 BC between the governor of Africa Nova, Titus Sextius, and the governor of Africa Vetus, Quintus Cornificius. Sextius was ordered by Mark Antony to remove Cornificius, so he took the troops available to him and invaded Africa Vetus, killing Cornificius in battle somewhere near Utica. Sextius governed both provinces for a while until ordered to give them up to Gaius Fuficius Fango, at which point Octavian made a play for power in Africa by seizing Numidia and parts of the provinces. Fango was appointed as his man in charge in the area, opposed at Mark Antony's behest by Titus Sextius, who eventually drove Fango into the hills northwest of the Roman holdings. It was there that Fango killed himself, apparently after mistaking a herd of wild buffalo on the move for a night attack by the Numidian cavalry.[54]

Having reestablished control over both provinces by 41 BC, Sextius was ordered by the Second Triumvirate to surrender control of them to Lepidus, who had been allocated Africa in a division of Roman territory (the settlement gave Octavian the western provinces, and Mark Antony the eastern). Lepidus governed as proconsul of both Africa Vetus and Africa Nova, with six legions given to him from Mark Antony's force. During his tenure in Africa, Lepidus appears to have encouraged donatives of land to be given to time-served veterans, possibly as an attempt to secure allies in the region whom he could call on if things went badly in the Second Triumvirate – although veterans were no longer active soldiers, they could be called on to fight when needed. However, in 36 BC, Lepidus made an ill-advised play to incorporate Sicily into his territory, which Octavian took offence to. By September of that year, Lepidus was stripped of his territories and every title except that of Pontifex Maximus (a ceremonial religious position), and the African provinces had been incorporated into Octavian's holdings.

Lepidus' rule over the Roman provinces in Africa had initially taken place alongside the rule of Arabio in the parts of Numidia which had not been incorporated into Africa Nova. During the conflict between the governors of the two provinces, Arabio ended up on the side of Sextius, although he may not have started there. When Fango arrived in Africa, it is not clear whether Arabio fought once more for Sextius or whether he simply remained neutral, but the result was that Fango had invaded Arabio's kingdom, forcing him to flee. This was a poor move on Fango's part, as Arabio had taken the forces he fled with to Sextius, strengthening the army that would eventually defeat Fango and drive him to his unusual death. However, despite Arabio having joined up with him, Sextius doubted his loyalty, and had him executed soon after. It is not clear what prompted Sextius' distrust of Sittius, but it may have been the result of a boundary dispute, with Arabio claiming territories that were formerly part of his father's kingdom, but incorporated into Africa Nova when Publius Sittius had been overthrown. With Arabio's death, the last independent Numidian king was dead. His region of western Numidia was absorbed into Roman territory, probably into the province of Africa Nova.

In 33 BC King Bocchus II of Mauretania died, leaving his kingdom to Rome/Octavian in lieu of a biological or adopted heir. For the time being, Octavian decided not to install another client ruler, but instead to administer it directly, adding significantly to his territorial holdings in Africa.[55] This would forestall protest from the local population should Octavian's choice of king not be popular with them; the civil war with Mark Antony was still at a delicate point in 33, and the last thing Octavian needed was a rebellion breaking out in Africa, especially as he had no spare troops to ensure matters went smoothly.[56] There was a potential heir, Juba the Younger (later Juba II of Mauretania) who *may* have been given the kingdom in Bocchus' will, but if so, the legacy was not upheld at the time.[57] Roman power in northern Africa was further bolstered by the acquisition of Egypt in 30 BC, following Octavian's victory in the War of Actium/Final War of the Roman Republic, against Mark Antony and Cleopatra. Egypt was a significant acquisition, bringing a wealthy and agriculturally fertile region under direct Roman control for the first time. It also established Rome's dominance over the entire North African coast, from Egypt in the east to Mauretania in the west.

Numidia after the Civil Wars

The creation of Africa Nova and the death of Arabio more or less put an end to the kingdom of Numidia, but it was partially revived one final time during the reign of Octavian/Augustus. When Juba I died in 46 BC, he left behind just one living heir, a son of the same name. This younger Juba had been taken to Rome as a young child by Caesar as part of his victory celebrations for the campaign in Africa, in place of his father who had committed suicide shortly after the Battle of Thapsus. He ended up living in Rome for a significant period, becoming a citizen in the process and receiving an elite education which led to a life of scholarship – he had published his first book by the age of 20 – that saw him dubbed *rex literatissimus*, 'most scholarly king'.[58] Sadly, none of Juba's works, which covered subjects from history and nature to language and theatre, have survived beyond citations or quotations in the work of later ancient writers. Initially part of Caesar's household, he was transferred to the care of Octavian after his first patron was dead, and once he was old enough was taken on military campaigns, establishing a loyalty towards Octavian from an early period. When war broke out between Octavian and Mark Antony in 32 BC, Juba the Younger fought for Octavian, and took part in the defeat of Antony and Cleopatra at the Battle of Actium (in 31). He was one of the most prominent non-Roman aristocrats loyal to Rome in Octavian's early reign, and the son of a former enemy who could, with the proper incentive, be coopted into the Imperial machine to mutual benefit. It was a general trend of Octavian/Augustus' early reign to win over the sons of those who had fought against him in the civil wars by offering them friendship and advancement, in an attempt to ensure that his reign was not ripped apart by internecine conflict. Although this action typically benefited members of the Roman aristocracy, it could also be extended to people like Juba where appropriate.

As a reward for Juba the Younger's loyalty, in 30 BC Octavian revived the Numidian throne and gave it to him (temporarily) in place of the province of Africa Nova. Such a territorial reversal was unusual, but Juba's loyalty to Octavian and Rome meant that it represented a minimal risk. Also, although a king in name, Juba II was a client ruler, protected by alliance with Rome but able to act only in a manner acceptable to Rome, and not as an independent monarch. Rome still held significant territory across the northern coast of Africa, now extending from Egypt all the way to the western border with the newly reinstated Numidia; it could well withstand losing direct control of the kingdom for a short period, especially if the ruler helped maintain security within the region. The civil war era taught Octavian that Africa was an important location in the Roman world, and not one which could be left under-managed any longer. Once his attention turned from events at home to the provinces, it was not long before the situation in Africa was addressed, and far greater levels of Roman control imposed. The changes were made for Rome's benefit and were not popular with the indigenous population of northwestern Africa. Another conflict was not far off.

Chapter 3

Northwestern Africa under Early Imperial Rule (30 BC–AD 16)

In a century or more of Roman occupation in northwestern Africa, their territorial holdings had not increased from those originally taken from Carthage in the second century BC. There had seemingly been little interest even in exploring the regions south of the settled coastline, let alone in bringing them under Roman administration. At the same time, Africa had played an ever more important role in the politics of Rome and the city food supplies had become increasingly dependent on imported African grain. After the final civil war of the Republic (between Octavian and Antony), in the early Imperial period, Rome's relationship with Africa began to change. In 27 BC, Octavian had been granted the name – and title – 'Augustus' and, along with it, an extraordinary range of powers that made him the first emperor of Rome.

Foreign politics in the early years of Augustus' reign were dominated by a series of conflicts outside northwestern Africa, particularly the Cantabrian Wars in Spain. Rome also needed to consolidate its territory in Egypt following its acquisition in 30 BC, and deal with problems which had erupted on the southern border with Meroë. However, it would not be long before new policies of exploration and administration were introduced to northwest Africa to provide greater security for Roman interests in the region. It would no longer be a kind of placeholder province, established mainly to stop Numidia (or someone else) taking the territory and becoming a new rival; it would now be administered like any other province, with all the ramifications – from the development of infrastructure like roads, to the introduction of taxation. Although it is not clear how far Roman control extended in the early stages of Augustus' rule, it soon became apparent that he wanted to increase it.[1] His changes would bring many of the indigenous peoples into more direct contact with Rome for the first time, while others were exposed for the first time to the negative side of Roman rule. Within a few decades, the region was supported by a permanent legionary garrison, although it is not entirely clear whether the unit had been in Africa from the start or introduced in response to conflict developing in the area.

Although northwestern Africa had not been an entirely peaceful place during the later second and first centuries BC, only the Jugurthine War saw direct conflict with Rome (as opposed to taking part in Roman civil wars) – and even that started as a domestic war of succession in which Rome chose to involve itself. There is no record of any rebellions or uprisings against Roman rule more generally; this is perhaps unsurprising given that the Empire had not expanded beyond the territory originally held by Carthage, and thus had not subjected any new populations. Rome was not particularly popular, as indicated by widespread indigenous support for Jugurtha during his war with Rome,[2] but there was much to lose and little to gain by open opposition. However, it was not long before problems began to develop as a result of Augustus' more invasive policies. The expansion of direct Roman administration of the region brought them into contact with more of the nomadic and transhumant populations, most of whom operated sufficiently far from the settled coastal regions to have been little impacted by the policies and politics of first Carthage and subsequently Rome. But as officials began to implement policies which appear to have introduced threats to indigenous territorial boundaries, such as roadbuilding across nomadic routeways, greater levels of conscription into the Roman *auxilia*, and – worst of all – the potential taxation of the nomadic population, it was likely only a matter of time before unrest broke out. There were several other conflicts between Rome and the indigenous population of the region before that led by Tacfarinas, resulting from an ever-increasing level of Roman activity.

Africa Proconsularis

The civil wars taught Augustus that firmer Roman control was needed in Africa and that major changes were required to ensure its security and prosperity. By the mid-first century BC Africa was already a major source of Rome's food supply, particularly grain, and a significant proportion of the land was already owned by wealthy Romans, many of them absentee landlords who still lived in Italy.[3] At some point, the short-lived provinces of Africa Nova and Africa Vetus, established by Julius Caesar, were reunited into a single territory that would come to be known as Africa Proconsularis. The unification has usually been dated to 27 BC and the reorganization of the provincial system under the new powers granted to Augustus in the same year, but it may have taken place as early as the governorship of Lepidus in 40–36 BC.[4] Its territory initially covered the same area as the earlier province of Africa, but it was soon expanded by absorbing the briefly revived kingdom of Numidia when Juba II was offered the kingship of Mauretania instead (see below) in 25 BC. From then on, Africa Proconsularis extended across much of central North Africa, from a border with Mauretania in the west to a border with the province of Cyrenaica in the east.

As part of the settlements of 27 BC, the Roman provinces were divided into two groups: those that would come under the direct jurisdiction of the emperor (Imperial provinces), and those that would be overseen by the Senate (Senatorial or public provinces).[5] Most of the newly-conquered territories were designated Imperial provinces, as were any in which a significant Roman military garrison was maintained. The civil war era had demonstrated to Augustus the inherent risks when provinces were governed by individuals who could win over the personal loyalty of their troops and use them as a private army against the state, as Julius Caesar had done – Augustus wanted to ensure that only trusted individuals were put in charge of militarized provinces. The Senatorial provinces, by contrast, were typically the more established territories, most of which were Republican-era acquisitions posing little risk of rebellion or invasion, and which typically did not have a permanent military garrison.[6] In Imperial provinces, the emperor would be in charge of appointing and instructing a governor (a *legatus Augusti pro praetore*, or 'legate of the emperor with the rank of a praetor'), who would serve as long as they were commanded to, typically but not exclusively for three years or more.[7] By contrast, Senatorial provinces were run by a *proconsul* appointed by the Senate, ostensibly selected by ballot (although there was no doubt manipulation in the system).[8] It was not expected that the *proconsuls* would have to deal with any military affairs during their year in office, although some of those who served in this role did have prior experience in the Roman army, in command of demilitarized provinces as part of their general progression up the career ladder (*cursus honorum*). Ostensibly, the Senate also had final say over the policies enacted in the province rather than Augustus, although in reality there is little prospect that they would decide either proconsul or policy against the wishes of the emperor.

Africa was designated as a Senatorial province, and renamed Africa Proconsularis in reflection of its status. The fact that it was given to the Senate strongly suggests it did not have a military garrison in the early Imperial period and there is no direct evidence for a legion being posted to Africa during the earliest years of the province's history. There are claims that a legion was present in Africa around 40–36 BC (during the Second Triumvirate), posted there with Lepidus and later defecting to Augustus, but there is no definitive evidence.[9] The earliest date that can be definitely associated with a legionary presence in the region does not come until AD 5 when the 3rd Legion Augusta can be placed here, their arrival likely linked to problems with the Gaetulians in the early first century AD, and they appear to have become a permanent presence from this period onward.[10] However, there was clearly some level of Roman military involvement prior to this, as a number of campaigns are attested in the period (discussed later in this chapter), against the peoples living to the south of the provincial territory.

A number of prominent individuals served as an early *proconsul* of Africa Proconsularis, including Gaius Sentius Saturninus, a distinguished military commander who was a senior officer under the future emperor Tiberius, and Lucius Domitius Ahenobarbus, nephew-by-marriage of Augustus and grandfather of the emperor Nero. Early in his career, Publius Quinctilius Varus – infamous for the loss of three legions in the Teutoburg Forest in AD 9 – also served for a year as *proconsul* in Africa (8/7 BC), his first provincial appointment.[11] The proconsuls would have been assisted in their role by the presence of a strong Roman ally in the region – Juba II, the former king of Numidia, who was given the kingship of Mauretania.

Juba II & the Kingdom of Mauretania

Having originally gifted Juba the Younger the kingdom of Numidia in 30 BC, Augustus changed his policy once again in 25 BC. The kingdom of Mauretania, in the western areas of North Africa, had been without a ruler since the death of Bocchus II in 33 BC, who had left it to Octavian in his will. Octavian had administered the kingdom directly for the next eight years, but in 25 decided that the time had come for a political reorganization of the region, perhaps in light of the changes introduced during the settlements of 27 BC. Numidia was taken back from Juba the Younger, who in exchange was offered the kingship of Mauretania as a client of Rome. Client kingdoms were ruled as technically independent of Rome, but at Roman pleasure.[12] The rulers of such kingdoms were often chosen by Rome, either directly or through military support that enabled them to take the throne, and were recognized by the Senate as *amicus populi Romani*, 'friend of the Roman people'. Client kingdoms in the early Imperial period were often established in territories where Roman already exerted considerable influence but which they did not yet want to take under direct control; they would have a strong influence on the client king's domestic rule, however. Client kingship would often be maintained in territories where the indigenous political society was set up in a way that Roman administration could exert control through existing structures; over time, the kingdom would change to a degree that direct Roman rule could be introduced.

Thus Juba II of Numidia became Juba II of Mauretania, the most loyal Roman ally in Africa since his ancestor Masinissa (his great-great-great grandfather). Juba did have a claim on the throne as one of Bocchus II's closest living relatives and may have been willed the kingdom in 33 BC.[13] Although related to Bocchus, Juba did not have any direct connection to Mauretania itself, but this was not particularly unusual in the context of client kingship under Augustus. Several of the major client kings in this period came not from the kingdoms they ruled, but from the aristocracy of a neighbouring realm – Archelaus of Cappadocia, originally from Pontus, and Herod of Judaea, who came from Idumaea, were other examples of this.[14] Juba had proved his competence during his time in Numidia and in warfare in Cantabria. He was also old enough to have some life and career experience, sufficient to demonstrate that he would not be a liability in Mauretania, yet was not old enough to have ambitions of acting against Augustus – the perfect choice for a client king.

The kingdom of Mauretania extended from the borders of Africa Proconsularis in the east (to the borders of what had previously been Numidia; modern central Algeria), to the Atlantic coast in Morocco. The kingdom may have been augmented by some of the Numidian territories, given to Juba by Augustus as part of his 'ancestral lands', but if this happened, it is not clear what areas might have been encompassed.[15] Even without these territories, Mauretania was the largest Roman client kingdom. Some parts of it had already been settled by Romans drawn to the area for commercial reasons, to the degree that some settlements were colonies in all but name. Augustus also directly founded three colonies during his reign, despite Mauretania being a client kingdom throughout.[16] It is not clear why the decision was made to give up Roman direct control in Mauretania in exchange for the Numidian territories. There were advantages to Rome in doing so, transforming their territory into a contiguous region without an independent kingdom between its two main holdings, and avoiding over-enlarging it beyond the point that it could be effectively controlled. Rome may have thought that an African king (albeit someone not from the kingdom itself) would prove more popular than their direct rule. If this was the hope, it would prove unfounded. Juba was disliked by many of the indigenous peoples who lived within or alongside his kingdom, partly because of his family connections – they had fought against his father, Juba I of Numidia, in the first century BC – and partly because of the closeness of his relationship with Rome.[17]

The animosity developed into conflict on multiple occasions during Juba's reign.[18] But nevertheless, the kingship of Juba also offered a measure of stability in northwestern Africa at a time when Rome was facing problems in Egypt, where the southern border with the Meroitic kingdom of Kush was beset by uprisings, border incursions, and skirmishes.[19] In 24 BC, a large Kushite army invaded lower Egypt when part of the Egyptian garrison was serving elsewhere, looting a number of towns of their treasures, including statues of Augustus. The ruler of Meroitic Kush, Queen Amanirenas (referred to as 'Candace' in the Roman sources, which was just the Kushite term for 'Queen'), later negotiated a peace by offering to return the captives and statues taken during the invasion; although at least one statue element, the Meroë Head now in the collection of the British Museum, was not returned.[20] If there was conflict in northeastern Africa, it was imperative that the northwest be kept as peaceful as possible – and with the installation of a client ruler there it became primarily his responsibility to ensure it, rather than Rome's.

Rome would find little to complain about in their decision to install Juba as king of Mauretania. He became a strong, reliable, and trustworthy ally and client who continued to assist Augustus through the early years of his reign. He sent Numidian troops to serve with the Romans in Hispania during the Cantabrian Wars and may have served there for a time alongside Augustus, who spent a year in the field during the war. The kingdom flourished under Juba's rule. He established a new capital city named Caesaria (modern Cherchell, Algeria) in honour of Augustus, and his kingdom became a great centre for arts and culture, as well as a wealthy trading nation. For the first decades of his reign, Juba ruled alongside his wife Cleopatra Selene, whom he had married around the same time as he became king of Mauretania.[21] Cleopatra Selene was the only daughter of Cleopatra VII of Egypt and Mark Antony. After the suicides of her parents following the Battle of Actium, Cleopatra Selene was, like Juba, taken to Rome and paraded in Octavian's triumphal celebration of his victory over her parents. She remained in Rome afterwards and was raised in the household of Octavia the Younger, Octavian's sister and Mark Antony's former wife. Octavia may have been instrumental in arranging the marriage. Cleopatra Selene went on to have two children by Juba II, a son named Ptolemy, born *c.*10 BC, and a daughter whose name has not been preserved.

Day-to-day security in the region, particularly on the southern borders, was probably the responsibility of Mauretania, particularly if a Roman garrison was not stationed in Africa Proconsularis during the first decades of Juba II's reign. One particular problem was bandit activity and the warbands who raided into Mauretanian and Roman territory from the semi-arid lands to the south, and one of Juba's primary responsibilities would have been to limit these attacks as much as possible. It was a task he appears to have struggled to fulfil. In many ways, frontier defence was a thankless and impossible task for Juba (or indeed, any client king). It required him to maintain security without disrupting internal or regional politics, technically operating as an independent agent while also trying to anticipate exactly what Augustus wanted him – and would permit him – to do. Not only was it thankless, it was also difficult, as client kings had 'little freedom of independent military action, but at the same time were expected to do what the Romans themselves often could not: keep the frontier zone secure, and defend their own territories.'[22] Many other such kings struggled with this balance.[23] Juba had to be careful not to misstep in his military actions, while also coping with some significant military problems, particularly with the Gaetulians (see below). He probably relied on significant Roman support, either through the secondment of troops or the training of his own army.[24] Whatever Juba's struggles with banditry and frontier security, Rome was evidently happy enough with his efforts to keep him in position for the rest of his natural life. Juba was still in power when Tacfarinas' war with Rome erupted – and indeed, may initially have taken charge of operations against him before a higher level of Roman involvement proved necessary.

Northwestern Africa under Augustus

The reign of Augustus was generally a period of expansion in the Roman world. But in northwestern Africa, Augustus appears to have been initially more concerned with consolidating and developing the territory Rome already possessed. With the conquest of Egypt Rome had established control of almost the entire northern coastline of Africa, aside from the part encompassed by Mauretania. The territories Rome held or indirectly controlled encompassed most of the agriculturally productive parts of the region. The desert interior was deemed to have little to offer in terms of farming or mineral resources until at least the 40s AD, when expeditions to the area began to show that there were better prospects than previously imagined.[25] There was little tangible advantage to increasing Roman direct control in the region at this time, but there was every benefit in strengthening Roman control as opposed to expanding it.[26] This was not as easy a prospect as it might sound, however. In many ways, northwestern Africa presented an especial problem for Rome, because there were not equal levels of development and pacification throughout the region. Policy decisions which benefited the coastal populations may have been detrimental to the interests of the other populations in the region that Rome now also had to consider; something which increased the prosperity in one area could cause conflict in another. Previously, any actions undertaken by the Roman administration would only really have impacted the 'Libyan' population living along the coast, which had been under Roman rule for at least a century. But from the reign of Augustus onwards, a larger group of people were impacted.

Those based in the territories that were formerly part of the kingdom of Numidia had only been under Roman control for a few decades, since the death of Juba I in 46 BC, and the degree to which they could be considered a pacified population is debatable. Some of the Numidians had served in the *auxilia*, giving them additional familiarity with Rome, although whether this was to Rome's advantage or not is debatable. The peoples living to the south on the desert fringes still lived largely as independently as ever, although they had potentially started to trade more with Rome by this stage. The differing levels of prior exposure to Rome would have affected the reception of Imperial rule in each sub-region, and the level to which new policies would impact their daily lives would vary. Although it has already been demonstrated that Roman writers underplayed the prevalence of permanent settlement and proto-urbanism among the indigenous population of northwestern Africa, the populations of Numidia and the southern pre-desert regions did maintain a level of pastoralist nomadism which was necessary for both groups to flourish.[27] Augustus may have hoped that indirect exposure to Rome would start to make both the Numidian and pre-desert populations more sympathetic to their rule, to become 'different without knowing it',[28] thus avoiding more armed opposition where possible. The aim was to tread lightly until the majority of the population was considered pacified, and although there were a number of second-generation revolts in the first century AD, the policy of slow change appears to have worked relatively well for Rome.[29] However, it was not always effective.

There was a lot of scope for increasing the level of Rome's administration in northwest Africa. Up until this point, the main responsibilities of the Roman authorities had likely been limited to ensuring basic security, overseeing and protecting the grain supply, and delegating responsibility for tax collection.[30] Under Augustus, a lot of this changed. There was almost certainly a survey of the region's land, often a precursor to either confiscations from the indigenous peoples or the introduction of taxation, neither of which would have been welcomed by those subject to them for the first time.[31] Plans to construct roads in the region were evidently put in place, although it may not have been until the reign of Tiberius that they were actually laid. Conscription levels probably increased, particularly among the Numidians who were still much in demand in the Roman *auxilia*. Some of these changes proved very unpopular – not just in Africa, but with many other recently conquered territories, such as Illyricum and Germany, being prompted into rebellion by their introduction.[32] From this point, northwestern Africa would be run like any other Roman province, not as a territory that was held to stop someone else from taking it.

The changes introduced by Augustus were not popular with much of the northwest African population, particularly those living in the former Numidia and the peoples based between the Atlas Mountains and the Sahara.

For much of the Punic period, there had been only limited conflict between the Carthaginians and the tribal peoples, and what fighting there was typically took the form of intermittent raiding rather than open warfare – not least, because neither side had the desire to actually take territory from the other. The non-Carthaginian peoples had their own settlements away from the coast, and the nomadic elements of the population typically spent most of their time in areas of little interest to Carthage, between the mountains and the desert. They drove their herds northwards for the summers, benefiting Carthage by providing an extra source of labour during the harvest. There was no doubt some raiding of Carthaginian settlements, but it appears to have been at a low level, not a big problem, certainly not enough to prompt Carthage into grand-scale action against the perpetrators. But the social and political relationships which had largely secured peace in the region between these peoples and Carthage now had to be renegotiated by Rome.

There were a number of conflicts in northwestern Africa in the early decades of Augustus' reign (and the years immediately prior to them), although few of them are narrated in the historical record.[33] On six occasions during this period triumphal honours were granted for Roman victories in Africa: Lucius Statilius Taurus (34 BC); Lucius Cornificius (33 BC); Lucius Autronius Paetus (28 BC); Lucius Sempronius Atratinus (21 BC); Lucius Cornelius Balbus (19 BC); and Lucius Passienus Rufus (AD 3). The award of such high-level honours suggest that the conflicts were fairly serious, as to qualify for triumphal honours there had to have been at least one battle which left more than 5,000 of the enemy dead.[34] Who exactly these conflicts were fought against, where, and what happened in them, is unknown. Some may have been prompted by wider political problems in the region, and the conflict overseen by Atratinus in particular may have been a response to Juba II being installed as king of Mauretania, against the wishes of some of the population.[35] Even without knowing the details, they indicate that northwestern Africa was far from pacified in the early years of Augustus' reign, which may lend support to an earlier date for the 3rd Legion Augusta being stationed there. There is a sense of gradually escalating hostilities in the 20s BC, leading to a conflict which is better documented than its predecessors – a war against the Garamantes.

The Garamantean War – 19 BC

One of the main populations in the region were the Garamantes, a well-established people based south of the province of Africa Proconsularis (within the modern Fazzān region in Libya and Tunisia).[36] Due to extensive archaeology in their territory in the last few decades a lot more is known about the Garamantes than any of the other peoples living in the region at the time, published extensively by David Mattingly and his collaborators on various excavations.[37] The Garamantes are documented as far back as the writings of Herodotus, in which they are described as a war-like people who use chariots to persecute the cave-dwelling Ethiopians.[38] Cave paintings from the Garamantean region, including their main settlement at Garama (modern Jerma, Libya) illustrate their connection to chariot warfare.[39] Some of the Garamanteans appear to have joined the army of Juba I to fight against Julius Caesar during the civil war between him and Pompey, ending up on the defeated side.[40] By the early Imperial period they were thought, by Rome at least, to have come under Imperial domination, even though their lands had not been territorially incorporated into the Empire, and they are referred to by Virgil as one of the peoples subdued by Augustus.[41] In the Roman sources, the Garamantes are portrayed as a barbaric people, eking out a living on the fringes of the desert – one of the victims of progressive barbarization in Roman ethnic writing.[42] They are presented as an intrinsic threat to Roman civilization – as hut-dwelling bandits, living in a lawless and nomadic society in miserable and savage poverty.

Scholarship in the nineteenth and most of the twentieth centuries largely followed this portrayal of the Garamantes as a predominantly nomadic and barbarous people. However, excavation in the 1990s and into the 2000s presented a very different picture. There was a significant level of sedentary settlement among the Garamantes, which probably comprised the majority of society. They had a developed agricultural economy based around oases, with three main areas of occupation in the Central Sahara: the Wadi ash-Shati to the north, the Wadi al-Ajal in the centre, and the Wadi Barjuj/Murzuq/Hufra depression to the south.[43] Most of the population lived in permanent, even fortified settlements. They grew cereals, dates, fruits, and vines, irrigating their crops with foggaras, an underground irrigation system which made the most of the limited groundwater resources available to them.[44] The heartlands of Garamantean territory were based around the largest and densest cluster of Saharan oases, which also brought a major path of communication under their control.[45] They were heavily involved in trade, including with Rome and the sub-Saharan populations (directly trading with each rather than as middlemen between the two). The Garamantes appear to have traded raw materials in exchange for Roman artefacts, as no provably Garamantean-made artefacts have been found in Roman territory.[46] Finds of amphorae indicate that they imported olive oil, wine, garum, and salted fish from the Roman world, in sufficient quantities that they do not seem to have been limited to elite consumption.[47] The Garamantes were also apparently quite heavily involved in the trade of enslaved peoples from as far south as modern Niger and Chad, likely raiding to acquire them and selling them to Rome where they were valued as household slaves due to their 'exotic' appearance.[48] The Garamantean population may have numbered in the tens of thousands, even up to 100,000 at its peak in the classical period. Anthropological studies of human remains from the region and period suggest that despite living on the fringes of the Sahara, their lives were no more difficult than other African populations of the same period.[49]

The Garamantes came into direct conflict with Rome in 19 BC. The proconsul of Africa Proconsularis, Lucius Cornelius Balbus the Younger, was put in charge of the campaign. Balbus came from a Punic family in Gades (Spain) and had not been born a Roman citizen. He won citizenship and honours after supporting Julius Caesar in the civil war against Pompey and had thereafter enjoyed a prolific career. Augustus appointed him proconsul of Africa in 21 BC, and it was not long into his tenure that the problem arose with the Garamantes. Hostilities were seemingly prompted by the Garamanteans charging Roman merchants (among others) high duties to move goods through their territory, likely coinciding with (excessive) Garamantean raiding of Roman settlements. Judging from the triumphs already awarded for conflicts in the region, this was evidently not Rome's first war against the indigenous population of the region, though it may have been the first directly against the Garamantes. Balbus led an army estimated at 10,000 soldiers into their territory, relying on gathering supplies as he went to maintain his army, and potentially aiming to reach and even capture the Garamantean heartlands. He covered a large area of their territory in the campaign, including the capital at Garama.[50]

The details of Balbus' campaign against the Garamantes are not well documented. There are indicators from other conflicts Rome had fought against them to give some idea of how the war would have been fought. The Garamantes liked to avoid pitched battle, similar to most provincial enemies of Rome, favouring rapid light-armed cavalry attacks which melted away into the desert. They would have attempted to exploit their superior knowledge of the landscape, of which the Romans could only have had the vaguest understanding by this stage, using it to restrict Roman access to resources. The Garamantes were said to fill wells along roads into their territory with sand, to restrict the availability of water to those they did not want to have it.[51] It is difficult to judge with any accuracy how many engagements were fought in the campaign, what scale they were, or what the casualties might have been. Balbus was awarded a triumph on his return to Rome, which indicates that there must have been at least 5,000 casualties.[52] It was apparently the first time such an honour was given to someone not born a Roman citizen – and the last time it was given to someone who was not a member of the Imperial family, although honours in lieu of a triumph continued to be awarded to others.[53] The Garamantes were not permanently pacified however, and within a few years, *c.*14 BC, they were fighting against Rome again, this time as allies of the Marmarides who lived to the east of them. The Roman campaign was led by Publius Sulpicius Quirinius, the governor of Cyrenaica, who might have had the honorific title 'Marmaricus' had he not downplayed the significance of his actions to the Imperial authorities.[54] There appears to have been a decade or more of relative peace in the region following this conflict.

The Gaetulian War – AD 3–6

Another major conflict broke out in northwestern Africa in the early first century AD. This time Rome fought the Gaetulians and the conflict dragged on for several years before finally being brought under control. The Romans used the term 'Gaetulian' to refer both to a specific people and collectively to all the tribes who lived to the south of Africa Proconsularis, Mauretania, and the former Numidia.[55] They are portrayed in the Roman sources as being one of the oldest populations in northwestern Africa, and were apparently known for their abilities in warfare.[56] The Gaetulians were said to have been ignorant of the existence of Rome before the Jugurthine War.[57] The ancient sources suggest that they were largely a nomadic population, but like the Garamantes, in reality they may have been far more settled than Roman writers acknowledge; as yet, there has not been sufficient archaeological research to decide the issue either way. Their centre of settlement appears to have been based to the west of the Garamantes, between the Atlas Mountains and the Sahara south of Mauretania and Numidia, although it was a fairly undefined area at this point. They appear to have technically fallen under the jurisdiction of Mauretania, as Juba II was referred to as their king.[58] The kingdom encroached on some of the territories traditionally used by the pastoralist nomadic elements of the population; as a result, they became one of the main security issues for Mauretania and the region more widely.[59] The Gaetulians had previously fought against Rome during the Jugurthine War, where they were used to make numerous irregular attacks on forces in the field.[60] Some Gaetulians also seem to have provided assistance to Gaius Marius when he was exiled from Rome by Sulla in 88 BC, receiving formal land grants in exchange, including in his veteran colonies at Thugga, Uchi Maius, and Thibaris.[61] Perhaps as a punishment, they were later put under the authority of Hiempsal II of Numidia by Sulla. Many of the Gaetulians sided with Julius Caesar during the civil war with Pompey, claiming that they owed him loyalty as the nephew of Gaius Marius – but apparently in part so they could fight against Juba I of Numidia. They were used by Caesar to try to convince other Africans to join his cause.[62]

Hostilities broke out in AD 3, when the Gaetulians evidently became discontented with the power balance in the region. Cassius Dio suggests that they disapproved of what they considered to be Juba II's servile relationship with Rome and decided to take preventative action lest they be forced to live under direct Roman control.[63] Whether this tells the whole story about the causes of the war is unclear, and unfortunately none of the other sources give any indication of what else might have sparked things off. Rome's growing activity and impact in the region no doubt put pressure on the relationship between them and the Gaetulians (as well as other indigenous peoples), although as yet some of the major symbols of Roman occupation, particularly roads, had not yet been established (the first Roman road in Africa was not built until *c.*AD 14). But there may have been other consequences of Roman rule which were harder to ignore. Half a century of expanding permanent settlements encroaching on their pastoral routes had put the Gaetulians under increasing territorial pressure; even worse, Rome had begun to campaign into the deserts, areas they had traditionally avoided.

In the period preceding the war (*c.*2 BC–AD 2) Juba was absent from Mauretania, travelling the eastern provinces with Augustus' heir Gaius Caesar, which may have been a further catalyst for growing indigenous incursions in this period. A number of other peoples joined in when the Gaetulians appeared to be gaining the upper hand, including the Garamantes, Marmarides, Naramones, and the Musulamii, who would later be ruled by Tacfarinas.[64] These were all lumped together by Rome under the term 'Gaetulian' i.e. (semi-)nomadic, underdeveloped tribes, and the name of the conflict refers to the overall coalition rather than one specific group. The Musulamii may have been particularly impacted by the Roman presence in the region, as it was in their territory that (part of) the 3rd Legion Augusta was garrisoned, at Ammaedara (modern Haïdra, Tunisia); at 9 hectares the fortress is not big enough to house an entire legion, suggesting that there were other bases elsewhere.[65] Although it is not certain exactly when the legion was permanently stationed in the region, the fact that they were placed in the territory of the Musulamii suggests this group was seen as a particular problem to the Roman authorities and thus needing direct oversight, regardless of whether that decision was made before or after AD 6.[66] The involvement of so many indigenous peoples suggests that this would have been quite a serious conflict, practically surrounding Africa Proconsularis and Mauretania, which may explain why it lasted for more than three years.

It is not clear who the Roman proconsul in Africa Proconsularis was at the outbreak of conflict in AD 3. The last known proconsular appointment prior to this is Gnaeus Calpurnius Piso, who was appointed in *c.*3 BC; so given that proconsuls typically served for a single year unless there was a pressing need for them to do otherwise, it is unlikely that he was still in position in AD 3. Lucius Passienus Rufus, who was awarded the title of *imperator* in *c.*AD 3 may have been in post – it is clear that he served as proconsul in Africa Proconsularis at some point around this time, although possibly slightly later.[67] Whoever it was, they were replaced the following year by Lucius Cornelius Lentulus, who led an expedition into the Libyan desert to confront the Naramones. Things went badly wrong for the Romans there and Lentulus was killed during the campaign, resulting in a major escalation of the conflict.[68] He was replaced by his brother, Cornelius Lentulus Cossus (possibly after Passienus Rufus in the interim), who saw the war through its final stages. He appears to have faced a difficult campaign, but brought matters to a conclusion in AD 6.

The nature of the fighting and the number of engagements are not documented in any of the surviving sources, although some Roman historians suggest that casualties were heavy for both the Mauretanian and the Roman forces.[69] Roman resources at the time were fairly stretched, with a lot of manpower gathered in Europe for a campaign against the German Marcomanni, which was subsequently abandoned due to the outbreak of a large rebellion in Illyricum in AD 6. Conscripts may have been ordered up from the indigenous population to bolster the manpower available to Rome;[70] Tacfarinas himself may have been part of this levy. The difficulty of the Gaetulian war may be indicated by the fact that Cossus was awarded triumphal honours afterwards; he received at least one victory memorial, set up in Leptis Magna.[71] He was also granted the honorific title 'Gaetulicus', suggesting that the victory was seen as of some significance. We learn elsewhere that the honorific was hereditary and passed to his son.[72] However, some sources suggest that the scale of operations did not justify the award of the title, which they argue was 'more extensive than his actual victory warranted.'[73] Juba II may also have received triumphal honours for this campaign; coins he issued in AD 6/7 depicted the objects he had been honoured with – a sceptre and a curule chair.[74] He certainly saw the conflict as a significant victory, also issuing coins showing the goddess Victory standing on a temple or, more rarely, on the head of an elephant, reinforcing both his role in this success and his dominion over (parts of) Africa.[75]

Despite the extent of the conflict, the Gaetulian War did not lead to a direct change in Roman policy in northwestern Africa. Although the main hostilities ended in AD 6 there may have been several months, or even years, of low-level fighting, subsiding *c.*AD 8–9. The conflict had shown the limitations of

Mauretanian military power in the region, demonstrating that although they may have been able to cope with small-scale bandit activity on the frontiers, they were unable to handle a full-scale war without significant Roman assistance. A permanent legionary garrison would be kept in the province from this point onwards (although it may well have been there already for several years, or even decades): the 3rd Legion Augusta, who were initially stationed at Ammaedara (modern Haïdra, Tunisia). The presence of the legion made Africa Proconsularis the only Senatorial province to come with a legionary command that, for several decades, fell under the direct control of the proconsul.[76] Evidently at the time, the need for troops to bolster internal security outweighed the risk of proconsuls using these troops as their own personal army. The conflict does not appear to have given Augustus any second thoughts about expanding Roman administration in the region.

Post-War Roman Administration

The Gaetulian War had demonstrated that the population of northwest Africa was far from completely pacified. What exactly sparked the conflict is unknown, but it is difficult to imagine there was no link between the growing Roman administration in the region and the outbreak of resistance. These were populations experiencing the negatives of Roman rule for the first time – potentially including land confiscations, conscription, and the threat of taxation – which were not offset by any obvious gains. It was not necessarily the case that there was a complete, irreconcilable difference between the sedentarism of Rome and the nomadism of the Africans, as the Roman sources seem to imply (and later scholarship typically followed). It is true that increased Roman control of the northwest African landscape, particularly the creation of large private agricultural estates, may have adversely affected the nomadic populations who seasonally drove their herds across the land. Without knowing the routeways used, however, it is difficult to assess how much of a difference it might actually have made. Furthermore, it would not necessarily have impacted a large part of the population. As discussed previously, the Garamantes (and others) were far more sedentary than the Roman sources suggest, and in many ways were no more 'underdeveloped' than some of the Gallic or Iberian peoples who had successfully been brought under Roman control.

Greater concern might have been prompted by survey of the land during the reign of Augustus, potentially for the purposes of either confiscation of productive areas or taxation (cadastration). However, current evidence indicates that this process began no earlier than AD 6, after the end of the Gaetulian War, suggesting it may have been an outcome of the conflict rather than a cause of it.[77] While there were probably surveys under Augustus and Tiberius, there was also one during the reign of Trajan, nearly a century later, suggesting that the process took some time to complete. Augustus' survey did not even affect all the people in the region at the time; the territory of the Musulamii, for instance, was probably not fully surveyed until the second century AD.[78] Road building had not quite started yet, although the land surveys conducted after AD 6 may have incorporated planning for their construction.[79] There certainly does not seem to have been any slowing of Roman activity in northwest Africa as a result of the Gaetulian War.

Nor does the war seem to have prompted any major changes in who served as proconsul in Africa Proconsularis either. Technically, the appointment was made at random from a selection of eligible individuals (a sortition), but it was recognized that in times of conflict someone with military experience was needed in the post. When Africa Proconsularis needed an experienced soldier in charge, that is what it got, even if it meant slightly breaking Senatorial selection protocols.[80] But there is no real evidence of this happening immediately after AD 6, with the known appointees being a mixed bag in terms of military experience, from those with practically none, to others with a significant amount. Lucius Caninius Gallus, *c.* AD 8–9, has little documented military experience and was more associated with legal matters and town planning in Rome; it may have been for the latter skill that he was sent to Africa, to work on the logistical development of the province. His successor(s) are not known until the appointment of Lucius Nonius Asprenas, who took office in AD 13/14, likely the first proconsul there during Tiberius' reign.[81] Asprenas possessed significant military experience, as well as Imperial connections. He was the nephew of Publius Quinctilius Varus and had served with his uncle as a military tribune in Syria, and as a legionary legate in Germany; during the Teutoburg disaster in AD 9, Asprenas was stationed on the Rhine with two legions, taking part in the protection of the frontier in the battle's aftermath.[82] He was replaced in Africa by Lucius Aelius Lamia in AD 14/15 (he was originally thought to have served as proconsul during the reign of Augustus, but epigraphic evidence has led to the revision of that date).[83] Lamia was an experienced administrator and commander who had previously served in Germany on the Rhine and in Pannonia.[84] After Lamia came Aulus Vibius Habitus, about whom little is known.[85]

These selections might suggest a gradual move towards the placement of individuals with greater military experience in Africa Proconsularis towards the end of Augustus' reign and in the beginning of Tiberius', but this is not necessarily the case. One of the next appointments, who was in position at the outbreak of Tacfarinas' revolt, was Marcus Furius Camillus, who had no significant connection with the military. The proconsular appointments do not necessarily suggest a province on the brink of war, but nor do they – especially combined with the legionary command they now came with – indicate an entirely peaceful territory. While their defeat in AD 6 may have temporarily pacified the indigenous peoples, there were likely tensions which grew stronger in the years afterwards, and violent action short of a war, particularly raiding and banditry, likely increased significantly over these years. Low-level border problems increasingly erupted into larger-scale conflicts which demanded – and received – a harsh response from the Roman authorities. After a period of calm, the cycle would then just start again.

By the end of Augustus' reign, plans were in place for the construction of the first Roman road in northwest Africa, running between the legionary fortress at Ammaedara and Tacape (modern Gabès, Tunisia). It was probably a military road, connecting Ammaedara with other strategically important sites in the region – possibly to military bases elsewhere, such as Tacape and Capsa, given that Ammaedara was not big enough to house the entire legion.[86] This road and its impact on the freedom of movement of the local population has been cited by some as the underlying cause of the Tacfarinas rebellion, although it is not clear how far activity was actually affected (discussed further in Chapter 4).[87] During the proconsulship of Lamia, another road was constructed, running 44 (Roman) miles south from Leptis Magna, suggesting further incursion into the interior of the region.[88] These roads – and many of those constructed later – seem to have been built with little consideration for their impact on the local populations, particularly the nomadic elements who drove their herds over them.[89] The construction process involved detailed surveying of the landscape, providing information that could also have been used to support the introduction of taxation to the region – something else unlikely to be popular with the local people.[90] Developments like the roads, colonies, and the legionary garrison, had to be paid for somehow, and the introduction of taxation was an effective way to make sure that the provincial population – *all* of them – paid their share.

The available evidence gives the impression that towards the end of Augustus' reign and the accession of Tiberius in AD 14, there was an intensification of Roman activity in northwest Africa which brought growing pressure to the region, as the physical presence of Rome, with all its consequences, became more visible. Rebellion in the early Empire typically broke out among the second generation to live under Roman control, as Rome abandoned diplomacy for development and the realities of subjugation began to sink in.[91] As a native of the region, even as the introduction of roads, large private farms, and military bases began to restrict your freedom, you were required to pay towards the upkeep of this infrastructure.

Full-scale conflict may have broken out again in *c.*AD 14/15, at the start of Tiberius' reign. Augustus' death in 14 prompted a period of political turmoil in the Empire, which in some areas (particularly Germany and Pannonia) had spilled over into military mutiny and rebellion. Although there is no historical record of problems in northwest Africa after Tiberius' accession, there are archaeological indicators that some of the indigenous peoples may have tried to take advantage of the situation to rebel against Rome once more. In AD 15 and again in 16 Juba issued more coins showing images relating to a military victory.[92] They are unlikely to refer back to the war in AD 3–6, so we can infer this was a new period of conflict and a fairly significant one, to merit commemoration in coins. There may have been an undocumented uprising or war at this period which the coins are referring to – or they may be the first evidence relating to the conflict against Tacfarinas, while it was still a relatively limited border issue that Mauretania was capable of dealing with alone. But within a year, Rome was forced to get involved, and the problem would develop from low-level banditry to a full-scale rebellion, lasting for more than seven years. The war with Tacfarinas had begun.

Chapter 4

Tacfarinas

Tacfarinas came into the historical record very suddenly, and disappeared just as abruptly. Establishing who he was and how he ended up leading a major war against Rome is not an easy thing to do. Much of his earlier life can only be partially reconstructed, working from the few biographical details recorded by Tacitus and extrapolating backwards from things he is known to have done or roles he took during the war. Tacitus gives no insight into his character, as though dubbing him a bandit told readers everything they need to know about him. There is also no physical description at any point. His portrayal by Tacitus is actually quite dehumanized and gives no sense of Tacfarinas as a real person, just a shadowy figure who was offered all the benefits of Roman friendship, rejected them and proceeded to make war against Rome. The only time there is some hint of his life outside the war is in a few references to family members. He was evidently not an only child, as Tacitus refers to the capture of his brother, and for the same reason it is clear that he had a son. He presumably spoke at least some Latin, indicated by his service in the *auxilia*, although whether he knew the language before enlistment is questionable. Other than these scant impressions, Tacfarinas is nothing more than a faceless enemy.

What definitely can be said about Tacfarinas is that he was the right man in the right place at the right time, at least as far as the northwest Africans were concerned. Just as increasing Roman interference in the region threatened to do them more serious harm, here was a man capable of taking on the Roman army – and inspiring many others to do the same. He had military experience and understood how to use irregular warfare against Rome in the field, exploiting the enemy's weaknesses while playing to the greatest strengths of his own men. Tacfarinas was identified by the Romans as the main protagonist in the conflict, much as Jugurtha had been over a century earlier, and it came to be understood that the war would not end until he was either captured or dead. This was not an African rebellion so much as it was the War of Tacfarinas, and without him it is doubtful that hostilities would have lasted as long as they did, or if indeed they would ever have begun at all. What is more difficult to understand is how he came to be in the position of leading a war against Rome, and whether he did so as just a bandit, a freedom fighter, or somewhere in-between the two.

Tacfarinas' Early Years

Little is known about Tacfarinas' life before Rome became involved in a war against him in AD 17. Like many anti-Roman rebels, his story was ultimately recorded only by his enemies, who had little interest in the backstory of an individual they considered little more than an honourless brigand. Minimal details about where he came from are given by Tacitus, who is now our only surviving source on Tacfarinas and who was writing almost a century after the events he describes. Nevertheless, it is possible to reconstruct a basic biographical framework providing some insight into our subject's early years.

Tacfarinas was clearly born into a family of one of the non-coastal indigenous peoples in northwest Africa. Tacitus identifies him as being a Numidian, but does not give any indication of the specific tribe or people he was associated with.[1] The fact that Tacfarinas later became the chieftain of the Musulamii complicates the issue slightly, because they were not Numidian but Gaetulian. The Musulamii were based in a desert territory south of Africa Proconsularis and Mauretania, in an area now known as the Chotts region, between Sicca (El Kef, Tunisia) and Theveste (Tébessa, Algeria). The Roman sources imply that they were still a largely nomadic people by the early Imperial period, although as with the Garamantes they may actually have had far higher levels of sedentary settlement than they were credited with. Tacitus identifies the Musulamii as living in the 'solitudes of Africa', noting that they were still 'innocent of city life' by the start of the war led by Tacfarinas, thus heavily leaning into the nomadic stereotype which characterized many descriptions of the northwest Africans in this period.

By the early first century AD, however remote their homeland had once been, the Musulamii now lived alongside Rome, with the fortress of the 3rd Legion Augusta at Ammaedara located in the territory of the Musulamii. This suggests that they lived in a strategically important location, or that they may have been viewed by Rome as one of the more problematic parts of the region's population. That Tacfarinas became their chieftain has led some to identify them as his people of origin, but as the Musulamii were Gaetulian rather than Numidian, this directly contradicts Tacitus' identification. Just because he became the ruler of the Musulamii does not necessarily mean that he was born among them. Some argue that Tacitus was right and Tacfarinas was Numidian and not Musulamian, others that he was Musulamian and therefore Gaetulian not Numidian.[2] There is even some suggestion that he was Musulamian, but that Tacitus in error thought they were a Numidian tribe and thus gave that as his ethnic identity, not Gaetulian.[3]

To complicate the matter further, it is not even certain that Tacitus would have used the identifier 'Numidian' literally, to mean that Tacfarinas came from a Numidia-based people or as an ethnic shorthand to indicate what type of people he was from. In the progressive barbarization model, being 'Numidian' would communicate a number of things to Roman readers: that he came from a semi-barbaric, nomadic background, and from a group whose loyalty could not be relied upon, but who also could also provide good service in the Roman *auxilia*. It did not necessarily matter to the Roman audience whether his people of origin actually were Numidian, all that mattered was for them to understand what type of people they were. Although Roman ethnic reference to inhabitants of northwest Africa had become more nuanced from the late third century BC onward,[4] such quick characterizations no doubt proved useful to ancient readers unfamiliar with the region. Tacitus himself may not even have known which people Tacfarinas came from, or whether they were Numidian or not. Elsewhere in the narrative, he incorrectly refers to other peoples as 'Numidians' (including the Cinithii and the Garamantes), suggesting that his ethnic knowledge of the region was poor.[5] Whatever Tacfarinas' actual origins, what can be understood is that he was not born in Africa Proconsularis or the urbanized coastal population, but was from one of the peoples who lived towards the interior and who maintained a certain (but not universal) level of nomadism. The only slight difference it makes whether Tacfarinas was Musulamian or not is that one of the potential causes of the war was the construction of a Roman road across Musulamian territory, which some suggest was the reason he took up arms against Rome (see Chapter 5) – but that road would be less of an issue if he was originally from elsewhere in the province.

It is equally difficult to work out when he was born, as Tacitus gives absolutely no indication of his age at any point in the narrative; and this is not a matter of policy, as when discussing the death of Arminius he gave his age as 37 years old.[6] The omission is unfortunate, but it is possible to put together an educated guess based on his later career. The fact that Tacitus makes no mention of his age suggests that he was not notably young or old at the time of the war. Elsewhere, Tacitus did comment on the young age of certain figures where he believed it related to flaws in their character, such as Ptolemy of Mauretania who was judged a 'heedless youth'.[7] An age range for Tacfarinas of 30–50 years old in AD 17 seems likely, which would place his birth at some point around the last three decades of the first century BC. It is possible to narrow this down slightly. We know that he served in the *auxilia* for a number of years. Most recruits and conscripts to the Roman army enlisted between the age of about 16 and 21, for a period of 25 years, unless they were invalided out earlier. Tacitus makes it clear that Tacfarinas deserted from the army without completing his full 25 years; the earliest possible date he can have enlisted was therefore 7/6 BC (this assumes he did not desert until AD 17 and had 24 years of service), and probably significantly later. Even if he entered the army at the age of 20, he cannot have been born much before 26 BC. But this date assumes a long career in the *auxilia* and desertion just before the war broke out, neither of which are necessarily the case (see below). Given that Mauretania seems to have been fighting Tacfarinas from *c.*AD 14–15, a few years before Rome got involved, Tacfarinas may have deserted as early as *c.*AD 13/14 (and potentially even earlier). For him to have enlisted, spent a few years (say five to ten) in service, and deserted by AD 14, he would have to have been born at some point *c.*12–7 BC at the latest (although the latter date would make him quite young when the war broke out). This gives a possible date-range for his birth of between 26 and 7 BC and in my personal judgement, the period between 20 and 12 BC is most likely.

Having failed to provide an unambiguous ethnic origin or age for Tacfarinas, Tacitus also fails to give any information about his social status, even as to whether he was part of the elite or not. This omission may be because he did not come from a particularly distinguished background – but the fact that he later became the chieftain of the Musulamii suggests the opposite. More than one modern scholar has posited that he came from the Musulamian elite and was given to Rome as a young child as hostage for the good behaviour of his family and people.[8] This would have meant he was part of the Roman system from an early age and may explain the sense of betrayal in Tacitus when he took up arms against them, as if he was an individual with more reason than most to be loyal to Rome. He evidently ended up joining the Roman *auxilia*, a common career pathway for hostages to Rome (as Arminius had done in Germany), but there is no indication that he did this as a member of the elite or as a unit commander.[9] There is no indication of what education or training he might have received in his younger years. A description of Jugurtha's youth may provide some insight, dominated by his learning to ride, run, throw the javelin, and potentially also hunt.[10] These were predominantly military activities, which would have endowed Jugurtha – and indeed, Tacfarinas – with valuable skills for the future.

Tacfarinas' upbringing may not have instilled in him a particularly high opinion of Rome. Whatever his actual year of birth, his formative years were lived in a period where there was not a particularly good relationship between Rome and the peoples of northwest Africa. There were multiple episodes of warfare in the 20s–10s BC, several of which Tacfarinas might have lived through. But some of his earliest negative experiences may have come at the hands of the Roman army, particularly if he did grow up in the territory of the Musulamii, where the 3rd Legion Augusta was at least partly based. If this group had been identified as a particular security risk in the region, they may not have experienced particularly good treatment at Roman hands. The presence of a Roman garrison was often detrimental to the lives of indigenous populations in the same area, who easily could find themselves at the wrong end of military brutalization. In a later period, documents from militarized zones like Hadrian's Wall give insight into the casual mistreatment of civilians and their struggles to gain redress.[11] The Roman author Juvenal gives some idea of how civilians could expect to be treated by soldiers, and how any complaint about military brutality would be treated by the authorities:

> if thrashed himself [by a soldier], he must hold his tongue, and not venture to exhibit to the Praetor the teeth that have been knocked out, or the black and blue lumps upon his face, or the one eye left which the doctor holds out no hope of saving. If he seeks redress, he has appointed for him as judge a hob-nailed centurion with a row of jurors with brawny calves sitting before a big bench … then the whole cohort will be your enemies; all the maniples will agree as one man in applying a cure to the redress you have received by giving you a thrashing which shall be worse than the first.[12]

This passage suggests that when Roman soldiers mistreated civilians – which they no doubt frequently did – there was no point in appealing to the army for justice, since it was designed by the military for the military. The treatment of civilians would be even worse if they were identified by the Romans as part of the barbaric 'Other' and thus only semi-human at best. If the soldiers stationed at Ammaedara and elsewhere in the region believed in even a fraction of the negative stereotypes put forward in the Roman written sources, then the people of northwestern Africa may have faced difficult experiences at the hands of the soldiers. Some of the nomadic population may have been able to avoid the worst treatment by simply staying away from the soldiers, but this was not possible for the sedentary communities, who made up the majority of even the indigenous population by this time. In his younger years, Tacfarinas would have seen first-hand how badly the locals could be treated by the Roman military. Although no direct evidence survives documenting Roman mistreatment of the indigenous nomadic population in northwestern Africa, incidents similar to those described by Juvenal are not unlikely to have taken place on a regular basis, particularly in the areas close to the legionary fortress. But before too long, Tacfarinas would find himself on the side of the potential oppressors, as a soldier in the Roman *auxilia*, the earliest biographical event in his life that can be identified with any certainty.

Northwest Africans in the Roman Army

Perhaps true to form, Tacitus does not provide any details about Tacfarinas' service in the *auxilia*, no indication of what unit he served in, for how long, or even whether he was an infantry or cavalry soldier. This information may not have been available to him, or may simply not have been considered relevant or of interest to his readership. Based on Tacfarinas' identification as Numidian (despite the associated issues), he has most commonly been assumed to have served in a Numidian unit – more specifically, as part of the Numidian cavalry. Tacitus does not specify this, and there were other auxiliary units raised from the region at different points, including the Ala Afrorum (Afri), the Ala Gaetulorum (Gaetulians), the Ala Maurorum (Mauri), and the Ala Musulamiorum (Musulamii), attested in the epigraphic record. As these were also cavalry units, it makes little practical difference whether Tacfarinas served in a Numidian unit or a different one, as his training and field operation would have been the same. Further, the Numidian cavalry may have long contained recruits who were not actually 'Numidian', but serving under this banner for practical purposes; the term 'Numidian' in this context is not necessarily an accurate ethnic identifier.

The Numidians had been known and admired as cavalry soldiers for several centuries by the early Imperial period, and they were arguably the most effective light cavalry in the ancient Mediterranean.[13] Their cavalry were lightly armed and wore no metal body armour, but were protected only by a light oval shield. Their weapon of choice was the javelin and they typically did not have swords, although may have had short daggers.[14] The battle techniques of the Numidian cavalry relied on excellent equestrian skills and wearing their enemy down. Their horses were controlled by a single rein attached to a basic neck collar made from hair or vegetable fibres, and were guided where necessary by a thin wooden rod.[15] Riders were trained to hurl javelins from horseback, advancing on the enemy and then retreating, repeating the attack over and over.[16] Their preferred method of engaging with the enemy was a quick darting attack followed by a rapid retreat before an effective defence could be put up, repeated multiple times as required.[17] A description of an attack on Roman troops by Numidian cavalry during the Jugurthine War gives an excellent summary of their methods:

> the Numidians cut down the rearmost Romans, while a part attacked them on the right and left, pressing on with vigour and energy and throwing the ranks into general confusion. For even those [Romans] who had withstood the charge with a stout heart were baffled by this irregular manner of fighting, in which they were only wounded from a distance, without having the opportunity of striking back or of joining in hand-to-hand conflict. Jugurtha's horsemen, following the instructions given them beforehand, whenever a squadron of the Roman cavalry began to attack them, gave way; not, however, in a body or in one direction, but dispersing as widely as possible. Thus even if they had been unable to check the enemy's pursuit, with their superior numbers they cut off the stragglers in the rear or on the flanks.[18]

The Numidians avoided being drawn into hand-to-hand combat whenever possible, attacking instead with light javelins deployed from a distance. They were not a heavy cavalry and did not inflict high casualties on the enemy in the way that cataphract units, for example, would. Nor were they mounted infantry. Instead, they were units of disruption in battle, targeting certain parts of the enemy formation to keep them from manoeuvring within the battlefield, or to lure them into an attack by heavier troops.[19] Their tactics reflected the low-intensity warfare origins of the Numidian forces, in which they were used for raiding, aiming to get maximum booty with a minimum of casualties, avoiding manpower losses which could prove unsustainable for individual tribes. However, their reputation for avoiding pitched battle where possible could be used to their advantage, as the enemy did not expect them to ever engage at close quarters and so could be surprised if they did.

The Numidian cavalry also played an important role off the battlefield. During the Second Punic War they were used to harass the enemy on the march, as well as to scout, raid enemy camps, burn crops, and attack enemy foraging parties, all important components of irregular warfare. They could put pressure on the enemy without having to set foot on a pitched battleground; Tacfarinas would make the same use of his men during his war with Rome. However, they were vulnerable if forced to fight hand-to-hand and/or on foot. During the Second Punic War, 500 Numidian cavalry were lost in a Roman surprise attack, when they could not reach their horses in time.[20] That said, catching them in such a position was difficult to do. Numidian soldiers were seen by the Romans as being exceptionally hardy,[21] and particularly adept at coping with hunger. The historian Appian suggested that they were able to survive on herbs or vegetables instead of bread and by only drinking water, while their horses fed exclusively on grass, without supplementary grain, and water.[22] The Numidians' stamina was also such that some cavalrymen apparently had two horses so that they could change mounts when one tired and immediately carry on with what they were doing, even in battle.[23] In the Imperial period, the horses used by the Numidian cavalry were still known for their stamina and speed.[24]

It is difficult to reconstruct what the Numidian cavalry looked like, although one can form some ideas based on the limited visual and descriptive sources. The soldiers themselves wore minimal armour and some accounts of the cavalry suggest that they were not necessarily always physically impressive. This impression can be found in a description given by Livy when the Romans and their auxiliaries faced an enemy army blocking a pass in front of them in 193 BC:

> At first nothing was more contemptible than their [the Numidians'] appearance: horses and men were tiny and gaunt; the riders unequipped and unarmed, except that they carried javelins with them; the horses without bridles, their very motion being the ugly gait of animals running with stiff necks and outstretched heads.[25]

However, they were clearly more capable in battle than looks suggested. Following the passage quoted above, Livy goes on to describe how the Numidians knowingly used their underwhelming appearance to lure the enemy into a false sense of security, and in fact further exaggerated it by deliberately falling off their horses and pretending to be unable to control them. Once their enemy had become complacent, the Numidians kicked into action and charged through the opposition's battle-line, causing them to break formation and flee. In art, Numidian cavalry appear to have distinctive visual characteristics, including their mounts having different head-shapes to Roman horses, with much longer necks and manes.[26] Trajan's Column, constructed in the early second century, contains a scene from the First Dacian War depicting horsemen who have traditionally been identified as either Numidian or Moorish cavalry (number 64).[27] The detail of the riders has been relatively well-preserved, showing them carrying short, round shields on their left arms, with ringleted hair, beards, and short tunics which seem to be tied over their shoulders. Although Trajan's Column theoretically only captures the appearance of the Numidian cavalry at a single point in time, it is likely that most troops would have resembled this portrait – not least as otherwise it may have been difficult for viewers of the monument to understand who they were looking at.

Not all Numidian soldiers were cavalrymen. A core unit of infantry was maintained to undertake tasks for which the cavalry were unsuited, such as defending forts and settlements. These troops were also predominantly lightly armed, mostly without armour (certainly without metal armour), using javelins like their mounted counterparts, and with light oval shields.[28] They were much more mobile than the general Roman infantry, and probably also avoided engaging in heavy hand-to-hand fighting, preferring to launch javelin attacks from a distance. Such mobility and flexibility made the Numidian infantry difficult to handle in some circumstances,[29] and they could not always be defeated by conventional methods. There was no inherent reason that Numidians could not make effective infantry fighting in a more disciplined manner and at times in the Republican period they had performed well in this role when trained by Roman soldiers.[30] Rather, they were just so pushed towards mounted warfare from a young age that they did not develop skills in infantry fighting, yet were more than capable of picking them up with the right training. However, it became a literary trope that Numidian soldiers (like many other 'barbarians') became especially competent soldiers when trained and commanded by Roman officers.[31] To Roman eyes, Numidians appeared disloyal to defeated commanders. During the Jugurthine War, Jugurtha was said to have been abandoned by all but his personal bodyguard, as 'not a single Numidian follows his king after a defeat, but all disperse whithersoever they choose, and this is not considered shameful for soldiers. Such are their customs.'[32] Evidently, however effective the Numidians were in warfare, Roman sources would find some way to disparage them.

The Numidian Cavalry

Tacfarinas was far from the first generation of Numidians to fight for the Roman army. Numidians had served as far back as the middle Republican period, before Rome even had a province in Africa.[33] Romans had first faced Numidians in the Second Punic War, when the latter fought as allies of Carthage. From the later stages of the Second Punic War Rome became increasingly reliant on allied Numidian cavalry units who, along with some Gallic tribes, provided a substantial part of their mounted troops. The alliance with Masinissa had greatly facilitated this; he had provided soldiers as part of their agreement, which probably won the Numidian king (and his successors) greater prestige and protection from Rome than they might otherwise have been given. Numidian cavalry fought for Rome in the Second and Third Macedonian Wars, and in Liguria, Gaul, and Spain.[34]

Given their value to the Roman military during the Republican period, it is unsurprising that Numidian cavalry in particular continued to be of importance during the early Imperial period.[35] However, the method by which they were incorporated into the Roman army changed as early as the reign of Augustus, from one of allies providing troops to help their 'friends', to a subject people providing troops on demand. One of the requirements made by Rome of subject populations during the Imperial period was the provision of troops to serve in the *auxilia*, often in designated ethnic units, and at some point Tacfarinas became one of these recruits, willing or otherwise. The recruitment – or conscription – of young men, particularly from newly subjected territories, provided several benefits to Rome. These included removing a part of the indigenous population most able to fight against Rome in any rebellion, taking them from their native communities where resentments might build up into resistance – it was thought better to have them inside the *auxilia* where a close eye could be kept on them. At the same time, hostility to Rome could potentially be neutralized during their period of service. If they completed a full 25-year period, an auxiliary soldier would be made a Roman citizen, with all the legal and economic benefits that brought. Unfortunately, this system was not always successful with the indigenous populations subjected to it, likely including northwest Africa during the reign of Augustus (see below). To try to avoid problems with auxiliaries deserting the army, wherever it was practical the units were sent to serve in a province far from their homeland, although this was not always possible, particularly for specialist units like the Numidian cavalry who had specific roles to play in certain places.

The cavalry of the Imperial Roman army was divided into two types of unit, the *ala* (purely cavalry) and the *cohors equitata* (mixed cavalry and infantry), both types either 500 or 1,000 men strong. They were sub-divided into *turmae* (singular *turma*) of 32 men, commanded by a *decurio*, sometimes from the same ethnic background as the troops.[36] The unit as a whole would be under a *praefectus equitum*, a citizen from the semi-aristocratic equestrian class. The majority of the Roman cavalry were heavily armed with both projectile weapons and swords, and were capable of fighting at close quarters as well as from a distance, in contrast to the style of the light and mobile Numidian cavalry. They, like other auxiliary units, served predominantly in the Roman frontier provinces, where their skills in patrolling and scouting played a vital role in security, but their battlefield skills meant that they were also used in campaigns of conquest and consolidation, and to put down rebellions where needed. The incorporation of Numidian cavalry into the Roman *auxilia* gave a new role to a group which also had a significant symbolic importance in northwestern Africa, perhaps even demonstrating how Rome and Numidia could viably integrate further in the future.[37] Not to have done this would have been to ignore a significant military resource available to the Romans, undoubtedly to their cost, and also to have potentially upset the social balance in northwestern Africa by excluding an important institution.

One of the inherent risks in the Roman auxiliary system in the late first century BC/early first century AD was that it relied on troops whose loyalty was not necessarily reliable, particularly among those forcibly conscripted. The Roman military took in these individuals, trained them to a high standard, taught them field operations, and promoted those with the right aptitude to positions of command – giving them a wide range of skills that could one day be turned back against Rome. Several rebellions in the early first century BC were led by ex-auxiliaries with insider knowledge of how the Roman army worked and what its weaknesses were, information they were able to put to good use.

Tacfarinas in the Roman Army

At some point before AD 17 – probably quite a while before – Tacfarinas became part of the Roman army. Tacitus does not give any indication of how old he was at the time, though he was almost certainly in his late teens/very early twenties; the standard age for new recruits seems to have been *c.*16–21 years old. Whether he was a willing recruit is unclear. He may well have been forcibly conscripted into the army rather than volunteering himself. Manpower resources would have been in high demand in the late first century BC and early first century AD with all the conflict in the region (and the Empire more widely), and Tacfarinas may have been part of a conscription drive in the early first century AD to boost the number of soldiers Rome had available.[38] There is no reference to what unit Tacfarinas served in, or where he was posted. Tacitus identifies him as an auxiliary soldier, but does not indicate whether he was a cavalryman or in the infantry. He is usually thought to have served in a Numidian (cavalry) unit, due to his ethnic identification by Tacitus, but it could have been one of the other African auxiliary units active at this time.

The Numidians were particularly prized as cavalry soldiers, but the other units were cavalry as well, so probably Tacfarinas was a mounted soldier, although later he proved adept at training his own recruits 'in the Roman style', suggesting that he may have been involved with the infantry. We don't know what rank he reached, or where his unit was based during his time in the *auxilia*. He may not even have left northwest Africa, as auxiliary units were typically only transferred out of their area of origin if their continued presence there would have represented a security threat.[39] Given that Numidians had been part of the Roman army for around two centuries, they may not have seemed an obvious threat, particularly if they had remained loyal during the Garamantean and Gaetulian Wars, as they seem to have done. Even if Tacfarinas did serve in a different unit, they may equally have been perceived as no threat and thus remained in northwest Africa. If it did stay in the region, Tacfarinas' unit was probably attached to the 3rd Legion Augusta, who would become his first and main opponent during the war – a personal connection to the legion may have made Tacfarinas' future actions particularly hard to take for his former comrades.

Although it is frustrating not to know more about Tacfarinas' military career, the omissions are not particularly surprising. Even in the case of other, better documented and more highly regarded ex-auxiliary rebels, such as Arminius in Germany, there is no historical evidence to tell us in which unit they served – either Roman historians did not know, or chose not to include the information, perhaps judging it of little relevance or interest to their readers. Further, Tacfarinas' status as a despised deserter from the army may have made it undesirable to record which auxiliary unit he had once been a member of, in case their association with him came to tarnish their reputation. As a result, his military career can only be reconstructed with the broadest of strokes, without any supplementary detail concerning where he served, with what rank, and for how long. During his time in the Roman army, Tacfarinas appears to have developed into a 'good' soldier, or at least someone with the skills of a good soldier, however he subsequently chose to use them. To a degree this is speculation, but arguably can be seen from his later actions against Rome as someone who understood the Roman military system, its strengths and weaknesses, who had not only learned how to engage in irregular warfare but was able to pass these skills on to his men.[40]

At some point, Tacfarinas deserted from the Roman army and returned to Numidia. How long he spent in the *auxilia* before that is not recorded. However, it was sufficient for him to pick up Roman training techniques that he later implemented with his own troops, suggesting he had remained for several years at least and potentially much longer. When exactly he deserted is another question, and the answer partly depends on whether he left specifically to go to war against Rome – which would suggest a date quite close to the outbreak of hostilities – or for another reason and subsequently ended up in conflict with Rome, in which case his desertion could have been at any time. Although the war broke out from a Roman perspective in AD 17, Mauretania was seemingly already fighting Tacfarinas as early as AD 14, indicating that he must have deserted before that year. A date as early as AD 10 has been suggested, on the basis that high levels of auxiliary soldiers did not need to be maintained in the region after this point, with the implication that reluctant soldiers would be allowed to slip away without too much Roman attention.[41] If he did desert this early, based on the probability that he spent at least a few years in the *auxilia* before leaving it, makes it more likely that he did serve in the Gaetulian War. In that case, the conflict would have given him really valuable insights into how the Roman army operated on campaign in the region, the general intelligence they had about the local topography and peoples, and what the weaknesses of both sides were in the field. The most likely date range for his desertion is *c.*AD 10–13 – but why it came about is far from clear.

There is certainly no indication in Tacitus of what led Tacfarinas to desert the Roman army. Desertion is a subject little discussed by the ancient sources, being mentioned mainly in the context of the punishment of men who tried to prematurely leave service – unsurprisingly, these punishments were often harsh, aiming to deter others from following the example of their former comrades.[42] How prevalent these punishments were in reality, however, is questionable, and desertion rates were probably consistently high.[43] Auxiliary soldiers were potentially more likely to desert, as they had no citizenship status to lose as a result, and they may have therefore been able to slip back into civilian life without undue attention. The likelihood of finding a welcome among the people you deserted (back) to probably also played a significant role in the decision to abandon the Roman military.

In terms of Tacfarinas, it is impossible to say for sure what prompted his desertion, or what he intended to do afterwards. He may simply have grown tired of military life and become part of a generalized drifting away of auxiliaries from military service in the years following the Gaetulian War, when they were no longer particularly needed by Rome, with many leaving at the same time as him and potentially becoming part of his force later on.[44] That he ended up in conflict with Mauretania and then Rome, initially through bandit activity, does not necessarily indicate that this was his intention in deserting. Many soldiers (and indeed, veterans) turned to banditry after leaving the Roman army, turning the skills they had developed in the army to their own benefit – they may even have been doing much the same as they did in the army anyway.[45] Banditry could be a lucrative new career for ex-soldiers, and both deserters and veterans may have had relatively few other options open to them.[46] Certainly, the material rewards of crime must have been tempting, in comparison to the relatively low (if steady) pay offered by the *auxilia*. Soldiers-turned-bandits would also be free of the negative aspects of being in the Roman army, which in addition to the usual rigours of military life and campaigning also included excessively harsh discipline and mistreatment by superior officers, including bribes being demanded to secure anything but the worst duties.[47] Tacfarinas and many of his comrades may simply have grown tired of such a life and decided that better prospects lay elsewhere. There may have been no specific intention of getting into a conflict with either Mauretania or Rome, at least initially, but simply the aim to enrich themselves through banditry for as long as possible.

Alternatively, Tacfarinas may have deserted for more political reasons, prompted by a desire to confront and resist Rome due to the mistreatment of some or all the northwest African peoples, and the growing threat to their way of life. In this scenario, the most likely prompt for his desertion is the construction of the Roman road between Ammaedara and Tacape, which ran through the territory of the Musulamii. This road has been viewed as one of the trigger-points of the rebellion, although it is far from clear how great an impact it would actually have had on the Musulamii.[48] If this was the cause of Tacfarinas' desertion, it pushes the date forward to AD 14 at the earliest, which is still consistent with Mauretania starting limited military operations against him around the same time.

Whatever the cause of Tacfarinas' desertion, the outcome was evidently the same: a growing campaign of banditry carried out against settlements in Mauretanian and Roman territory. The war did not suddenly erupt, but escalated from a conflict that looked like just another example of border banditry into full-scale war against Rome. For several years it was seemingly the responsibility of Juba II to deal with the problem, but further escalation led Rome to take direct action in AD 17.

Chapter 5

The Road to War (*c.*AD 12–17)

A lot happened between Tacfarinas deserting the Roman army and Rome declaring war on him and his army in AD 17. For several years before this declaration, Tacfarinas had been recruiting and training an army, conducting settlement raids, and gradually developing a political reputation among the people of northwest Africa. In this phase of activity, Tacfarinas was probably seen initially as little more threatening than any other marginal bandit, of which there were no doubt many in the region. In the years from *c.*AD 13 (or earlier) to 17, responsibility for dealing with Tacfarinas probably rested with Juba II of Mauretania, as part of his remit to maintain border security in the region on behalf of Rome. Over time, however, Tacfarinas developed a much more well-organized army and drew support not just from bandits and other deserters, but from those who wanted to (re-)establish their independence from Roman rule. Whether he intended to lead an actual rebellion against the Romans – or indeed, fight them at all – is debatable, but the notion he was no more than a bandit does not really fit the evidence, even in this period. Ultimately, Juba would fail to suppress Tacfarinas, despite evidently claiming a series of victories, so that by AD 17, Rome was forced to step in and lead the war effort directly.

Tacfarinas' Army

After deserting the Roman army, Tacfarinas either headed back to or remained in northwest Africa. He may have taken many of his fellows with him. Although Tacitus does not specify that any of the men who later served in his army were also from the Roman army, it seems reasonably likely that at least some of those he knew in service followed him rather than stay enlisted.[1] Roman deserters were not the only men to serve under Tacfarinas, but they may have been the first. Initially he seems to have commanded a relatively small force, which was used to raid settlements, perhaps particularly along the southern border(s) of Mauretania and possibly Africa Proconsularis. Tacitus gives no details at this stage of the war about where Tacfarinas' main area of operation was, but it was not until much later that he attempted anything near the more settled coastal area. Suppressing these early banditry-style operations would have been the remit of Juba II rather than Rome.

However, Mauretania was also going through a politically sensitive period when Tacfarinas entered the scene. Juba turned 60 around the same time, and although there are no references to any illness or infirmity, he was already starting to pass power on to his son, Ptolemy of Mauretania. Ptolemy probably became co-ruler with his father *c.*AD 11, and was made formal regent by about AD 17.[2] The co-rulership may have been introduced to try to convince Rome to let Ptolemy inherit the kingdom after Juba's death, or to enable him to earn support among the population, with whom he does not appear to have been popular. The Mauretanian response to the developing conflict with Tacfarinas might not have been as strong as it would have been in the past, when Juba's attention was not partially diverted towards the issue of his succession.

According to Tacitus, the initial recruits to Tacfarinas' army were 'gangs of vagrants, accustomed to robbery',[3] whose primary desire was to violently plunder the richer communities of northwest Africa. There were undoubtedly some deserters among them, and indeed possibly some discharged veterans finding that retirement was not as exciting or economically bountiful as they might have hoped, but Tacitus makes little reference to these groups and their numbers may have been limited.[4] Instead, he focuses on the more contemptible (from a Roman perspective) recruits, those who were not settled in a particular area and had previous experience of banditry. As discussed in the Introduction, banditry was a common phenomenon in the Roman world and one which most of Tacitus' readers would have feared. The only effective way to deal with bandits was through military discipline and force – either a campaign against them, or by recruiting them into the Roman army where they could be controlled. In a passage from Cassius Dio, the Imperial advisor Maecenas guides Augustus through the benefits of recruiting into the army those who might otherwise become bandits:

> The hardiest of them and those most in need of a livelihood should be enlisted as soldiers and given a military training. For they will fight better if they devote their time to this one business, and the rest will find it easier to carry on their farming, seafaring, and the other pursuits appropriate to peace, if they are not compelled to take part in military expeditions but have others to act as their defenders. Thus the most active and vigorous element of the population, which is generally obliged to gain its livelihood by brigandage, will support itself without molesting others, while all the rest will live without incurring dangers.[5]

This speech is a literary construction of Dio's rather than an accurate account of an actual conversation between Maecenas and Augustus and was written two centuries after it was supposed to have taken place, but it raises some particularly interesting issues. The impact of banditry is illustrated by the peace that will fall on the settled communities if their activity were stopped, and the increase in productivity that will result from them not having to serve in the army any more. But of most interest is the tacit acknowledgement that many of these bandits did not engage in such activity to become wealthy, but just to earn a living. A career in the Roman army would allow them to support themselves without resorting to banditry. Yet even if some Romans were aware of these wider issues, the majority of Tacitus' readers would have understood that identifying Tacfarinas and his men as bandits from the start of the conflict would lead to their being viewed in a particularly negative way.

Whether or not Tacfarinas' army was originally mostly composed of vagrant bandits, he took early steps to train them into a much better force. He took the recruits and organized them in the manner of a formal field army, dividing them into units and different troop types, perhaps using military theory he had picked up in the *auxilia*. These arrangements alone would have started to make his warband a much more daunting prospect to face in the field; bandit raids were organized, but never on this scale. What his men thought of the change is unknown – they had enlisted in the hope of plunder and violence, only to then find themselves subjected to Roman-style military discipline. Presumably, had this idea appealed to them they would have enlisted in the *auxilia* themselves, suggesting that the development may not have been entirely welcome. This early army seems to have been predominantly used for settlement raiding prior to AD 17, so it might appear that Tacfarinas' ambitions in this period were largely limited to banditry. However, the level of organization of his troops suggests that something more was going on, even if it still fell far short of any ambition to free northwestern Africa from Roman rule.

It was not long before Tacfarinas' army began to win him political recognition. At some point he became a leader of the Musulamii; Tacitus uses the word *dux*, which literally meant 'leader' but had a range of possible meanings related to military command, for both Roman and non-Roman individuals. In the context of Tacfarinas it seems to imply that he became the chieftain of the Musulamii, but it is possible that he became a military leader without any responsibility for domestic politics.[6] Tacfarinas does not seem to have been born into the ruling family of the Musulamii, not least because his rise to that position would not have been remarkable had he just inherited it. Whether he had harboured any such ambitions when he began recruiting and training his army is unknown. But the fact that he came to lead his tribe suggests that he was a competent, even shrewd, political operator – in addition to clearly being an excellent military commander capable of transforming a band of marauding warriors into a coherent and disciplined military force.

Under Tacfarinas' leadership, the men continued their raiding and plundering against settled populations in the region. As their influence spread, Tacfarinas was able to make a form of alliance with the Mauri of eastern Mauretania, whose chief was named Mazippa. The additional manpower and command allowed Tacfarinas to further develop the operational effectiveness of his forces. He was able to hand-pick the most promising recruits and focus on training them in the style of Roman soldiers. He equipped them with Roman weapons, and focused particularly on developing their discipline and obedience.[7] The less capable soldiers formed a more lightly-armed warband under the command of Mazippa, who used them to wreak 'fire, slaughter, and terror' on the civilian population, raiding and pillaging the more settled areas of the region. It was not a new idea to train non-Roman troops with Roman methods to produce a better fighting force, having been done as far back as the Second Punic War for Syphax of Numidia. Tacfarinas recognized that better organization, training, and discipline, combined with the best equipment, could turn his recruits into excellent infantry soldiers, capable of matching anyone in battle. However, he would likely also have been aware of the dangers of meeting larger armies in pitched battle, no matter how well-drilled his soldiers were – if he needed any examples, the Jugurthine War, fought by Numidia against Rome just over a century earlier, would have provided plenty.

Tacfarinas' army was bolstered at various points through alliances with other peoples in the region, or through the ability of his existing force to compel others to join with them. It is difficult to judge the size of the army and it likely fluctuated over time, probably at its largest at the start and end of the war with fewer recruits in the middle years. The Mauri (Moors) fought with Tacfarinas in AD 17 and 24, but not in the intervening period, while the Cinithii were forced to join him in AD 17, but not later on; in the latter case, it appears that Tacfarinas was employing enforced conscription, just as the Romans had probably done previously. Some from the Garamantes and Gaetulians also fought with Tacfarinas at various points. His force at the start of the war was said to have outnumbered that of the Roman army sent to face him, which could have been 10–20,000 men or more, suggesting that Tacfarinas' army was far from inconsiderable. It was almost certainly the largest force ever assembled against Rome in this part of Africa.[8]

The Initial Response

In these early years, suppressing Tacfarinas would have fallen under the remit of Juba II of Mauretania, who was responsible for maintaining security in northwest Africa. Tacitus suggests that the Mauretanian army only became involved in the last stages of the conflict, after the death of Juba II and the accession of Ptolemy. However, coinage of the time suggests that Mauretania was engaged with Tacfarinas before Rome was, when the situation was still one of banditry, and continued to be from the earliest stages of the actual war right through to the end.[9] Although the 3rd Legion Augusta was stationed in Africa Proconsularis by this point, they were probably not involved, at least not as a complete unit, although detachments may have been sent to assist Juba in his efforts. From a Roman perspective, there probably seemed little to worry about, as banditry was so endemic on the provincial borders (indeed, as it was everywhere in the Roman world) that the emergence of a new gang would not have been particularly unusual. What actions (if any) Juba took against Tacfarinas are unknown, although an indication of their potential scale may be illustrated by the fact that he issued victory coins in AD 15 and 16; if these were connected to Tacfarinas, it would strongly suggest that substantial efforts were already being taken by AD 14 at the latest to suppress his depredations.[10]

However, Rome did not get directly involved at this stage. It may not have felt the need to intervene by engaging in an all-out war until the scale of Tacfarinas' operations became apparent, potentially years after the early skirmishes. Roman inaction was certainly not the result of an inability to get involved. The proconsul of Africa Proconsularis at this time was probably Lucius Nonius Asprenas, a highly experienced commander who had previously served as an officer in Syria, Germany, and Pannonia. Asprenas would have been more than capable of leading a campaign against Tacfarinas should such a move have been deemed necessary. He also did not lack the manpower resources, with the 3rd Legion Augusta already garrisoned in the province, partly based in Musulamian territory, over which Tacfarinas now claimed military authority. There is no indication that the 3rd mutinied around this time, suggesting they would have been available to go into the field, although if there had been mass desertions a few years earlier when Tacfarinas left, their supporting *auxilia* might have been a little light in numbers.

There were good reasons for Rome to avoid getting involved in a war in northwest Africa. Deploying military resources there and potentially opening up a new war front was not much in Rome's interests at this particular time. The Empire had gone into crisis in AD 14 with the death of Augustus and accession of Tiberius. The new emperor was seemingly unwilling to accept the power he had inherited and was not particularly decisive during his first months in power.[11] In documents discovered after his death, Augustus had urged Tiberius to not extend the Empire beyond the territory it already held.[12] Aside from making the eastern client kingdoms of Commagene and Cappadocia into Roman provinces, Tiberius appears to have obeyed this injunction, relying on the pre-existing fear of Rome to keep the other territories under control.[13] Multiple legionary mutinies had broken out in the period, particularly in Germany and Pannonia, threatening the internal security of the Empire and limiting the amount of reliable manpower available to deploy in a new war.[14] The Roman military was still recovering from the Great Illyrian Revolt (AD 6–9) and the loss of three legions in the Battle of the Teutoburg (AD 9) in Germany. There were ongoing problems in Germany, with Arminius still on the loose and liable to make war with Rome, and early in Tiberius' reign plans were put in place for a new military expedition to restore security in the region. For a combination of these reasons, Juba II was left in charge of operations against Tacfarinas in the years preceding AD 17 – Rome might get involved in the future, but only at a time that suited Rome.

Tacfarinas' auxiliary experience would have given his army an additional edge, even when they were just facing the Roman-supported Mauretanian army in the early stages of the conflict; any deserters in his army would have had their own military training and experience to add. The ex-auxiliaries had had the opportunity to learn at first-hand what Roman military protocols were in particular situations, such as ambushes or surprise night attacks, and what were the operational weaknesses in the responses. This type of insider knowledge had enabled the German rebel Arminius to orchestrate a devastatingly effective ambush of three Roman legions in Germany in AD 9, using his insight into field operations under attack to pre-empt any moves the Romans would make to escape, ultimately leaving them trapped and helpless.[15] Tacfarinas also presented a unifying figure, able to bring together a wide range of tribes into what became a fierce force of opposition. Revolts against Rome in the first century AD were typically led by individuals from a Romanized class, who managed to bring together disparate groups previously too busy fighting amongst themselves to band together against their overlords.[16] Tacfarinas clearly fell into this group, but whether he intended to lead a rebellion against Rome from the start, or whether this ambition developed later, is another question.

An Area Ripe for Rebellion?

What was the real nature of Tacfarinas' conflict with Rome? Was it, as Tacitus suggested, simply a campaign of banditry which had escalated far beyond acceptable limits? Or was there a wider political element to it (disguised by disapproving Roman sources under accusations of bandit activity), making it a rebellion with the aim of removing Roman administration from certain regions of northwestern Africa? One of the problems in answering these questions is that they contain implicit assumptions that, i) everyone in Tacfarinas' army was fighting for the same reasons and with the same aims, and ii) that these reasons and aims did not change over the course of the conflict. Another is that raiding was a common military field strategy in northwest Africa, particularly in the context of an irregular campaign, and it is almost impossible to distinguish banditry from legitimate warfare under such circumstances.

Rebellions in the Roman world were not uncommon and there were a significant number in the first century AD. In some cases, Roman writers did explain the causes for the unrest breaking out – or at least, what they understood to be the causes, although how accurate they were is unknown. Tacitus often did give at least some partial explanation of most rebellions discussed in his works, and usually portrays them as the result of existing discontent at Roman rule turning rapidly into rebellion after a specific outrage (social, political, or financial).[17] In the case of the Boudican Revolt in Britain, for example, the violent abuse of the tribal queen and her daughters after the death of husband/father Prasutagus was the outrage, but the treatment of the Iceni people by the Roman authorities is portrayed as the overall cause of the uprising, including the loss of their land.[18] The poor treatment of local populations leading to revolt is identified by Tacitus not as an inevitable part of Roman occupation, but as a result of bad behaviour on the part of the administration, from the soldiery up to corrupt officials.[19]

Without a certain level of discontent among at least parts of the population more widely a single event might not be enough to lead to rebellion against Rome – it did not have to be universal among a people, but sufficiently widespread that a large armed force could be raised. But while Tacitus seemingly accepts that some rebellions were prompted by genuine grievances, the perpetrators being victims with no other choice, in the case of Tacfarinas and other leaders identified as bandits (such as Julius Civilis during the Batavian Revolt in AD 69) he does not acknowledge sufficient motivation for their actions. This presentation fits into a wider habit in Roman historiography to pass off crises caused by systemic flaws in the Imperial system as the fault of the individuals involved.

Background Discontent

Certainly, there was political discontent with Roman rule in northwestern Africa, which had only recently developed into full-scale conflict (the Gaetulian War).

The lack of detailed narrative of that conflict sometimes masks its seriousness, but the few references there are suggest it was a major challenge for Rome. Not only did the hostilities last for more than three years, a proconsul of Africa Proconsularis was killed during the campaign – it was relatively rare by this time for someone in his position to be a casualty of war. The Gaetulian War had been fought less than a decade before Tacfarinas began his operations in the region, and in many ways both conflicts can be seen as different phases of a much longer war between Rome and the peoples of northwest Africa. The relationship between Rome and the indigenous population may never have been particularly good. The Romans' initial presence was probably only a result of the defeat of Carthage and the desire to stop another power (most likely Numidia) emerging as a new rival in the region.

During the Jugurthine War, some of the Numidian population had been treated badly by Rome, including entire communities suffering enslavement and slaughter because of perceived links to Jugurtha. The town of Capsa was burned to the ground, its adult population killed and the rest enslaved and sold for the soldiers' profit, all because it was a strategically important location to Jugurtha and Rome could not bribe or terrorize the population into loyalty to them.[20] The Roman sources seem to express some unease about the treatment of Capsa, but evidently judged that military necessity outweighed other concerns. And Capsa may have been one among many Numidian settlements treated in this way. Losing their independence when Julius Caesar summarily turned Numidia into a Roman province (Africa Nova) in 46 BC may have done little to improve relations, and the reorganizations under Octavian/Augustus would not have helped. Unfortunately, not only does Tacitus not provide any details about why the conflict broke out, he also omits to give any insight into Roman activity in the region during the years immediately before the war, making it difficult to assess what might have led to the discontent. All the 'causes' of unrest that preceded the war have come from subsequent scholarship, looking at the limited evidence of Roman activity in this period and putting their own interpretation on events.

There was a longstanding trend in earlier scholarship about the Tacfarinas War to attribute the tensions leading to it to an incompatibility between the sedentary lifestyle of the Romans and the nomadism of the northwest African population.[21] But by the early first century AD the local population was not entirely nomadic, and even the elements that were did not have an innate hostility to sedentary peoples.[22] Each actually needed the other – the settled needed the nomads for trade and pastoralism, the nomads needed the settlers to be their partners in a 'trade-or-raid' lifestyle that gave the necessities they could not find elsewhere.[23] Rather than thinking of them as two different groups, it might be better to imagine them at different points on a scale of agro-pastoralist lifestyle. There is little evidence that Rome tried to force the nomadic elements of the population to become sedentary. Nor are there any grounds to think that significant changes in social and cultural life were imposed on the population, the process known as 'Romanization' – which has become a loaded and often rejected term.[24] Under this model, rebellion could be prompted by over-rapid change being forced on unwilling populations by provincial authorities. However, archaeological research across the provinces suggests that there was no such process, that elements of Roman culture were made available to the local inhabitants without any obligation to adopt them, and that many people, particularly the rural poor, lived under Imperial rule in more or less the same way as they had before.

A land survey under Augustus may have provoked some worry among the population about the potential outcomes. Increased Roman activity in the region had led to greater competition for agriculturally productive land, and the wider population may have feared that the surveys were a preliminary to the confiscation of their best lands in exchange for others that the Romans did not want. The nomadic element of the population (albeit probably a minority) would have increasingly found the traditional routes they drove their flocks along blocked by new farming estates, which also reduced the amount of wild pasture available to them. People would have felt threatened by the large private estates established near their territory, which started to encroach on the land they could claim for themselves.[25] These changes were backed up by military force, with the 3rd Legion Augusta garrisoned nearby, based at Ammaedara but with detachments elsewhere, most likely at Capsa and Tacape.[26]

The land surveys could also have provided the information needed to introduce taxation to the region, which would have impacted settled and nomadic populations alike. The administration of a province, especially one with a military garrison, was an expensive business, and the more that could be extracted in local taxes to pay for it, the better. Taxation caused significant discontent in many provinces and was identified as a cause of unrest among the British during the Boudican revolt.[27] Some identify this as a primary concern of the population in the period leading up to the Tacfarinas War.[28] The 3rd Legion Augusta may even have been stationed in Africa Proconsularis specifically to collect tax from the more isolated parts of the provincial interior where civic collectors could not be expected to work.[29] The early Imperial tax system is not well understood, but evidently it could be levied on land, property, annual produce, and possibly *per capita* as well.[30] There was probably no uniformity of tax collection throughout the provinces in the first century AD, and the rates levied from each population may have varied – but would still have had a significant impact on people who had not previously been expected to pay them.

The garrison itself may have presented a further issue, as the burden of supplying the troops with food, fodder, and other necessities would have impacted the territory around the fortress at Ammaedara – once again this meant the Musulamii. Many garrisons sustained themselves as much as possible on local produce, and the surrounding population was often required to provide grain and other foodstuffs (surplus or otherwise) to the military, placing strains on their resources. Alternatively, land belonging to locals could be confiscated and given to the legion to supply itself (*territorium*, or *prata legionis*).[31] The legionary garrison likely needed at least 1kg of wheat/grain per soldier per day, for up to 5,000 men (though likely fewer most of the time). Calculations made for a later legionary fortress in the region (at Lambaesis) suggest that an area of 91km^2 was needed to meet basic needs, the equivalent of a surplus of at least 650 tribal households.[32]

Increased levels of military conscription from the population of northwest Africa may have provoked further discontent; it was a cited cause in other rebellions of the first century AD.[33] Conscripts potentially became active participants in the exploitation of their homeland and suppression of their people. The treatment of the auxiliaries themselves may also have proved an issue, particularly if the first time-served generation of veterans found the material rewards of service were insufficient – more particularly, if they did not receive the retirement bonuses they expected. Some have even suggested that the rebellion began as a kind of military revolt, which the wider population joined in with as a way to express their own discontent with Roman rule.[34] Rome did not take much of an active role in frontier security at this time, leaving Juba II in charge of the area, and he appears to have struggled on occasion – so the population of the region did not even get greater protection from banditry and raiding in exchange for everything they were losing. As for the population outside Numidia, they may have been spared some of the worst by the fact they did not live in areas that the Romans campaigned in during this period. However, increased Roman exploration brought more of the people living away from the provincial territories, particularly those in the mountains and on the edges of the desert, into more frequent contact with Rome. They evidently knew enough about its consequences to fear Roman rule being extended to them – one of the reasons Juba II faced opposition in Mauretania was the inhabitants' fear that this would effectively make them subjects of Rome in all but name.

These various sociocultural, economic, and military factors combined to create a state of discontent among the parts of the population of northwest

Africa coming under direct Roman rule for the first time. The people who were not yet impacted would have seen what would happen, probably only a short time in the future, when they came under Roman rule themselves and may have been keen to take action to delay this happening for as long as possible. The background conditions were certainly ripe for a rebellion in northwest Africa in the early first century AD, but there would need to be a spark-point, probably *c.* AD 14/15, the point at which conflict broke out once more in the region.

The Spark Point: A Road from Ammaedara to Tacape?

There are several possible events that brought about the transformation of provincial discontent into an actual conflict. One of the prime candidates is the construction of a road from Ammaedara to Tacape in AD 14. It was the first major Roman road to be constructed in the region. There were some Punic-era routeways in northwest Africa but in that period, with their territory largely on the coast, boats would have been an efficient way to move things around. Rome may have used largely the same system in the second to first centuries BC but this, like so many things, would change in the early Imperial period. Roads were an important part of provincial infrastructure, particularly for the military, and it is no surprise to see them being constructed in northwest Africa once Rome had become more interested in the areas away from the coastline. There were no major rivers there suitable to move large amounts of men and goods by boat, meaning that everything going in or out of the provincial interior would have to go by road. In many ways, it is surprising that road building started as late as it did. But while the exact course of the road is known, it is less clear how it physically interacted with land owned by the indigenous populations.

For some, the road was the main cause of discontent and subsequent rebellion in the region, so it became a symbol of the power struggle between Rome and the nomadic population.[35] The route took the road through the territory of the Musulamii and impacted the freedom of movement of the nomadic pastoralists. This has become a popular explanation and might be thought of as the 'traditional' view, particularly among those who view Tacfarinas as having been a rebel leader from the start. The road may have forced the pastoralists to drive their herds through limited parts of the landscape, potentially redirecting them away from traditional routes towards those which were convenient for Rome. It would potentially have also enabled a level of Roman surveillance of the nomadic peoples of the region and brought them into more direct contact with the Roman army, with all the negative impacts – such as mistreatment and theft – that could bring.[36] But this division of Musulamian land, and the consequences it may have had, were hardly the intention of the Romans. The road may simply have been constructed to link Ammaedara up with Tacape for strategic reasons, perhaps to connect two bases of the 3rd Legion Augusta.[37] It happened to cut through the territory of the Musulamii, but this may have been for convenience only, perhaps also in ignorance (or ambivalence) about any impact it might have on the locals. The construction of the road may simply have been judged a military necessity at this point, due to growing problems with raiding on the southern borders of the province and a resurgence of conflict in the area *c.*AD 13/14. Although Mauretania was supposed to take the lead in border security, perhaps the Roman authorities were already anticipating that they would need the road to facilitate their own campaigning in the near future; if so, it would be ironic if the road they constructed to deal with a future war actually provoked one.

And yet, whether the road would have had a really significant impact on the nomadic pastoralists in the region is debatable. Although it ran through the territory of the Musulamii, it did not necessarily hinder their freedom of movement – not least because roads alone do not really function as barriers to herds in that way – and besides that the land taken to build it was minimal.[38] Any restriction on movement that there was may only have affected a small proportion of the Musulamian population, since the prevalence of nomadism may have been limited by this point, as it was for the Garamantes and likely other peoples in the region.[39] Others point out that if the road was so hated by the local population it makes little sense for them to have waited until it was finished to launch an uprising – if it was the cause of rebellion conflict would surely have broken out sooner.[40] This is a reasonable argument, but it does not address the fact that there was conflict in the region from *c.*AD 13/14 linked to Tacfarinas, and although this has typically been identified as settlement raiding, there could have been attacks on the road construction as well. The road alone, however, is not sufficient to explain why peoples other than the Musulamii got involved in the initial stages of the conflict, as they would have been unaffected by this particular development. The fact that Tacfarinas drew recruits from across the region suggests there were wider fears about Roman activity, either because others were also already being directly affected, or they expected to be in the near future if they did not take action to prevent it.[41]

The road may have contributed to people's discontent for other reasons and may have damaged the Musulamii and others in different ways. The construction period would potentially have had a significantly negative impact, requiring substantial quantities of material resources and labour (human and animal), and putting significant strain on local food and – particularly – water supplies.[42] Some have suggested that it was viewed as a problem because of the impact it would have on trade in the region, with Roman merchants entering the field and affecting the income of local elites[43] and merchants using this new road instead of the traditional routes controlled by the Musulamii.[44] This is difficult to quantify as not enough is known about trade in this part of the world in the early Imperial period, but evidence from Garamantean territory not too far away indicates bustling Saharan commercial networks that may have been replicated elsewhere.[45] Perhaps the road was a factor, but more like a symbolic 'final straw' in an already deteriorating situation, as the Musulamii and others came to a better understanding of their future with Rome.[46]

A move to introduce taxation is an alternative candidate for the event which sparked off a rebellion. It seems clear that Rome did want to tax the region, preferably sooner rather than later, and had already implemented the surveys which would have provided the information needed to initiate tax collection. The army was in place to help quell any disturbances potentially expected by the Roman authorities (although if the Tacfarinas War did erupt from this, the scale of the resistance was seemingly underestimated).

Tacfarinas: A Rebel or a Bandit?

The conditions may have been ripe for rebellion, but that does not necessarily mean that Tacfarinas intended from the start that his actions would be any more than a campaign of banditry. It may have developed into rebellion once elements of the local peoples started to ally themselves to Tacfarinas as a result of their widespread discontent, but again that does not necessarily indicate that Tacfarinas himself had intended this. There is no evidence that he deserted from the *auxilia* specifically to lead a rebellion, and the likely spark-points seem to post-date his time in the army by several years. Banditry was rife throughout the Roman world in this period and was one of the most profitable post-army careers for deserters and retired veterans alike.[47] There may have been no motive in the early stages except the desire to loot as much as possible from Roman and Mauretanian settlements, and the campaign appears to have attracted many to it. Tacfarinas himself was clearly a capable and no doubt charismatic leader who managed to gather a large force around him – one which would be very useful if it could be coopted into a rebellion, even if that is not why it was originally formed.

So, in some ways Tacitus' characterization of Tacfarinas as a bandit may at least partially reflect the truth for the earliest stages of his operation c.AD 12/13. However, the lack of effective Mauretanian response and the wider discontent among the population of northwest Africa may then have combined to transform banditry into rebellion, and Tacfarinas from an outlaw into a political and military leader. The fact that he trained his forces so well, far beyond what would be necessary for raiding, backs up the idea that the campaign grew into something different from its original purpose. Over the course of the conflict several of the peoples of northwest Africa allied with Tacfarinas, particularly at the start and end of the conflict (AD 17 and 24). For some of these, especially the Mauri, freeing themselves from Roman rule was their aim, and Tacfarinas certainly leaned into this by the late stages of the war.[48] Many different groups united under him to fight their common enemy, not just to plunder their settlements (although the booty acquired from raiding was no doubt appreciated). Tacfarinas became increasingly concerned with gaining territory in which he and his men could live free of Roman oversight – an aim later extended to freeing the entire region from Roman rule. These were not the actions of bandits, but of a group fearing the complete appropriation of their territory and loss of their way of life.[49] This transformation may have been what prompted Rome to take the conflict more seriously in AD 17, having previously tolerated what must have appeared to be just another instance of border banditry, albeit on a much larger scale than usual. Tacfarinas may initially have been dismissed as nothing more than a local thug, part of the general background of low-level misbehaviour that plagued the Roman world. Only when he developed ambitions beyond raiding did Rome's response to him change.

It seems likely therefore that Tacfarinas started off as a bandit, and the actual rebellion developed over time. At what point this happened – whether it had already taken place by AD 17 or built up during the course of the war – is unclear. Despite Tacitus' characterization, Tacfarinas is now generally regarded as the leader of a rebellion against Rome. In early twentieth-century scholarship he was compared favourably with leaders like Viriathus and Boudica, and some argue that he was one of the major rebels in the early Imperial period.[50] But though he was an African leader who took on Rome under his own agency, it is important not to get swept away by the desire to see him as some sort of ancient Robin Hood or Lawrence of Arabia. Tacitus was probably wrong to dismiss Tacfarinas as nothing more than a bandit for the entire course of the war, but it seems very likely that this was how he started off. Nor does his becoming a rebel leader necessarily mean that Tacfarinas completely abandoned the pursuit of gaining illicit wealth, or that none of his recruits were drawn towards him because of the material rewards of service. The problem may lie in making the choice lie between two binary and mutually exclusive positions: that Tacfarinas was *either* a bandit *or* a rebel leader. In reality, he was doubtless a bit of both, with his priorities shifting over time, and with an army that contained both elements at all times.

There are several reasons why the 'bandit' label may have stuck so closely to him in Tacitus' work. The irregular tactics he used against Rome did share many characteristics with banditry and the Romans clearly struggled to handle an enemy who fought them exclusively in that way. His refusal to engage in pitched battle, the ambushes in the field, and the attacks on settlements did not help to dispel the impression of banditry – although this style of fighting cannot have been much of a surprise to Rome, given that northwestern African armies had been using such tactics since the Second Punic War. The Jugurthine War had been fought in this manner, as had actions in the region during the first century BC civil wars – so Rome should not have expected anything different from Tacfarinas. Bandit-like activity went hand-in-hand with warfare in northwest Africa in this period, and there was overlap in outcome as well as field strategy.

It is clear that Tacfarinas' army did take a lot of booty, so much so that it became impossible to transport in the middle years of the conflict, suggesting that he and his men had acquired serious wealth by their methods. But elements of Tacfarinas' character and biography may also have prompted Tacitus' unfavourable characterization of him. His status as a deserter from the *auxilia* would not have helped his reputation. The fact that he was probably not from a Numidian royal family may also have compromised him in Roman eyes.[51] Further, he had become ruler of the Musulamii as a result of military strength (not political justification), usurping the position by means of his private army – this would have been an uncomfortable reminder to Rome of the chaos of the Late Republican civil wars, when individuals like Sulla, Pompey, and Caesar (and indeed, Octavian) had done exactly the same thing. Once this negative image had been established everything he did could be interpreted through it, so even when Tacfarinas offered to negotiate with Rome it would have been seen as insulting rather than a genuine and legitimate attempt at diplomacy. Still, the fact that Tacitus bothered to record his name – unlike, for instance, any of the commanders in the Gaetulian War – suggests that he was recognized as someone of importance. What the Roman commanders who faced him at the time made of him is not known, but even if they thought of him as a mere bandit, they had to engage with him as a rebel.

Rebelling against Rome in the First Century AD

Rebelling against Rome was not an easy thing, and entering into conflict was not a step to be taken lightly. The first century AD was an era of rebellions for Rome, with other uprisings against their rule erupting in Illyricum, Germany, Britain, Batavia, and Judaea. There may have been even more localized revolts which have not made their way into the historical record. With the exception of Germany, these rebellions never succeeded in permanently ending Roman rule of a conquered territory, but that did not stop people trying. The writings of historians like Tacitus suggest that while Rome did not relish facing revolt, they accepted it as an inevitable part of the Imperial system. At least part of the Roman political class recognized that their rule was not welcomed by some among the provincial populations and certainly was not of benefit to them. The impact of conquest could be dramatic and the loss of freedoms and traditional lifestyles under Rome was one of the main rallying points for resistance. During Julius Caesar's Gallic Wars, the Gallic leader Critognatus implored his men to resist Rome lest they fall under the same repression that other Gauls were already experiencing:

> what other motive or wish have the Romans, than, induced by envy, to settle in the lands and states of those whom they have learned by fame to be noble and powerful in war, and impose on them perpetual slavery? For they never have carried on wars on any other terms. But if you know not these things which are going on in distant countries, look to the neighbouring Gaul, which being reduced to the form of a province, stripped of its rights and laws, and subjected to Roman despotism, is oppressed by perpetual slavery.[52]

This passage came from Caesar's own account of the Gallic Wars, either repeating a speech he heard from Critognatus, or creating one – either way, it illustrated the knowledge even on the Romans' part that conquest severely reduced the freedoms of newly subjected populations. In many ways, this should have prompted some sympathy from a Roman perspective, as liberty was also a quality they valued (at least, when it concerned their own). However, Caesar's narrative presents the idea that some individual liberties had to be surrendered by certain populations in the interests of the greater good; war first, and worry about the nature of the peace later.[53] A similar theme is seen in a well-known speech from Tacitus' *Agricola*, put into the mouth of the Caledonian leader Calgacus when facing a Roman army at Mons Graupius, during Agricola's attempt to conquer Scotland in the AD 80s. The speech (almost certainly an invention of Tacitus, who would have had no way of knowing what was said by Calgacus, if indeed anything ever was) highlighted some of the negative aspects of Roman conquest from the perspective of the conquered, and made it clear why provincials might be provoked into rebellion:

> Robbers of the world, having by their universal plunder exhausted the land, they [the Romans] rifle the deep. If the enemy be rich, they are rapacious;

> if he be poor, they lust for dominion; neither the east nor the west has been able to satisfy them. Alone among men they covet with equal eagerness poverty and riches. To robbery, slaughter, plunder, they give the lying name of Empire; they make a solitude and call it peace. Nature has willed that every man's children and kindred should be his dearest objects. Yet these are torn from us by conscriptions to be slaves elsewhere. Our wives and our sisters, even though they may escape violation from the enemy, are dishonoured under the names of friendship and hospitality. Our goods and fortunes they collect for their tribute, our harvests for their granaries. Our very hands and bodies, under the lash and in the midst of insult, are worn down by the toil of clearing forests and morasses.[54]

Tacitus gave Calgacus this speech in the context of inspiring his warriors to resist, lest they suffer the consequences of Roman subjugation, but it gives us an insight into the Roman perspective of how their imperialism was experienced from the point of view of the conquered. Like Critognatus, Calgacus highlighted the costs of living under Roman rule, with no indication that any 'benefits' would be experienced or recognized as such. Many of the issues cited in the passage proved to be motivations for rebellion in the Roman period,[55] demonstrating that Tacitus did have some insight into the discontent of recently conquered populations.

Tacfarinas' war with Rome came in an era where there was widespread discontent – and not infrequent conflict – on the frontiers of the Empire, predominantly (but not exclusively) in territories which had only been conquered by Rome in the preceding few decades. Most aimed to re-establish their independence, preferably by forcing Rome to abandon the province. They commonly took place in the early adulthood of the second generation to live under Roman rule, who had grown up under its harsh realities and who were less affected by any tribalism or old enmities. They usually occurred after Rome believed an area to be generally pacified, meaning that a limited military presence was maintained there, and could be either localized or spread across an entire province.[56] The leader was often a member of the elite who had previously had a close working relationship with Rome (as a client ruler say, or an auxiliary soldier) which had gone wrong, drawing them into conflict. Most of the rebel armies conducted an irregular campaign against the Romans, using guerrilla-type tactics and avoiding pitched battle whenever possible. The Romans, in turn, would try to pressurize the rebels into a battle, eroding their popular support by attacking settlements, and denying them resources through slash-and-burn destruction. Tacfarinas was far from unique in his field strategy against Rome.

With the exception of the revolt led by Arminius, whose actions did ultimately start the process of Rome abandoning the German territories east of the Rhine,[57] all the first century AD rebellions failed. Many of the leaders did not survive, variously betrayed and executed by their own men (Bato the Breucian, Arminius), or committing suicide to avoid capture (Boudica). Others were captured and taken to Rome for further punishment, where some were judged too dangerous to live and executed (Simon bar Giora), which had been common practice for rebel commanders in the Republican period. Others were allowed to live in Italy under close Roman watch, including Bato the Daesitiate, although he was not permitted to leave the country. Some of these rebel leaders received a relatively sympathetic portrayal in the Roman sources, even winning a grudging respect despite the damage their actions had done. They were recognized as freedom fighters (*liberatores*), who were taking on Rome not just out of their own personal interest, but in response to genuine grievances and for the good of their people. Rome could accept they were fighting for good reasons, although this did not stop them supressing the rebellion with as much force as required. Mercy could even be shown to some rebel leaders who expressed appropriate levels of contrition, though this was rare for leaders who posed a particular threat because of their ethnicity, religion, or gender.[58] It was not even always necessary to capture the rebel leader, so long as they could be thoroughly defeated in the field and left powerless, as happened in the case of Arminius.

But Rome looked much less sympathetically upon those who took up arms purely with the intention of personal financial or political gain. Tacfarinas, accurately or not, was firmly put in this group in Tacitus' account, potentially reflecting previously established judgements about his aims and permanently influencing the way that he was viewed by subsequent commentators. This does not, however, mean that they give an accurate representation of Tacfarinas' motives and objectives, and may reveal more about Roman sensibilities than about Tacfarinas' character.

It is perhaps not surprising to see inconsistencies in Roman historiographical attitudes to provincial rebels, with some cast as legitimate freedom fighters and others as bandits even when there was little real difference between their actions. Provincial rebellions were problematic from a Roman perspective, never able to satisfy the criterion of a 'just' or legitimate war, which was a purely ritual definition in the Roman context, concerning the proper conduct of pre-war religious rites in Rome rather than a moral or legal ruling over the legitimacy of the grounds for conflict. The rituals, which included the throwing of a ceremonial spear from the Temple of Bellona, had to be carried out before any fighting started in order to confer 'just' status on the conflict. As this was not possible in cases of provincial rebellion, their status was never as sound as wars fought at Roman instigation. Further, irregular wars were psychologically problematic by their very nature, even though Rome increasingly faced this type of warfare from the first century BC onwards, as it expanded outside the core Mediterranean world. Even worse were cases where due to circumstance the Roman army itself had to adopt irregular tactics (something which again likely happened far more than the historical record would suggest).[59] From a Roman perspective, provincial uprisings were politically, militarily, and ritually problematic. While the motivations of the rebels might be understandable from an objective perspective, any Roman sympathy for a rebel leader would rely on them being recognized as a freedom fighter aiming only at the liberation of their lands and people.

Chapter 6

Marcus Furius Camillus and the First Stages of the War (AD 17–18)

By AD 17, Tacfarinas' actions in northwest Africa had intensified to the point that Rome felt it needed to be more involved in the situation. What had started as a typical case of local banditry had escalated to a regional rebellion, prompted by significant background discontent on the part of the local population. Juba II of Mauretania had probably tried to repress Tacfarinas to the best of his ability but had been unable to do so, and the raiding was becoming more frequent, more damaging, and probably reaching closer towards the settled coastal area, where the majority of the province's wealth was concentrated. Rome could tolerate a certain amount of low-level unrest, particularly when its impact on the regime was minimal, but when it became in their interests to take an active role in suppression, they would act.

The commander in charge of the first stages of the war with Tacfarinas was Marcus Furius Camillus, the recently arrived proconsul of Africa Proconsularis, with the 3rd Legion Augusta and their associated auxiliary units as his main army. He was probably not sent to Africa specifically to conduct the first moves in a war, but while in post received instructions from the Senate (with the tacit approval of Tiberius) to take action against Tacfarinas. He would have required an official mandate (*mandatum*) to act, as provincial officials did not have the authority to initiate a campaign like this; he may also have received directions on how to conduct the war and what his aims in the field should be. The challenge offered by the conflict was significant, even in geographical terms alone, with a front potentially stretching from modern Morocco to Libya, and involving terrain such as deserts and mountains in which the Roman army often struggled to campaign effectively. Nevertheless Camillus, and Rome in general, probably expected this to be a relatively easy campaign brought to a swift and conclusive ending: instead, it became a conflict that would drag on for seven years, dominate the tenure of four different proconsuls, and require the doubling of Roman military manpower in the region.

Marcus Furius Camillus

Marcus Furius Camillus came from a high-ranking family, one with a distinguished heritage but which had faded into relative anonymity. He was a scion of the *gens* (clan) *Furia*, one of the oldest aristocratic families in Rome, more specifically the branch *Furii Camilli*. The *Furii* claimed descent from another Marcus Furius Camillus, who in the early Republican period was said to have protected Rome from being sacked by the Gauls after they had inflicted a devastating defeat on the Romans at the Battle of the Allia (*c.*387 BC). This earlier Camillus was appointed Dictator five times, celebrated four triumphs, and was called by some 'Second Founder of Rome' – although, it was noted, he never held the highest political honour of all, a consulship.[1] The details of the earlier Camillus' life are preserved in one of Plutarch's biographical *Parallel Lives*, in which he is paired with the Athenian general Themistocles. However, historians have since cast doubt about the authenticity of the first Marcus Furius Camillus, suggesting that either the deeds of others were incorrectly attributed to him for the sake of historical narrative, or even that he was entirely fictional.[2] Whatever the truth about him, the family through to the Imperial period promoted the story and emphasized their connection with this important figure in Rome's history. But the family had fallen into relative decline by the later first century BC, as had many of the older aristocratic families in Rome, with none of their number holding more than minor political offices after the third century BC.

The Marcus Furius Camillus who oversaw the first stages of the war against Tacfarinas was born in the last decades of the first century BC, probably around 26 BC just after Augustus was acclaimed first emperor of Rome. He grew up after the near-century of civil wars which had brought ruin on Rome, in an era when the Imperial regime was open to the advance of men from families which had not previously been prominent on the political scene. If he followed the standard aristocratic career ladder (the *cursus honorum*) Camillus would have entered public life as a military tribune around the age of 20. There is no indication of where he served his tribuneship, implying that his military experiences were not substantial in this period. After returning to Rome, Camillus almost certainly would have held a series of administrative positions, including a quaestorship, aedileship and praetorship – but again no details are known about them, they were just part of the standard career progression.

Camillus' career must have gone well, for in AD 8 he was elected consul for the first half of the year[3] at the age of about 33/34 – too young under the Republican system, but more than acceptable under the Imperial regime. Although the establishment of the regime had reduced the consulship to a largely honorific post by the first century AD (as opposed to it being the pinnacle of a career during the Republic), appointment to it was a sign of approval at the highest state level. Camillus' co-consul was Sextus Nonius Quinctilianus, who himself had significant connections. Quinctilianus was the nephew of Publius Quinctilius Varus, a long-time friend of Augustus and Tiberius, a member of the Imperial family by marriage (to Augustus' great-niece, Claudia Pulchra), and a key figure at the heart of the regime. Varus would become infamous just the following year through the loss of three legions in Germany, but at the time when Camillus and his nephew were appointed as consuls, his star was still riding high.[4] The prestigious appointment indicates that Camillus had won the attention and approval of the Imperial regime, and made him eligible for a range of other political positions in the Empire.

What happened to Camillus over the following years is unknown. It is particularly unclear whether he gained any further military experience in this period; his effective response to Tacfarinas suggests he might have done, but he was specifically known as someone with little military background, suggesting that his role was mainly administrative. Either way, the next point at which Camillus can be definitely identified is in AD 17 when he became proconsul of Africa Proconsularis. In theory, he would have been selected by sortition from a group of eligible candidates and there is no indication of any special treatment in his appointment. He replaced a fairly obscure individual named Aulus Vibius Habitus, judging by archaeological evidence placing him in the province around this time.[5] Prior to Habitus, the proconsulship had been held by Lucius Aelius Lamia, a man of administrative and military experience gained in Germany and Pannonia. His predecessor was Lucius Nonius Asprenas the Younger, whose father was a close friend of the emperor Augustus, and his mother a sister of Publius Quinctilius Varus. He was also the brother of Sextus Nonius Quinctilianus, who had served as co-consul with Marcus Camillus in AD 8. Asprenas the Younger had been a prominent commander, serving with his uncle Varus in both Syria (4–1 BC) and Germany (AD 7–9), and protecting survivors of the AD 9 Teutoburg attack as well as helping to secure the Rhine frontier in the aftermath of the battle.

The proconsuls who served prior to Camillus evidently did have some military experience, but in some cases no more than would be expected of any individual on the aristocratic career path. There is no sense, however, that Africa Proconsularis was felt to need the presence of a highly experienced soldier and commander in charge, as provinces like Germany and later Britain did, but that someone with the typical mix of administrative and military background would be suitable. It is unclear whether Camillus knew before being sent to Africa that one of the main tasks in his proconsulship would be to make war on Tacfarinas, whose bandit-rebellion had been ongoing for several years by that point. It may or may not have been obvious to Rome that outright war with this troublemaker was imminent, making it difficult to tell whether Camillus was specifically selected on the basis of his background. Although Tacfarinas was clearly already a problem, Rome may still have felt that Juba II would be able to deal with him – or perhaps they simply hoped that he would give up or die before they had to get involved. If a full-scale war was anticipated by Rome, Camillus would not seem to be an obvious choice for the person to be in charge of it. He appears to have had neither much military experience, nor a particularly prominent reputation. Tacitus notes that he was 'not regarded as a soldier',[6] and that he came from a family without much in the way of recent military credentials. (All the same, this lack of reputation would save Camillus from suffering from Tiberius' personal jealousy later on, unlike many others.) Someone like Lucius Nonius Asprenas, proconsul just a few years earlier, would have made more sense than Camillus if military intervention was anticipated. As it is, there is no light either way on whether or not he was expected from the start to go into the field against Tacfarinas.

Preparing for War

Camillus would have arrived in Africa at some point in the first half of AD 17. Whether he went straight into the war with Tacfarinas is unclear. The typical Roman military campaigning season ran from spring to autumn, roughly March to September/October, but it is not necessarily the case that Camillus was in Africa and already waging war by March, only that this is the earliest likely date. Later in the conflict, some of the proconsuls did not withdraw from the field for the winter but fought through, contrary to expectation (as Marius had done during the Jugurthine War), but this did not happen under Camillus. Certainly within a few months, or even weeks, of his arrival, plans were being made for the Roman troops in the province to go to war with Tacfarinas.

Clearly Tacfarinas' power was growing, as was the danger he represented. He may have been active in the region for five years by this point – possibly even longer – and from posing a minor threat in the borderlands had developed into the leader of a large army. The Cinithii, a powerful people who lived within the territory of Africa Proconsularis (around modern Lesser Syrtis/Gulf of Gabes in Algeria), were forced to submit to Tacfarinas and contribute men to his army. He now constituted a direct threat to Roman interests in the region, and potentially threatened parts of the provincial population more than Rome itself did. His army was now substantial, including allied troops from the Mauri, Cinithii, and Musulamii, as well as those who had deserted the

A Numidian coin depicting either Masinissa or Micipsa, issued in the second century BC (© cngcoins.com)

A Roman denarius minted *c*.56 BC depicting the Mauretanian king Bocchus I kneeling before Lucius Cornelius Sulla and offering an olive branch, with the Numidian king Jugurtha kneeling with his hands tied behind his back (© cngcoins.com)

The ruins of Roman Ammaedara, the base of the 3rd Legion Augusta during the war against Tacfarinas (© Astiosaurus via Wikimedia Commons, CC BY-SA 3.0)

Statue of Juba II in the guise of a Greek hero, found in the West Baths of Caesarea Mauretania (© Carole Raddato, CC BY-SA 2.0)

A Roman sestertius issued during the reign of Augustus, found in Africa and countermarked APRON for Lucius Apronius during his proconsulship and his part in the war against Tacfarinas (© cngcoins.com)

A denarius minted in Caesarea, featuring portraits of Juba II and his son Ptolemy of Mauretania (© cngcoins.com)

The Royal Mausoleum of Mauretania in Algeria, alleged burial site of Juba II and Cleopatra Selene (© Carole Raddato, CC BY-SA 2.0)

A fragment of an inscription from Leptis Magna, referencing a 'Scipio' – likely Lentulus Scipio, who commanded the 9th Legion Hispana in the region during the proconsulship of Junius Blaesus (© Marco Prins/Livius, CC0 1.0 Universal)

A monument erected to Gaius Gavius Macer in Leptis Magna, probably for his role in the Roman victory against Tacfarinas (© Marco Prins/Livius, CC0 1.0 Universal)

The so-called 'Mausoleum of Tacfarinas' (Mausolée de Tacfarinas) near Bouira, Algeria (© Hynox. qualaty via Wikimedia Commons, CC BY-SA 4.0 International)

The ruins of the Roman city of Ammaedara, at Haidra, Tunisia (Adobe Stock 1279524789)

Ammaedara, one-time base of the 3rd Legion Augusta (Adobe Stock 1279519353)

The ruins of the Roman city of Leptis Magna (Adobe Stock 151549144)

Leptis Magna, with the later Arch of Septimius Severus at the southwest entrance to the city (Adobe Stock 363626171)

Roman army with him, and any individuals drawn by the economic prospects of raiding. The implication of Tacitus' description is that Tacfarinas' army was 10–20,000 strong, probably the largest force raised in the region that Rome would ever face.[7] The Roman authorities – technically the Senate, albeit with the approval of Tiberius – at some point issued a command to Camillus to take his own army into the field and confront Tacfarinas.[8]

It is not obvious from Tacitus' account what exactly had changed to make Rome take direct action in AD 17. It may have been the sheer size of Tacfarinas' army that prompted them – perhaps they (rightly) suspected that the limited forces allowed to Juba II would be unable to impose control against so large a foe. Even if Tacfarinas was still merely raiding for his own benefit, the size of his force made the situation far more dangerous than the average banditry problem.

Events elsewhere in the Empire may also have conspired to make this a good time to confront the issues in northwest Africa. The problems with legionary mutiny following the death of Augustus had been resolved and the loyalty of the Roman army largely restored. Major military operations elsewhere had also recently ended, potentially freeing up manpower and economic resources which could be transferred to Africa if needed. Until AD 16, Rome had been engaged in a war in the former German territories, directed against the tribes who had been involved in ambushing and near-destroying the three-legion army of Publius Quinctilius Varus in AD 9. As well as punishing the tribes, Rome hoped to secure the German situation by diminishing the power base of Arminius, the Cherusci chief who had masterminded the AD 9 attack; an ex-auxiliary, he had used his insider knowledge of the Roman army against his former allies. That campaign was led by Germanicus, Tiberius' nephew and potential heir, and proved a successful one. Over the course of three years, culminating in three known pitched battles (Pontes Longi, AD 15, Idistaviso, and the Angrivarian Wall, AD 16), the German tribes were subdued. Arminius was left alive, but no longer in a position of power or a threat to Rome and he was ultimately assassinated by his own men a few years later. Germanicus returned to Rome a victorious commander, holding a triumph in AD 17 to celebrate his successes; he had also recovered two of the three legionary eagles lost with Varus, a feat widely celebrated in Rome.[9] Germanicus left Rome soon after for the eastern provinces, with the intention of putting plans in place for an invasion of Parthia in the near future, but died in AD 19 before any such campaign could be launched.

Thus the year AD 17 was a moment when Rome was not actually involved in a large-scale war, meaning that manpower and financial resources could be drawn upon for the campaign against Tacfarinas as necessary, and it would have made sense to secure as much of the Empire's frontier as possible prior to getting involved in a campaign against Parthia. From a purely military perspective too, AD 17 was as good a time as any and better than most, to direct attention towards quelling the developing problems in northwest Africa. Although they were evidently not expecting a serious campaign, it was wise not to open too many fronts at once if it could be avoided, but there may have been an expectation that the fighting would be over quickly.

A growing negative impact on the grain supply may also have played a role in Rome's intervention, particularly as Juba was proving unable to stabilize the situation. Rome had become increasingly dependent on grain from North Africa to feed both the city and the Empire. The city alone needed to import 150–200,000 tonnes of grain a year to feed its population.[10] Since the days of Masinissa, grain from northwest Africa had flowed into the Mediterranean world, and this continued into the Imperial period. By the mid-first century AD, Africa could meet the needs of the city for eight months a year.[11] Any disruption to that supply could have severe consequences, including riots. The Garamantean War and Gaetulian War had both led to grain shortages in Rome, and officials were doubtless keen to minimize disruption to agriculture in the region.[12] When Tacfarinas' actions reached a level that posed a threat to the supply, action had to be taken before things got too bad.

The overall impression given by Roman preparations for the campaign against Tacfarinas is that while Rome had found it necessary to act in northwest Africa it was not anticipating a difficult campaign. At this point, Tacfarinas was a regional annoyance rather than a serious threat to the internal security of the Empire, and action was being taken before he and his army became a major problem. The 3rd Legion Augusta and their associated auxiliaries were evidently considered sufficient to handle the campaign, far fewer troops than had been needed to suppress other recent provincial uprisings. The Great Illyrian Revolt, a decade earlier, had required between 10 and 15 legions in total to quell it. Rome had experienced a series of problems in provinces such as Illyricum and the German territories east of the Rhine, and really should have learned not to take them too lightly. The same problems had the potential to teach Tacfarinas a thing or two about how to successfully oppose Rome, both in battle and in a wider campaign – and he certainly put some of these tricks to use in the field.

The Armies

The first thing Camillus did after the decision was made to go to war against Tacfarinas was to gather his troops together. His main force was the

3rd Legion Augusta, based at Ammaedara, with additional outposts at Tacape and Capsa.[13] At the start of the revolt, the 3rd was the only legion stationed in Africa, so there was no support close by to call upon in the case of military disaster. Its paper strength was 5,000 men, although in reality most legions probably operated below this level much of the time. The legion was supported by the *auxilia*, the number of whom appears to have been high in Africa Proconsularis, particularly when it came to cavalry, who were probably needed to oversee large areas of sparsely populated landscapes and distant, indistinct desert borders. Some estimates reach as high as 15–20,000 auxiliary soldiers, meaning that Camillus would have had a field army of some 20–25,000 men.[14] However, this figure seems high given that, later in the war, the addition of a single extra legion to the provincial army made a considerable difference to Roman field operations, so it's possible the original may have been more modest in size, perhaps 10–15,000 soldiers. This force would likely have been supplemented by Mauretanian troops, who appear to have been involved in the war throughout, rather than just in the last stages as implied by Tacitus. Juba seems to have contributed not just men, but war elephants as well, to judge by coins he issued during the conflict.[15]

Whatever the exact number, it is clear that the Roman army put into the field against Tacfarinas was not enormous, but neither was it inconsiderable. The fact that Rome did not think it necessary to transfer additional troops into North Africa suggests they felt the existing garrison, supplemented by the Mauretanian troops, would be able to cope with the level of threat posed by Tacfarinas. There is no evidence at this stage for an emergency levy of troops, nor for a transfer of units into the province, both of which did happen later in the war. Even so the Roman troops were almost certainly outnumbered, with Tacfarinas' force potentially standing at 20,000 or more (an exact figure is difficult to estimate with any accuracy), although only some of these soldiers would have been trained, organized, and equipped in the Roman style. Tacitus notes that the Roman army posed 'a modest array in view of the multitude of Numidians and Moors'[16] when the two forces first approached each other prior to battle, suggesting the numbers were not balanced.

But while Tacfarinas' army might have been bigger than the Romans', not all of it was better trained. He clearly had some capable soldiers, who were equipped, trained, and deployed in a 'Roman' manner by Tacfarinas personally – if there were fellow deserters among his recruits, their quick moulding into a Roman-style unit becomes more understandable. These troops, presumably infantry, were consequently heavily armed in a way quite different from the traditional Numidian infantry (or cavalry). But the rest of Tacfarinas' army was probably far below this standard. These men were under the command of Mazippa, a Mauri rebel who joined Tacfarinas early on. They were lightly armed and were used to raid settlements and bring down 'fire, slaughter, and terror' on them, in a manner typically associated with the Numidian cavalry in the past.[17] Tacitus gives no indication of how many men were in either group, or what the balance of infantry to cavalry was. The mounted soldiers were highly mobile in the field, and very effective in scouting, harassing the Romans on the march, attacking settlements and military installations, and generally causing disruption and chaos. There is no indication of whether Tacfarinas had any war elephants, but it remained a formidable force even without pachyderm support. If the Senate or Tiberius had thought that this would be an easy victory, they would soon discover their mistake and their vulnerability in the face of provincial rebellion – and not for the first time even in recent years.

Campaigning against Rome: Some Recent Lessons

Although Rome liked its enemies to think of it as ultimately unbeatable – that however many battles you won, you would lose the war – there were vulnerabilities in the Roman military system that could be exploited by those with the knowledge and training to do so. As a former auxiliary soldier, Tacfarinas was in a prime position to know the operational methods – and more importantly, weaknesses – of the Roman army in the field, and how to exploit them to his advantage. It is not difficult to see how he would have an understanding of the value of irregular warfare and surprise attack against the Roman army, and how to use insider knowledge of a landscape hostile in population, terrain and climate, against an enemy with little understanding of it. He may even have been aware of others who had done the same thing in recent years. Former auxiliary commanders had been prominent in the Great Illyrian Revolt, and Arminius' service in the *auxilia* had probably been a factor in his victory in the Battle of the Teutoburg (AD 9).

Unfortunately, not enough is known about the transmission of military intelligence between soldiers stationed in different provinces, or indeed how aware the population of one area was of conflict at the other end of the Empire. It is impossible to be certain that Tacfarinas would have been aware of the damage other ex-auxiliaries had inflicted on Rome, still less whether he would have been able to draw useful parallels between their situation and his own. But he may well have still been an auxiliary when some of these events happened, particularly those in the Teutoburg, and it seems likely that soldiers would have had more opportunity than most to find out this kind of intelligence – even if it was in the form of a warning about something they might themselves face one day.

As well as highlighting the dangers posed by auxiliaries going rogue against Rome, several recent conflicts had demonstrated that the Roman army was not invulnerable, and shown how its enemies could effectively challenge it on the battlefield and in a campaign more widely. In AD 6, the Great Illyrian Revolt (also known as the Pannonian Revolt and in antiquity referred to as the *Bellum Batonianum*) had broken out in the province of Illyricum. Under the command of two native chieftains, Bato the Daesitiate and Bato the Breucian, the Revolt raged for more than three years, with numerous setbacks for Rome during the conflict.[18] It became a massive drain on the financial resources of the Empire and a significant amount of manpower had to be diverted to it, including 15 legions and a corresponding force of auxiliaries; it was said even in antiquity to have been the most serious military challenge Rome had faced since the Punic Wars.[19] The Great Illyrian Revolt was only brought to an end when the Roman commander in charge of operations there (in fact, the future emperor Tiberius) abandoned the strategy of trying to defeat the enemy on the field of battle in favour of a scorched-earth approach – the starving rebels surrendered the following year.

Not a month after the end of the Great Illyrian Revolt, Rome suffered another massive military setback at the hands of provincial malcontents, this time in recently occupied German territories east of the Rhine. A German tribal coalition had gathered under the command of the Cherusci chief Arminius with the intention of attacking Publius Quinctilius Varus and his army. Arminius was a former ally of Rome, who had been raised in the city from a young age as a hostage for his tribe's good behaviour, learning Latin, gaining Roman citizenship, and serving in the *auxilia* as a cavalry commander.[20] However, once back in Germany ostensibly an allied chief, he began to plot against Rome, using his insider knowledge of the field operation of the Roman military to devise a plan that would wreak devastation on the enemy. Varus had received warning about the plot from a German ally named Segestes, who urged him to act before it was too late. But Varus dismissed the intelligence as unreliable, assuming that Segestes was simply trying to make trouble for Arminius, as there had been poor relations between the two. Arminius had married Segestes' daughter Thusnelda without permission, incurring her father's anger, and also enjoyed a privileged position in Varus' staff as a trusted advisor and frequent companion – an elevated status which Segestes appears to have envied.

What happened was that Varus and his men were lured into an ambush while on the march between their summer campaign headquarters and the

Rhine, diverting from their planned route to deal with reports of discontent in a distant German settlement. The attack came while they believed themselves still in safe territory and were advancing without maintaining a semblance of battle-array, relying on local guides to conduct them safely through a largely unknown landscape. The soldiers had been marching amongst the wagons of the baggage-train, with the women and children camp-followers – the unofficial families of the soldiers – mixed among them. When the German attack came, the Romans had a struggle to restore order in the early stages of the battle but were able to do so after a short period, even managing to build a camp to shelter in overnight. They burnt their surplus baggage and wagons, and attempted to outpace the German attacks, hoping to break free into open country where they would be better able to defend themselves They were ultimately hoping to reach the safety of a Roman fort, or the Rhine – despite the fact that they likely had little idea of where they were, their scouts having defected to Arminius.

However, on the third or fourth day after the attack, the discipline of the Roman army collapsed. They had faced increasing problems trying to fight in the midst of marshes and dense forests and an autumn storm brought winds and heavy rain, making it hard to use their weapons. At a late stage in the battle Varus and his officers committed suicide, and many of the Roman soldiers followed their example, some casting down their weapons and waiting to be killed without resistance. Archaeological investigation of the battlefield suggests that at least part of the army was funnelled into a narrow pass between a marsh and a mountain, and penned in by a turf rampart that had been constructed by the Germans in advance of the battle.[21] Varus and his men had performed exceptionally by managing to maintain cohesion and discipline for as long as they did, but in the end their efforts proved insufficient.

The Great Illyrian Revolt and the Battle in the Teutoburg demonstrated several uncomfortable truths about the Imperial Roman army and the potential risks of auxiliary troops. They highlighted the army's vulnerability in the field to ambush and irregular warfare more generally, particularly at times when they were not in a state of battle-ready vigilance. The risk of ambushes was well-known to the Roman political as well as military authorities. Augustus experienced at first-hand this type of warfare when he served in the Cantabrian Wars in Spain, the stresses of which soon forced him to leave.[22] A decade earlier, a Roman army on the march in Spain had been caught in an ambush and overrun before they could construct a camp from which to defend themselves, an engagement which is documented archaeologically if not historically.[23] Nor was vulnerability to ambush a phenomenon uniquely associated with the post-Augustan army. In Julius Caesar's *Gallic Wars*, a

Roman legion had been ambushed during the uprising of the Eburones, and forced to flee back to their recently abandoned camp, sustaining significant losses along the way.[24] Surrounded by the enemy, the Roman soldiers had fallen into despair and decided to commit mass suicide rather than try to fight their way out. However, while ambush had been identified by the Romans as an operational risk and there were procedures for how to handle such attacks, in reality there was little that the army could do to prevent them.

The Roman soldiers had struggled to adapt to the irregular terrain they encountered in the Teutoburg, unable to find sufficient open ground to adopt battle-array amidst the trees and marshes. Although a later commander would argue that their kit was eminently suitable to fighting in this type of terrain – stabbing spears, short swords, and close-fitting body armour[25] – Varus' soldiers clearly did not find this to be the case. The weather did not help them, the rain making their bows and spears difficult to use, and soaking their shields so they were too heavy to wield.[26] The battle had shown that the Roman army could struggle to operate in certain types of terrain, particularly when it found itself the victim of a surprise attack. Extremes of climate were also a problem, particularly when the effectiveness of their weaponry was lessened.

Events in Germany had further highlighted one of the inherent weaknesses of the auxiliary system – that potential enemies were being recruited into the military, equipped, and trained, giving them inside knowledge of the operation of the Roman army which could be used against Rome in the future. Arminius had been a perfect example of this, using his experience as a cavalry commander in the *auxilia* to effectively predict Varus' response to an ambush and allowing him to take measures to render the Roman actions ineffective. Varus' former friendship with Arminius complicated matters, demonstrating that Roman officials and officers could be blinded to potential threats by assumptions about the loyalty of their auxiliary comrades. Rome could not afford to abandon the auxiliary system as the manpower resources it provided were too valuable, but a reminder had been given of its inherent risks – some of which would reemerge under Tacfarinas.

Low Morale in the Roman Army – a Good Time to Fight?

The early years of Tiberius' reign were a good time to rebel against Rome, as a significant part of the army was still recovering from upheaval and mutiny during the early months after he succeeded to power. Not only had he been a reluctant heir, Tiberius had also anticipated that his accession would not be universally welcomed by the military; he had particular doubts about the German and Pannonian legions.[27] His fears were soon recognized. In AD 14, the Pannonian legions mutinied, aggrieved about the length of their service (30–40 years, instead of the 20 they were supposed to serve), the harshness of military discipline, and the low wages they received.[28] Tiberius was forced to send his son, Drusus the Younger, to try to quell the unrest, a move that nearly backfired when the soldiers complained that he lacked the authority to act on their grievances. Some order was restored following a lunar eclipse which alarmed many of the superstitious soldiers, following which the ringleaders of the mutiny were rounded up and many of them executed.

The German legions stationed on the Lower Rhine had also rebelled at the start of Tiberius' reign.[29] They cited much the same reasons as their Pannonian counterparts – the over-long service, harshness of military duties and discipline, and the bribes they were forced to give their commanding officers. Some troops attacked and lashed their centurions, 60 strokes each (one for every centurion in a legion) before throwing them out of the camp. It fell to Germanicus, Tiberius' nephew, to handle the situation on the Lower Rhine. He initially struggled to contain the mutiny, but found that the sight of his wife, Agrippina the Elder, and son, Caligula – both beloved by the troops – being forced to flee the violence temporarily calmed affairs enough for Germanicus to restore order. The 5th and 21st legions, garrisoned a short distance away, were then threatened by these loyal troops, and it was established that the majority of the soldiers in these legions were willing to end their rebellion. After this the German mutiny was effectively over, leaving a sense of shame and a renewed fervour to attack the enemy.[30]

Although only the Pannonian and Lower Germany legions went so far as to mutiny at this time, their actions likely reflect a wider institutional problem in the Roman army. The system introduced by Augustus and later refined by him was showing some cracks. Particular grievances included soldiers being forced to serve long past their original term of enlistment, the harshness of military discipline, and the backbreaking labour they were forced to undertake. There was also a perceived lack of adequate financial reward for their service, in terms of both pay and discharge bonuses for those fortunate enough to be able to retire.

Tacfarinas had probably long since deserted the Roman army by the time these mutinies took place, and he and some of his men may have been induced to leave by the same problems the soldiers in Germany and Pannonia experienced. Banditry was a far more lucrative prospect than soldiering and there may have been a continual flow of deserters to Tacfarinas throughout the years of the conflict. Although the mutinies themselves had been quelled by the time Tacfarinas launched his first attacks in AD 17, military discontent probably remained a volatile issue, with an ongoing impact on the morale of the Roman military. In many ways the first years of Tiberius' reign were an excellent time for Tacfarinas to launch operations: the Roman army was overstretched and fragile, while the emperor was unwilling and lacked authority.

Camillus Against Tacfarinas

Camillus appears to have adopted a conventional approach to fighting Tacfarinas, no doubt assuming that the ordinary methods of Roman military field operation would be sufficient to end the conflict. The Roman army had become increasingly adept at fighting irregular warfare over the previous century – indicated through archaeology rather than historical sources[31] – but nothing in Tacitus' account suggests that Camillus used such a strategy against Tacfarinas. Presumably his aim, therefore, was to meet Tacfarinas in open, pitched battle, by force if necessary, where the numerical, organizational and technological advantages of the Roman army would lead to sufficient destruction that continuing the revolt was no longer possible. However, the reason Roman militia had had to become skilled in irregular provincial warfare was that their enemies were increasingly refusing to meet them on the battlefield, recognizing the advantages the Romans had in such a situation. It was far from certain that Tacfarinas would enter a pitched battle if the prospect of victory seemed slight – perhaps Camillus hoped that the numerical inferiority of his army, outnumbered by two to one (or even more) would help lure the rebels to the battlefield. As a result, Tacitus notes, Camillus had to appear not over-eager to engage Tacfarinas, in case the rebels took fright and ran away before battle could be joined. If this were to happen Roman interests in the region would be little improved, security would remain problematic, and both Tacfarinas and Mazippa would be free to continue the banditry and pillage which had led Rome to act in the first place. For Camillus, it was imperative that Tacfarinas be confronted in pitched battle as soon as possible.

At first, the campaign went well. Camillus was able to ascertain the location of Tacfarinas' army and advance towards it. The rebels did not run away and Tacitus suggests that their numerical superiority was the deciding factor for their decision to remain in place to meet Camillus. Once he was close to them, Camillus drew his troops up in battle-array, putting his legion in the centre, flanked by two cavalry *alae* (wings) and an unknown number of light infantry cohorts also on the wings. Tacfarinas accepted the challenge and for the first time led his men into pitched battle against Rome. Typically, provincial leaders (whether rebels or bandits) recognized that in a pitched battle their inferiority in training and weaponry would almost certainly lead to defeat.

They had to be forced into it through measures such as denial of resources and attacks on civilians or tricked into it by overconfidence (particularly when they significantly outnumbered the Romans). That Tacfarinas was willing to engage in pitched battle so early in the campaign seems unusual, but he had a much larger army than the Romans did, and was much more familiar with the landscape and territory than his enemy. He may also have welcomed the opportunity to test his troops in the field against Rome, to judge their ability in battle – particularly those he had hand-picked to train and equip in the Roman style. Whatever his reasons, Tacfarinas was to find that the engagement did not go his way. His army was comprehensively defeated by the Romans, forcing the survivors to flee into the desert.

Unfortunately, almost nothing is known about the battle. It was clearly a Roman victory, sufficiently comprehensive that Rome at the time believed it would effectively end Tacfarinas' activities (or at least, minimize them to the degree that they would no longer be a problem). But beyond this, details of the engagement are thin. There is no indication of where it took place, though it seems likely to have been fought in an area where Tacfarinas felt confident; perhaps somewhere in the territory of the Musulamii, or a spot where they had already been engaged in banditry. It also had to be somewhere that the Roman army was comfortable to fight. Tacitus gives no description of the battle, although this is not particularly unusual in his work with regard to engagements fought decades earlier in far-flung regions. Even if he had included such a narrative, it would likely have been composed with literary conventions in mind rather than an accurate record of what happened on the day.[32] There are no data for the respective casualty figures. Statistical analysis of casualty figures in Roman battles (albeit based on potentially flawed numbers in the ancient written sources)[33] suggests that the victors could expect to sustain between 4 and 6 per cent in casualties, while the defeated could suffer three or four times as many losses, more under disastrous circumstances.[34] If these figures were played out in the engagement between Camillus and Tacfarinas, Roman casualties could be estimated at 400–600 men, while Tacfarinas' losses would potentially be in the region of 2,400–4,800 (assuming a force of *c.*20,000 men and a casualty rate of 12–16 per cent), but could have been higher. In fact, Camillus was later given triumphal honours, indicating that at least 5,000 of the enemy must have been killed. However, there is no indication of the battle being a complete rout, so Tacfarinas' losses were unlikely to have been wildly beyond the norm; he was able to field another army the following year, suggesting his casualties were not devastating. Still, the Numidian losses were clearly sufficient for Rome to feel that the battle had been a comprehensive victory, and had effectively ended the rebellion, or banditry, that Tacfarinas had been waging.

In recognition of the victory, Camillus was awarded triumphal honours by the Senate and highly praised by Tiberius, bringing the military glory back to his family which Tacitus noted had long been missing.[35] He was the only Roman to be awarded honours for the battle – no ordinary soldiers were singled out for acts of bravery, as did happen several times in later phases of the war. Camillus receiving triumphal honours tells us his victory was seen in Rome as significant – they were not given to leaders simply for suppressing banditry.[36] The award suggests that the conflict had already developed into a rebellion, despite any impression given by Tacitus.

Before going to Africa, Camillus had not had any particular reputation for skill in warfare and, as previously discussed, may not have been appointed with the intention of going to war against Tacfarinas. But he seemed initially to have done an excellent job and achieved all that Rome could have wanted, a textbook response to banditry or the early stages of a rebellion.[37] He had acted quickly and decisively, using only the troops made available to him, and had managed to engage the enemy in pitched battle, inflicting what he must have hoped would be a decisive defeat. Certainly, this setback was sufficient to stop Tacfarinas from ever meeting the Roman army in set-piece battle again. The impression of a great military success was emphasized further in northwestern Africa by Juba II minting coins that year, which referred to the victory and his role in it.[38] At the end of the campaigning season, both Camillus and Rome would have been satisfied with the outcome. We do not know how the war would have been referred to at this point, for instance on any dedicatory inscriptions set up to commemorate Camillus' victory – would it have been another Gaetulian War, a Numidian War, or would it already be intrinsically associated with Tacfarinas?[39]

Yet, whatever the war was called in Rome at this point, it was not over. From the Roman perspective, one of the most significant problems of the day was that Tacfarinas was not captured or killed on the battlefield, but had escaped, along with an unknown number of his men. Rome may have felt that the danger he posed had been ended, at least for the time being and potentially permanently. As they soon found out, this was not to be the case. Tacfarinas had fled defeated, but there followed only a brief hiatus in hostilities while he regrouped his forces – and within a year, Rome had to begin a new phase in this war.

Chapter 7

Lucius Apronius and the Renewal of War (AD 18–21)

When Marcus Furius Camillus inflicted a decisive battlefield defeat on Tacfarinas, Rome clearly believed that their problems in northwest Africa were over. At this stage, Tacfarinas was probably still regarded as little more than a bandit leader who had grown over-powerful and who in defeat would drift back into an acceptably low level of activity. The Romans may have hoped that much of his army would desert their unsuccessful leader, fearing he would no longer be able to offer them substantial financial rewards. One of the things the Romans believed they knew about Numidian troops was that they would desert a defeated commander without a second thought. But they underestimated the situation, failing to recognize the ongoing severity of the conflict. The fact that Camillus was awarded triumphal honours for the victory implies that Rome recognized it was something more than the repression of banditry – but also that with that single battle they believed the threat had been vanquished. That it was the opening action in what would develop into a significant regional rebellion was not appreciated. Whether or not Tacfarinas planned at this point to lead a campaign of resistance against Rome might be debatable – but either way, some elements of his army certainly intended to fight in one.

It must have been an unpleasant surprise for Rome to discover that Camillus' victory over Tacfarinas was not the decisive success they had expected. Tacfarinas had certainly been driven into the desert interior for the winter, but had no plans at this point to cease raiding Roman and Mauretanian settlements – again, regardless of whether he was acting as a mere bandit or a rebel leader at this point. Camillus' victory had been nothing more than the end of the beginning of the war, the opening action in what would become a much longer conflict. Tacfarinas had learned valuable lessons from his defeat, in particular that his army was no match for the Romans in pitched battle, and he would never fight with them in this type of engagement again. He returned to raiding soon after, and the conflict was inherited by Camillus' successor in office, Lucius Apronius.

Over the next few years, Rome would fight an increasingly gritty irregular war with Tacfarinas, in which he refused pitched battle in favour of ambushing Roman marching columns, attacking settlements and military outposts, and causing chaos and terror among the population at large. He became a figure of fear among some of the Roman troops, so that in one case they fled from his army at the first sign of fighting, for which they were punished with one of the last documented instances of decimation (the execution of one in every ten men in a unit, chosen by lot). During Apronius' proconsulship Tacfarinas would become an increasingly thorny problem in the region and the Roman leader ultimately proved unable to bring the war to a conclusion. Apronius' time in Africa might be thought of as the middle years of the conflict and he stayed in post for two or three years, rather than the standard single year. It soon became necessary to introduce more manpower to the province in the hope of ending the conflict, but the longer the war dragged on, the more expansive and political Tacfarinas' ambitions appear to have become. By the end of Apronius' consulship, what had initially been understood by Rome as mere banditry had developed into something far more dangerous.

A Surprise Return for Tacfarinas?

Did Rome really think that the conflict against Tacfarinas was over after a single season in the field? The evidence is mixed. The fact that Camillus was summoned home from Africa after the standard proconsular year of office seems to suggest that the authorities believed the war to be at an end, with therefore no need for continuity of command. Although proconsuls typically only served for a single year in office, their tenure could be extended if circumstances justified it. It could be inefficient, even dangerous, to replace them with new personnel who had no prior experience of the situation on the ground, and who would have to be familiarized with the conflict and its combatants. Camillus may not have had much military experience before his time in Africa, and may never have been intended to lead a campaign against Tacfarinas – but once events had put him in that position, he evidently performed well. There was no need to replace him as proconsul if Tacfarinas had still been considered a threat, but the Senate evidently felt it unnecessary to delay his recall. That Camillus was also given triumphal honours, typically associated with the end of a campaign, may mean that Rome thought the immediate danger in Africa had passed.

However, there is another way to look at the situation, which may indicate that the authorities in Rome were well aware of the on-going risk that Tacfarinas posed, and decided that someone with greater military experience was needed in Africa Proconsularis. Rome may well have expected – or at least, allowed for the possibility – that the problem of Tacfarinas was not over and they must prepare as best they could for his return. Although Camillus had dealt with Tacfarinas effectively, he would not necessarily be suited to a drawn-out provincial campaign. Camillus had won a battle, but had no experience (that we know of) of ongoing irregular warfare – and having been so easily defeated previously, Tacfarinas was unlikely to be tempted into pitched battle again. That Camillus was awarded triumphal honours does not necessarily indicate that Rome believed the conflict to be over. In the early Imperial period, this type of award could be made even in the midst of an ongoing campaign. Just the previous year several other prominent Roman figures had been given triumphal honours in the middle of a campaign in Germany, including Germanicus and Camillus' successor in Africa Proconsularis, Lucius Apronius.[1] The fact that their enemy was still at large and the war not over did not prevent the honours from being awarded. The winter of AD 17/18 offered the opportunity to change personnel while Tacfarinas was still in hiding, so that Rome could bring in someone with more military experience who could handle an extended irregular provincial campaign. As far as Rome was concerned, Tacfarinas might or might not return, but there was no harm in preparing for the worst while hoping for the best.

When Camillus was replaced, it was not by someone whose career prior to the proconsulship had predominantly been administrative. They chose Lucius Apronius, a veteran military commander with experience in fighting irregular warfare. Whether or not the Senate believed that the conflict against Tacfarinas was over, they appear not to have taken any chances when appointing a new proconsul to replace Camillus. It turned out to be a wise decision in the light of events of the following years.

Lucius Apronius

When Lucius Apronius replaced Camillus as proconsul, it was the second time in his career that he had succeeded him. Apronius had been suffect consul in AD 8, replacing Camillus halfway through the year. Apronius' career following that year appears to have differed from Camillus' – certainly involving a lot more direct military activity – but the close parallel between the two men's appointments to both the consulships and proconsulships in Africa suggests that their careers were on a comparable trajectory, albeit specializing in different fields.

It is not clear from the sources when Lucius Apronius was born, but it was likely in the last decades of the first century BC, most likely the 20s/10s BC.

Little is known about his family background or earlier career prior to the suffect consulship. After this, he went on to become a distinguished military commander and served in the Great Illyrian Revolt (AD 6–9) under the overall command of Tiberius, still then the heir to the Imperial throne. Apronius may have earned triumphal honours for his actions during that conflict, having conducted himself with 'distinguished valour' throughout the campaign.[2] He appears to have fought particularly alongside Gaius Vibius Postumus, the governor of Dalmatia,[3] who through his 'repeated services and careful vigilance' did win triumphal honours.[4] Apronius was already known to Postumus prior to the Illyrian Revolt, as his co-suffect consul in AD 8 had been Aulus Vibius Habitus, Postumus' brother. The campaign would have given Apronius first-hand experience of irregular provincial warfare against an enemy who avoided pitched battle wherever possible, and used their intimate knowledge of the landscape to repeatedly gain advantages over the Roman army. Whatever Apronius' experience before this, the Illyrian campaign was a key part of his military development. As well as an opportunity to display his military capabilities, the war also allowed him to make an impact on prominent figures in Rome, particularly core members of the Imperial regime. Since the campaign was led by Tiberius, Apronius was able to demonstrate his potential to the future emperor, which would no doubt have benefited his career prospects.

In the first years of Tiberius' reign, Rome undertook a campaign in the German territories east of the Rhine, aiming to reduce Arminius' power in the region, to take revenge for the defeat in the Teutoburg in AD 9 and (if possible) to recover the legionary eagles which had been lost in the battle. The campaign was led by Germanicus, under whom Apronius had likely already served in Illyricum during the rebellion there. Apronius was given several key roles during his time in Germany. In an advance against the Chatti, he was put in charge of constructing the roads and bridges which would be necessary for a Roman army to progress safely through the landscape.

Constructing roads and bridges was vital for the swift movement of troops and during the campaign parts of the Roman army had struggled to operate in areas where it had not yet been possible to build them.[5] Germanicus had taken advantage of a drought to advance with part of the army despite the absence of this infrastructure, hoping to surprise the enemy.[6] Splitting their force like this posed an operational risk, but it was one which paid off in this instance, and Apronius and his men were later able to rejoin Germanicus. It is not clear whether they had already done this by the time Germanicus came across the Teutoburg battlefield and buried the remains of the dead there, or the frantic pursuit of Arminius which followed,[7] but Apronius was no doubt aware of both if not. The Teutoburg would have offered a sobering demonstration of what could happen to a Roman army at the hands of a rebellious provincial enemy.

As the German campaign continued, it provided Apronius with further experience of gritty irregular warfare, building on what he had already learnt in Illyricum a few years earlier. Descriptions of the military engagements give some insight into the dreadful conditions with which the Roman soldiers were faced – struggling with the weight of their armour and equipment on ground that had become too slimy and oozy to stand fast in, and too slippery to advance over.[8] Although the Romans did not suffer any disastrous defeats in this campaign, they came close to doing so on more than one occasion – and the ghost of Varus even made an appearance in the dreams of one commander, reaching out his hand and calling to them.[9] It was a gruelling campaign that would have prepared Lucius Apronius for most aspects of irregular provincial warfare.

At the end of the first phase of campaigning in AD 15, Lucius Apronius, along with several other commanders, was awarded triumphal honours for his role in the conflict.[10] It is unclear whether he returned with Germanicus the following year for the second, more decisive phase of the German campaign. But whether he was actually present or not, the end of the campaign may have influenced Apronius' own strategy against Tacfarinas. Germanicus inflicted several decisive defeats on Arminius and his allies, by forcing them to engage in pitched battle. Despite the Germans sustaining heavy casualties in these battles Arminius survived, but with his power hollowed out to the degree that he was no longer considered a threat. Rome was not incorrect in this assumption and Arminius never again caused problems for them. He was eventually murdered in AD 21 by members of his own tribe, who felt he was becoming too powerful in their domestic politics.[11]

From Apronius' perspective, the episode with Arminius taught him that a formerly powerful enemy leader could safely be left alive at the end of a campaign so long as their support among the people had been minimized. Obviously it was more desirable to kill or capture them, but if this was not possible or practical a secure victory did not depend on the death of the enemy commander. When they were no longer able to call on reliable reserves of manpower, the threat posed by a leader could be considered neutralized. This 'lesson' may go some way to explaining the attitude not just of Apronius, but of both his predecessor and successor in office regarding Tacfarinas – and the fact that all three were satisfied to leave him alive following what they believed to be decisive victories.

A few years after his service in Germany, Lucius Apronius was appointed proconsul of Africa; although the dates provided by Tacitus for his tenure in office are vague, numismatic evidence dates it to AD 18–20/21, with his successor taking over in the early part of AD 21. Apronius brought much more military experience to Africa than had Furius Camillus, as might be expected of an appointment in a province which had recently been a warzone. But he found his abilities tested over the following years, with Tacfarinas proving a skilled opponent more than capable of matching Apronius in the field.

Return of the Raiders

Before too long, Apronius had to begin his own operations against Tacfarinas, in either AD 18 or 19. The initial impression from Tacitus is that Tacfarinas re-emerged in AD 18, as he describes the events under Camillus as having happened the 'previous summer' (*priore aestate*).[12] However, Tacitus also states that the war was renewed in the same year that Germanicus died, which would place them in AD 19. How Tacitus made what seems to be such an obvious narrative error is unclear, although this is not the only time a mistake like this crept in.[13] The date has narrative implications – both in understanding how long it took Tacfarinas to resume operations after his defeat by Camillus, and how long it took for Rome to respond to his return. If events resumed in AD 18, it suggests that Tacfarinas was able to recover fairly quickly from the defeat to Camillus, renewing the conflict at the next available opportunity, while Apronius was still a relatively new figure in the region. However, Tacitus only really covers what seems to be a single campaigning season against Tacfarinas under Apronius, and at the end of it the rebels were not left in such a bad state as they were after their defeat by Camillus, making it problematic to imagine that nothing happened the following year. AD 19 is also the year in which more troops were introduced to the province, which again makes little sense if Tacfarinas had been defeated once more in the summer of AD 18. If the war was renewed in AD 19, several of these issues are resolved, on the understanding that Tacfarinas took nearly two years to recover from the defeat, but was subsequently able to field a large army which was not so easily dealt with by the Romans. There may be a compromise position, as Tacitus suggests that the early stages of Tacfarinas' return were quite minor and inconsistent – it may have been these operations which restarted in AD 18, without much Roman response, before the situation escalated again into one of active warfare in AD 19. This is pure speculation, however, my attempt to reconcile the two mutually exclusive date references provided by Tacitus.

What is known for sure is that by either the year 18 or 19, Tacfarinas was back. He had probably lost some of his troops, particularly the Mauri who had chosen to fight with him in AD 17, and the Cinithii who had been forced to.[14] There is no further mention of Mazippa, his second-in-command who had been in charge of the raiding elements of the army – he was from the Mauri people and may have returned to them. The distinction between Tacfarinas' hand-picked troops trained in the Roman style and the rest, whom Mazippa had previously commanded, may no longer have been strictly maintained, with Tacfarinas now in sole command of the entire army. His operations were probably correspondingly smaller, at least in the first stages of his return, and he was clearly wary of ever engaging with the Romans in pitched battle again. He returned to the style of warfare which had worked best for him and which was fairly traditional in the region, relying on light-armed troops who could move quickly through the landscape to devastating effect.

During this time Tacfarinas and his men resumed banditry-style operations, initially making sporadic and inconsistent raids on settlements, much as they had been doing in the years prior to AD 17.[15] These sorties were presumably directed primarily towards Roman and Mauretanian settlements rather than those of the tribal populations, which may have been an effort to keep the 'hearts and minds' of the latter group, but likely they were also spared because they would offer fewer material rewards. Although Tacitus is quite dismissive of these raids, it is worth remembering that they would not have been easy to organize, particularly in a region where the population expected such trouble and were potentially trained and armed themselves. Anthropological studies on raids in northwest Africa during the early twentieth century demonstrated that they were labour-intensive and required a good deal of planning, often several weeks in advance.[16] Indeed, the raiding by Tacfarinas is seen as a precursor to the phenomenon of the *razzia* which was practised in the region from the Islamic period onwards.[17] So while it is easy to dismiss this activity as 'just' raiding, they were probably quite significant operations. They were also no doubt terrifying for the people caught up in them, and over so quickly that there was little opportunity for defence or reprisal.

Emboldened by these successes, Tacfarinas stepped up his activity, moving on to the destruction of villages and larger-scale plunder. At this stage, he probably switched from attacking settlements on the borders of Mauretanian and Roman territory to richer pickings closer to the wealthier settled coastline region. This brought his operations into close contact with outposts manned by the Roman military. While Tacfarinas would not face the Romans in pitched battle again, he was certainly willing to fight them under other circumstances, where he judged the odds to be more in his favour.

A Roman Defeat at the Pagyda

Tacfarinas' operations were clearly mounting, and he and his men growing in confidence. After successes in larger-scale raiding, they approached a Roman military installation on the river Pagyda (a position not yet identified in the modern landscape) at which a cohort of *c.*480 men was garrisoned.[18] Whether they were a general outpost or a unit specifically placed there to guard against Tacfarinas is unclear. Either way, they were drawn directly into the war when Tacfarinas and his men lay siege to their camp. The Roman forces were under the command of an experienced and decisive commander named Decrius, who did not take well to being surrounded by the enemy in such a way and determined to break the siege as soon as possible. The Roman army was reasonably adept in sieges, but primarily when they were the attackers. When defending a siege it suited them better (if possible) to sally out of the defensive position and fight in the open, and this is evidently what Decrius intended to do. He drew the men of the cohort together, gave them a rousing speech (the content of which is sadly not even guessed at by Tacitus), and marched them out of the camp. They formed battle-lines directly in front of it, and prepared to engage.

In theory, this was a shrewd move on Decrius' part, but for one thing: his soldiers were afraid of Tacfarinas and his army. They were not psychologically prepared to face him and this was to have devastating results. In the early stages of the battle, seemingly as the two sides were still exchanging missiles prior to a clash of battle-lines, the cohesion of the Roman troops shattered. They began to flee the field, seemingly before they had even engaged with the enemy at close quarters. The impression given by Tacitus is of complete blind panic overtaking the Romans right at the start. The shock of the Imperial battle-line failing so early must have been extraordinary – and to Decrius at least, unbelievable. One of the greatest strengths of the Roman army was its fighting discipline and the organization of its battle-lines, enabling them to maintain their integrity under all but the most dire of circumstances. While it was not unknown for Roman troops to flee from a battlefield, this was almost exclusively when it became clear that they were losing – on some occasions, units were even able to recover their combat morale after a short period and return to the fray, sometimes to snatch victory from defeat. Even under irregular attack, Roman units were usually able to maintain order. In the Teutoburg in AD 9, Roman soldiers had remained disciplined through three days of German ambushes, finally giving up only when they were encircled, trapped and numerically overwhelmed. Yet here, against Tacfarinas, their combat cohesion had disintegrated from the first moments.

Unsurprisingly, the outcome of the battle was not in Rome's favour. When he saw his men abandon the lines, Decrius tried to intercept the fleeing soldiers, darting among the African projectiles trying to reimpose discipline. He cursed the standard bearers who, rather than using their position of authority to restore order, merely watched as the cohort fled from the 'horde of undrilled men or deserters'. Decrius refused to flee the field. He sustained some serious wounds, including a pierced eye and a severe wound to the chest, and was killed soon after, abandoned by his men but fighting to the last. Tacfarinas and his men were no doubt delighted and inspired to see a Roman cohort run from them at the first moment of engagement. Their morale must have been as positively impacted as the Romans' was negatively, and it likely emboldened them for the next stages of the war.

Although not a major battle, the incident on the Pagyda was evidently a shameful episode. Disaster had not been inevitable, even once the soldiers had abandoned the battle-lines and started to flee. They appear to have gone back into the safety of their camp, where they would have been protected. At this point, it would have been theoretically possible for them to regroup, restore their discipline and rejoin battle; this was not an unusual action in Roman warfare when things started to go wrong. Instead of which they completely abandoned their commander, and any soldiers who had not fled, to an inevitable death, handing Tacfarinas one of the easiest victories he would ever win.

There is no real indication in Tacitus of why the Roman cohort at the Pagyda reacted in the way they did. There was clearly a generalized background fear of Tacfarinas and his army, which may have been the result of their earlier methods of campaigning – the rapid raids that came out of nowhere and disappeared just as quickly, leaving death and destruction in their wake. Modern studies have demonstrated how fear of the known can be a significant combat stressor for soldiers, becoming heightened in irregular conflicts such as the Vietnam War.[19] Soldiers are particularly vulnerable to disintegration on their first entry into battle. Tacitus doesn't mention how long the soldiers of the cohort had been in the Roman army, but they may have been relatively inexperienced and psychologically unprepared for their first battle against a feared enemy. Experienced or not, they had certainly been in the region for a while, however, since at this point no new troops had been transferred in to deal with the situation, so they undoubtedly already knew about Tacfarinas and his methods. Their response suggests that his raids were particularly brutal – a detail skipped over by Tacitus – and had earned him a fearsome reputation.

Some further insight into the impact of Tacfarinas' reputation on the Roman soldiers can be gained from looking at the response of French soldiers during the nineteenth-century conquest of Algeria.[20] The nature of that war, with little in the way of pitched engagements but in constant anticipation of a surprise attack, took a heavy psychological toll on the French. The effects were exacerbated by the deprivations of the campaign, including the unfamiliar climate and a lack of food, as the soldiers carried few supplies in the interests of rapid movement. It was not the war they expected, nor what they had been trained to face, and many struggled to cope. One can imagine that the Roman soldiers at the Pagyda found themselves in exactly the same type of situation. Their shameful conduct was contrasted by Tacitus against the courage of Decrius, one of the few Romans singled out for praise in his account. The description of Decrius fighting on, despite having sustained multiple serious wounds (including one to an eye), evokes a heroic figure who embodied the admired quality of *virtus* (masculine virtue).[21] Individuals who continued to fight despite sustaining massive injuries are found elsewhere in Roman historical writing. Marcus Cassius Scaeva fought on in the Battle of Dyrrhachium with one eye lost and with javelins through his shoulder and thigh – and he even survived the battle.[22]

Disgrace and Decimation

When news of the defeat reached Lucius Apronius, his reaction was rapid and harsh. According to Tacitus, he was not overly concerned about the fact of Tacfarinas' victory, likely judging it to be of minimal impact, but was agitated by the fact that Roman troops had disgraced themselves by fleeing as they had.[23] He was no doubt concerned that such actions might be copied by other Roman units who found themselves in a similar situation. To punish the cohort involved at the Pagyda, and to deter repeats elsewhere, Apronius decided to revive a severe and unusual Republican-era punishment: decimation. The cohort would be subjected en masse to the selection of one man in every ten, chosen by lot, who would then be executed by the rest of the unit, usually by being beaten, flogged, or stabbed to death (a process known as *bastinado* or *fustuarium*). The surviving men, having killed their unlucky comrades, would be put on barley rations (i.e. animal fodder) and forced to stay outside the safety of the camp until the stain of their disgrace was cleansed.[24] It was intended to be a more terrifying prospect than facing Tacfarinas in battle and would have sent a strong message to the rest of the provincial garrison.

Decimation was one of the cruellest punishments of Roman military discipline and among the most feared. It was not issued lightly, being reserved for the most severe cases of mutiny or disobedience on the battlefield, where there had been a mass (not necessarily universal) infraction. The shame of the action was sufficient that soldiers were willing participants in the slaughter of their comrades, for acts they themselves had likely also committed. By drawing lots for who should be executed decimation punished the guilty and innocent alike, but also allowed for the collective guilt of the unit to be erased.[25] Indeed, some units in the Late Republic even 'volunteered' for decimation for disciplinary lapses on the field, although probably in the hope that their offer would not be accepted.[26] This cruel punishment was intended to ensure through fear that such actions were repeated as infrequently as possible – statistically, soldiers were almost twice as likely to die in decimation than they were on the battlefield – and its rare use seems to align with periods when the Roman authorities were concerned about the prevalence and spread of low morale among the troops.

In practice, decimation was extremely rare, particularly by the Imperial period. Just eleven instances are known in the entirety of Roman history, the majority dating to the civil wars of the first century BC.[27] It started to become obsolete in the earliest stages of the Imperial period, and its last attested use was in AD 69 under the short-reigning emperor Galba.[28] Decimation was not in fact suited to the Imperial Roman army. This type of collective punishment may have helped to instil battlefield discipline through fear in the levied Republican armies, but in the professionalized Imperial force, it threatened to do more harm than good by undermining the social bonds that were deliberately encouraged between the career soldiers. Forcing soldiers to kill their long-term comrades, who had been selected by arbitrary lot for 'crimes' they may not even have been part of was problematic and could well have incited the indiscipline and mutiny it was intended to prevent; in such cases, or where the unit's discipline could no longer be restored, disbandment of the legion was preferred over decimation.

Thus Lucius Apronius would not lightly have made the decision to decimate one of his cohorts. Prior to this, the punishment had not been used for over fifty years, since Octavian had imposed it on troops who abandoned their posts during a campaign in Illyria in 34 BC.[29] To have employed such a drastic (and now antiquated) method of punishment, Apronius must have been seriously concerned about the morale of his soldiers, and to have questioned their determination to face Tacfarinas on the battlefield unless a greater punishment awaited if they fled from him. Evidently Apronius did not feel the circumstances justified such a breakdown of discipline and that his only appropriate response was a decimation – both to punish the cohort and to try to prevent any repeat of the incident elsewhere.

A cohort had a paper strength of 480 men, although these units were often undermanned and some casualties would have been sustained during the battle. The 10 per cent selected for decimation would thus have numbered

40–45 men – not a large number in absolute terms, but the impact of losing so many of one's comrades over a single disciplinary issue would have been substantial. Although Tacitus devotes only a sentence to the decimation, the use of it despite the rarity of the practice by the reign of Tiberius suggests that Apronius believed Rome to be in a dangerous situation in northwest Africa. He could not take the risk of the desertion at the Pagyda being repeated elsewhere, and was willing to go to extreme lengths to prevent that.

A New Approach from Tacfarinas

Tacfarinas' success attacking the Roman camp near the Pagyda, and the apparent ability of his army to inspire blind panic among the enemy simply by its presence on the battlefield, can only have emboldened him. Prior to this he and his force had limited their attacks to settlements and, aside from the pitched battle against Camillus the previous year, had not faced the Roman army in combat. The situation now changed. Although still unwilling to engage in pitched battle again, Tacfarinas clearly felt his army was more than capable of challenging them in other circumstances. It is not clear from Tacitus whether the siege of the Roman camp was the start of a new strategic approach from Tacfarinas to target military installations, or an ad hoc tactical decision made because he found himself close to a vulnerable target. Either way, the incident at the Pagyda evidently convinced Tacfarinas that attacking Roman military installations could be an effective new approach and it was not long before he launched an assault on a different stronghold – that located at Thala (Tunisia), garrisoned by a force of *c.*500 experienced soldiers.[30]

Tacitus refers to the unit at Thala as a *vexillum veteranorum*, which suggests they were soldiers who had served 20–25 years in the legion and had not yet been released from service – a special category of soldiers known as *veterani*.[31] These men could form their own unit which served in addition to the overall provincial garrison. Those at Thala were *veterani* of the 3rd Legion Augusta and at nearly 500 men constituted a force almost a tenth the size of the legion itself. Not all the soldiers in the unit were necessarily veterans. The one named from the battle, Helvius Rufus, is described by Tacitus as a *miles gregarius*, the lowest ranking soldier, but an inscription relating to his wider career suggests that he achieved the rank of *primus pilus* ('first spear') during his service.[32] This complicates the status of the unit slightly, as if he was only a *miles gregarius* after 20-plus years of service, it is difficult to understand how he rose to one of the highest ranks in the unit within just a few years of the battle. More likely, he was a younger member of the unit who went on to a distinguished career, possibly helped by the honours he won in the battle at Thala.

Unfortunately for Tacfarinas, the Roman garrison at Thala was a very different prospect from that at the Pagyda, and they proved more than capable of fighting off his attack. Tacitus does not describe the battle beyond saying it was a comprehensive Roman victory. There is no reference to the size of Tacfarinas' force. The Romans are numbered at about 500 men, although this figure seems to be given to emphasize how few soldiers it took to achieve victory against Tacfarinas and is not necessarily reliable. The only detail Tacitus records from the engagement is that an ordinary rank-and-file soldier named Marcus Helvius Rufus distinguished himself by saving a Roman life during the fighting, for which he was rewarded by Apronius with a ceremonial collar and spear, the traditional awards given for exceptional bravery in battle. On hearing reports of Rufus' bravery, Tiberius further granted him the civic crown (*corona civica*), an oak-leaf wreath for the head and the second highest military decoration which could be awarded to a soldier.[33] It was within Apronius' power to award the civic crown himself, which Tiberius evidently felt he should have done – but fortunately for the proconsul, Tiberius was saddened rather than angered at having to step in and make the award himself.[34]

The civic crown seems to have had a positive impact on Helvius Rufus' future career, to judge by an inscription found in Vicovaro (northeast of Rome) which appears to refer to him. He adopted the cognomen Civica in reference to his award and went on to become the most senior centurion (*primus pilus*) in his legion, surviving his service and retiring to Varia (now Vicovaro), where he paid for a bathhouse to be constructed for the community. The fact that Rufus was in a position to win the civic crown suggests that the battle at Thala was no walkover for the Roman troops caught up in it, but the result was clearly a comprehensive Roman victory. There is no indication of what the casualty figures for either side might have been.

Tacitus suggests that the use of decimation after the debacle at the Pagyda had succeeded in shoring up the courage of the soldiers, although the fact that they were highly experienced legionaries probably played a significant role in their combat hardiness. Nevertheless, it seems that Apronius' gamble in using an antiquated and severe disciplinary technique for the first time in more than fifty years paid off. All the same, it is just as likely that the garrison at Thala would have stood their ground anyway, regardless of what had happened at the Pagyda.

A Return to Irregular Warfare

The defeat at Thala appears to have had a significant negative impact on the rebels' morale. Tacfarinas' men 'lost heart and disdained sieges', rejecting the newer strategy in favour of a return to raiding. Tacitus only refers to two sieges of Roman camps (Pagyda and Thala) which does suggest that the strategy was abandoned fairly quickly. However, there may have been other attacks which went undocumented – Tacitus very much gives the sense of Tacfarinas' men becoming weary of sieges, so there might well have been more than those two. In some ways, it seems surprising that Tacfarinas would have abandoned this approach after just two engagements, one of which he had won, but if his men were unwilling to fight in this way he may have had little choice. The change to attacking Roman camps had been a bold one; whether it had been adopted as a new strategy deliberately or not, but with the exception of the Pagyda it had not paid off. It would have been clear by now that the rebel army was effective in irregular warfare but unlikely to overcome the Romans in either open battle or in sieges against experienced soldiers. Despite having trained at least some of his men in the Roman style and equipping them in the same fashion, Tacfarinas' army was simply not a match for the Imperial troops on the battlefield. A return to their old tactics, abandoning the attempt to play and beat the Romans at their own game, offered the rebels their greatest chance of success at this stage in the conflict.

The resumption of irregular warfare and raiding proved a success from Tacfarinas' perspective. They accrued a large amount of material reward, eventually more than his army could easily transport. The heavily-armed Roman troops, particularly the legionaries, were unable to match their enemy for speed and adaptability, which became two of the most important factors in this stage of the war. Tacfarinas led his forces through northwest Africa, raiding and pillaging settlements as he went. The Roman army tried to chase him down, no doubt aiming to try to force him into pitched battle which they would be likely to win. But whenever they got close Tacfarinas would yield the ground and withdraw a short distance away, reappearing after a brief pause to launch a rapid attack on the rear of the marching column. There was no way for the Roman army to effectively respond. Even Tacitus recognized the success of Tacfarinas' approach at this point, noting that 'so long as the African adhered to this strategy, he befooled with impunity the ineffective and footsore Roman.'[35] It was no doubt dispiriting for the Romans to be caught in this situation, but they had no choice but to continue trying to chase him down, unless they intended to abandon the settlements to endless raiding.

Tacfarinas' tactics closely resembled those used by enemies and rebels in other parts of the Empire, including in Illyricum during the Great Illyrian Revolt and in Germany against Arminius. Lucius Apronius was as experienced as anyone in the Roman military at facing this type of campaign, but he does not seem to have been able to find a way to render it ineffective in Africa. While there is no evidence of large-scale disasters for the Romans during this period of the war (none that Tacitus documents, at least), it would no doubt have been a frustrating time for them, unable to make any impact on an enemy they could not pin down. While Tacfarinas maintained his approach of avoiding battle and launching low-level attacks on the Roman marching columns, there was seemingly little they could do to stop him, except to hope that at some point he would make a mistake they could capitalize on.

The disruption caused by this war was starting to have an impact on the wider Roman world, in particular its grain supply. Tacfarinas' actions had seemingly led to problems in getting grain from Africa to Rome, with potentially all points in the supply chain being adversely affected – from the growers actually being able to plant and harvest it, through to its transfer to the coast and on to Italy. Conflict in northwest Africa had negatively affected grain supplies on two previous occasions (23/22 BC and AD 5–7).[36] Shortages in supply in AD 19 led to increases in price, which in turn sparked off riots in Rome.[37] Tiberius was forced to step in and subsidise the prices to calm the disturbances. There was no doubt also some war profiteering going on behind the backs of the authorities, including some merchants who sold grain to Tacfarinas instead of supplying it to Rome. A few years later (AD 23) two merchants, Carsidius Sacerdos and Gaius Gracchus, were put on trial as public enemies, accused of supplying grain to Tacfarinas; in both cases, the accused were found innocent.[38] Gracchus in particular seems to have been lucky to get away without conviction. The son of Sempronius Gracchus, banished from Rome to Africa by Augustus, Gaius Gracchus had a famous name but little wealth, despite which, Tacitus notes, he still came in for the accusations often levelled against the elites in Rome during this period. It took the intervention of two former proconsuls in Africa – Aelius Lamia (in office AD 14–17, Camillus' predecessor) and Lucius Apronius – to clear his name.

Although the two merchants were cleared of wrongdoing, it is evident that illicit grain trading was going on in Africa at the time, with Tacfarinas purchasing supplies that would otherwise have gone to Rome. Whether this was done for a political reason, suggesting at least a modicum of popular support for Tacfarinas in Africa,[39] or simply because the rebels were willing to pay more than Rome did, is impossible to say. Whatever the realities of the illicit grain trade, the unrest in Rome prompted by food shortages, combined with the growing suspicion that all was not right with the supply chain, gave the war in northern Africa a social and economic relevance as well as a political and military one.

It was seemingly around this point that Rome recognized there was a need for additional manpower in northwest Africa. While there is no record of an emergency levy of soldiers in response to the conflict, we know that troops were transferred in, suggesting that the Roman authorities were taking the threat posed by Tacfarinas far more seriously than before. In AD 19, the Jews living in Rome were exiled from the city, with 4,000 being drafted to the army for military service, ostensibly to deal with brigandage in Sardinia.[40] They may actually have been sent to Africa or, more likely, they replaced in Sardinia a unit of Lusitanian auxiliaries, who were transferred to Africa Proconsularis.[41] Such levies were rare and typically only carried out when there was a pressing need – in AD 19, the only active warfront that might have needed an influx of men was northwest Africa.[42] Other units, including the 2nd Cohort Gemella Thracum (a unit unattested anywhere outside Africa) and the 15th Cohort Voluntariorum, were likely also transferred to the region.[43] Their movement is not documented by Tacitus, but inscriptions from the region indicate an increase in the presence of different military units at this time. There were also plans to transfer a new legion, the 9th Legion Hispana, to Africa Proconsularis from Pannonia.[44] All these troop movements suggest the situation in northwest Africa was felt to be far more dangerous than Tacitus' narrative would lead one to believe.

A Decisive Moment for Rome

Rome's patience finally paid off. Tacfarinas shifted from raiding settlements on or near the fringes of Roman and Mauretanian territory to attacking those in the wealthier regions on the coast. His army looted an even more significant amount of booty as a result – so much so that it was no longer possible to transport it with the army whilst moving rapidly. Tacitus gives the impression that the quantity of loot would have compared to a standard Roman baggage-train, meaning dozens, even hundreds, of wagons-full. Even if Tacfarinas had the mules to transport such a substantial treasure, it would have slowed down his army, making them as slow and ponderous as the Romans and taking away one of the key advantages they had over their enemy. The only option was to find somewhere to store their loot so it did not have to be transported wherever they went. To do this Tacfarinas was forced to establish a fixed camp – and once he had done so, understandably, he did not want to venture too far from it. This development gave Rome its advantage: Tacfarinas was now pinned down to a known region and unlikely to flee very far. The Roman army finally had the opportunity to catch up with him and force him to fight the pitched battle he had been avoiding.

Lucius Apronius ordered his son, Lucius Apronius Caesianus, to march against Tacfarinas. Apronius Caesianus was evidently very young at this point, as indicated by a votive dedication he later made at the temple of Venus Erycina in Sicily, which referred to the fact that he had not even reached manhood by the time he was sent out against Tacfarinas.[45] He was directed to move as quickly as possible, to try either to catch Tacfarinas in battle or capture his treasury.[46] Speed was essential to avoid intelligence of their approach reaching Tacfarinas, or to allow reinforcements to join him. Apronius Caesianus took a limited force with him, concentrating his strength mainly in troops who could move rapidly through the African landscape: the cavalry, light-armed auxiliaries, and the most mobile of the legionary troops. This is the first point at which the Roman command adapted their conventional tactics for a situation-specific reason, something which would become more common in the later phases of the war. One of the greatest advantages Tacfarinas had had was his ability to move much faster than the Romans, but this change would help to even things up. It was a good decision, and the Romans were able to reach Tacfarinas before he had the opportunity to evacuate either his army or the booty from the area around their encampment.

Unfortunately, Tacitus gives no details of the battle, only saying that the Romans were victorious. The engagement evidently did not involve the entirety of the Roman army in Africa, just the part which was sufficiently lightly armed to move quickly – and Lucius Apronius does not appear to have been present, having delegated command on the field to his son. The bulk of the legion was almost certainly absent, Rome relying instead on its cavalry and lighter-armed auxiliaries, supplemented by a smaller number of the most mobile legionaries. Indeed their force may have resembled Tacfarinas' own more than a 'traditional' Roman field army. It can be surmised, therefore, that the engagement may not have taken the form of a conventional pitched battle, with two heavily-armed battle-lines facing off against each other, but potentially a more mobile fight with each side trying to outmanoeuvre the other. Tacfarinas appears to have known that the attack was coming (while being unable to leave the area to avoid it), but what preparations he might have made are not reported by Tacitus. Again, there are no indications of the size of the forces involved, and nothing is said of the respective casualty rates, although they were probably not particularly high.[47]

The Roman victory was sufficiently comprehensive that Tacfarinas and his men were forced to flee the field without their booty. After their previous defeat, to Camillus, they had sought sanctuary in the desert, where they could be fairly sure that the Romans would not be willing or able to follow them. Tacitus makes no comment on how damaging this new defeat was to Numidian manpower, and gives no indication of possible casualty figures. However, it was clearly viewed in Rome as a significant victory, and it resulted in Lucius Apronius being granted triumphal honours.[48] His son, Apronius

Caesianus, received a priesthood from Tiberius (he was too young for any other honours) and he dedicated spoils from the campaign at the temple of Venus Erycina in Sicily in his own name; he also dedicated a statue to his father, and father and son jointly dedicated another to Tiberius.[49] The awards did not necessarily mean that Rome believed the war was over – Camillus had also been given honours when the outcome was far from clear – but does mean they recognized the scale of the achievement. For the time being, Tacfarinas had been defeated again, but once more he had been left alive. Rome may have hoped that this second major setback would start to impact the morale of both Tacfarinas and his men, and consequently either he would decide not to resume the conflict or would struggle to recruit replacements for the casualties sustained. That Tacfarinas was not killed seems not to have been viewed as a significant problem and no effort was made to chase him down or entrap him once he had fled.

The Aftermath

The events above probably took place in the summer of AD 18 or 19, within Apronius' first year or so as proconsul in Africa. AD 19 seems most probable, but it is impossible to be certain. Unlike Camillus, Lucius Apronius did not leave Africa in the immediate aftermath of his victory, but remained in position until *c.*AD 20 (or possible early 21). He served for at least double the standard proconsular term, but this is not surprising under the circumstances, particularly if the events above did happen in 19; it would make little sense to replace a proconsul in the middle of a military campaign. Tiberius obviously trusted Apronius in the role and it seems he was right to do so. Although the narrative for these years is very sketchy, in Tacitus' account there do not appear to have been any major Roman military setbacks, and indeed, the tide may have turned against Tacfarinas. But this period did not necessarily see a complete cessation of hostilities between Rome and Tacfarinas. At a later stage, Tacitus refers to Tacfarinas as having suffered 'many repulses' at the hands of the Roman army,[50] which does not really fit the narrative of the war in his own account. It suggests that even after the capture of his treasury Tacfarinas continued operations, perhaps on a lower scale, throughout Apronius' proconsulship. The fact that additional troops were sent to the region, and evidently kept there for some time, indicates ongoing conflict through (the rest of) AD 19 and into 20. Tacfarinas' army evidently succeeded in maintaining its numbers during this period, which also supports the idea that raiding continued.

Rome may still have felt that it was gaining the upper hand, particularly if they continued to see Tacfarinas as more of a bandit leader than a rebel.

However, the threat posed in northwest Africa did not go away, and there was a renewal of intensive hostilities towards the end of Apronius' tenure, the rebels making serious inroads into Roman territory.[51] This development prompted the search for a replacement proconsul. As well as re-emerging as a threat, Tacfarinas now began to develop ambitions beyond the acquisition of wealth (assuming he had not done so already), aiming to seek not just loot from his raids, but land – somewhere he and his men could live free of Roman oversight. The change heralded a shift in the tone of the conflict, as Tiberius became more invested in seeing it brought to an end. Lucius Apronius was finally called back to Rome and replaced by the third proconsul to take on the war against Tacfarinas.

However, the threats posed in northwestern Italy did not go away, and there was a [illegible] towards the end [illegible] the [illegible] into Roman territory. This development [illegible] may begin to develop [illegible] already [illegible] change [illegible] a shift in the [illegible] of the conflict [illegible] to Rome [illegible] against Tarentum.

Chapter 8

Quintus Junius Blaesus and a New Approach to the War (AD 21–23)

Under Lucius Apronius, the war with Tacfarinas had reached a state of stalemate. There was no obvious prospect of resolution, as the nature of the conflict made it unlikely that either side would be able to inflict a decisive blow on the other. The heavily armed Roman forces could defeat Tacfarinas in pitched battle, but he simply avoided engaging with them under such circumstances. But the nature of the war meant that Tacfarinas could not inflict a major defeat on the Romans either. The transfer of additional troops into the region had evidently not proved decisive for Rome and they must have started to despair of finding a way to end the conflict. Lucius Apronius had competently managed the campaign and prevented any serious Roman military defeats, but seemed unable, at least with the resources allowed him, to bring the war to an end. Tacfarinas continued to attract recruits, some of whom may have followed him purely for money, while others may have been drawn to his cause as rebels. The war was having a growing negative impact on the rest of the Empire, and it was becoming increasingly desirable to bring it to a conclusion. The existing provincial garrison was proving insufficient to handle the conflict and the additional units transferred in, while necessary, were a drain on the resources of the province. The grain riots in AD 19 demonstrated that the repercussions of war could affect even Rome itself.

By this stage, the war had clearly passed the point of being mere banditry. If it is debatable in the early stages whether Tacfarinas had any ambitions beyond looting, during this next phase it became clear that he was no longer satisfied with the proceeds of raids. He may also have started to consider the realities of his situation. The stalemate could not continue indefinitely and, while he had held his own against the Romans for a number of years, he may have begun to wonder how long the situation could last: to stay in the game he had to be lucky every time, while Rome only had to be lucky once. A new proconsul, Quintus Junius Blaesus, was selected by agreement between the Senate and Tiberius, but before he could set out for Africa there was an unexpected development. For the first time, Tacfarinas now attempted to negotiate with Rome, albeit in a typically over-the-top manner. He did not come through the channels of the provincial authorities, but made moves to establish a dialogue with Tiberius himself, offering a cessation of hostilities in exchange for a land grant. Rather than leaping at this opportunity to end the war (or perhaps disbelieving Tacfarinas' sincerity), Tiberius was enraged by the proposal. Blaesus was authorized to renew hostilities and to do everything necessary to bring matters to a head. He adopted an innovative field strategy, incorporating many of the irregular tactics which had proved so effective for Tacfarinas, and took major strides towards ending the conflict for good.

The Search for a New Proconsul

It had become increasingly important that the conflict be handed over to someone with the experience and ability to end hostilities for good. As Africa Proconsular was a Senatorial province, it was the Senate that had the responsibility of selecting the proconsul, theoretically independently of the emperor (though it is unlikely they would ever have chosen a candidate he disapproved of). But in appointing the next proconsul the Senate decided to request that Tiberius become directly involved in the selection process: why is unclear. Both Marcus Furius Camillus and Lucius Apronius had been chosen by Senatorial sortition, and neither had proved a bad choice. Getting Tiberius involved was not the easiest of matters at this point either. By AD 21, the emperor had withdrawn from Rome to Campania, ostensibly to improve his health, but apparently also to get the Senate accustomed to what he hoped could become a permanent absence.[1] It was not a complete withdrawal, however. He was serving as consul for the year (AD 21) alongside his son, Drusus the Younger, and still received Imperial correspondence about events in the wider Empire. Through this system, he was informed that Tacfarinas was once again causing problems in northwest Africa, in a renewed phase of activity.

Tiberius did not return to Rome to deal with the issue, but wrote to the Senate to ask them to select a new proconsul to replace Lucius Apronius.[2] He advised them to select someone with significant military experience, and who was physically fit enough to take on the challenge of the conflict. In the subsequent debate, the Senate failed to decide on a candidate. Tiberius' preferred choice appears to have initially been a man named Marcus Aemilius Lepidus, but there was severe opposition to his appointment among the Senators, some of whom attacked him as a 'spiritless and poverty-stricken degenerate'. Unable to make a decision, the Senate nevertheless requested that

Tiberius himself appoint someone to replace Lucius Apronius as proconsul in Africa. By the next meeting of the Senate, Tiberius – after criticizing the Senators for forcing him to make the decision – had narrowed down the field to two candidates: Marcus Aemilius Lepidus and Quintus Junius Blaesus. Both candidates met the criteria he had specified for the next proconsul and both had served as consuls at an earlier stage in their career.

Marcus Aemilius Lepidus was an ideal choice for the appointment. He was a distinguished member of the Roman aristocracy, described as 'a man who in name and in fortune approaches the Caesars'.[3] He had served as consul in AD 6, making him one of the more senior members of the political circle at the time, and eligible to serve as proconsul in either Africa or Asia. He was also a minor member of the Imperial family by marriage.[4] He is probably the same Marcus Lepidus referred to by Augustus on his deathbed as 'capable but disdainful'.[5] He had military experience, having commanded a legion during the Great Illyrian Revolt (AD 6–9), and at one point during that conflict was given command of the entire army.[6] After the war he served as governor of Dalmatia or Pannonia. At the time of Augustus' death in AD 14, Lepidus was in northern Spain as the governor of Hispania Tarraconensis (also known as Hispania Citerior), a role which came with the command of three legions (none of which revolted when Augustus died, as their counterparts on the Rhine had done).[7] However, when Lepidus returned to Rome in AD 20, he became embroiled in the controversial trial of Gnaeus Calpurnius Piso, the man accused of murdering Germanicus in late AD 19 in Syria, and he spoke publicly in Piso's defence.[8] This may have won Lepidus the gratitude of Tiberius (who was suspected by many of involvement in Germanicus' death), but had made him enemies among the Senate and it was some of these individuals who spoke out against his appointment as proconsul.

At a hearing of the two candidates in the Senate, Lepidus withdrew himself from the selection process. He cited his health and the needs of his children, particularly a daughter who had recently become of marriageable age. Many suspected, however, that these were excuses to hide the real reason, which had more to do with the family connections of his rival, Blaesus – in particular, his relationship to Lucius Aelius Sejanus, a confidant of Tiberius who came to rule the Empire in all but name during the AD 20s.[9] Lepidus was subsequently appointed proconsul of Asia (*c.*AD 26),[10] and Quintus Junius Blaesus was offered the proconsulship of Africa. He declined at first in what is presented by Tacitus as a demonstration of false modesty, allowing the flattery of the Senate to change his mind for him. The decision about the next proconsul had been made.

Quintus Junius Blaesus

Little is known of Blaesus' early life. Given the dating of his later career, he was likely born in the 30s–20s BC and first appeared on the political scene as suffect consul in the latter half of AD 10, serving alongside Servius Cornelius Lentulus Maluginensis. Although there is little evidence about his political career, he did have a significant amount of military experience, particularly in frontier warfare – certainly enough to qualify as a viable candidate to lead the next phase of the campaign against Tacfarinas. When the Illyrian legions had threatened revolt and Tiberius' son Drusus the Younger was despatched to deal with them, he had been assisted by Blaesus, who was praised as 'no ordinary helper' and so capable in both military and civic affairs that it was unclear whether he was 'more useful in the camp or better in the toga' (i.e. on campaign or in the Senate).[11] The picture given by the sources is of a man who was a most efficient field commander and politician – exactly the kind of person Tiberius might want in charge of the ongoing war in Africa.

However, in addition to these undoubted talents, Blaesus also had something of even greater value – political connections to Tiberius at the highest level through his nephew, the infamous Lucius Aelius Sejanus. A prefect of the Praetorian Guard from the earliest days of Tiberius' reign, Sejanus had become a trusted confidant of the emperor in the years thereafter. He came to exercise growing influence over the Imperial regime and by the early AD 20s played a significant part in the governance of the Empire – so much so that Tiberius even referred to him as the 'partner of his toils'.[12] Various members of Sejanus' family inevitably profited from his rise to power, including his uncle Blaesus.[13] The influence of Sejanus no doubt contributed to Blaesus being considered for the proconsulship, though he was undoubtedly qualified for it – the war against Tacfarinas was too important to be entrusted to someone not up to the job. Blaesus had sufficient military, political, and administrative experience in his own right, and Rome could rest assured that the next stage of the conflict was in good hands.

Destabilization in Africa

Lucius Apronius had managed to keep things stable in northwest Africa, but proved unable to force a permanent defeat on Tacfarinas. He had made little change to the field operation of his army in the region, although he had at least partly recognized the importance of deploying light-armed mobile troops in certain situations. The additions to the provincial garrison suggest that he was struggling to cope with the troops he had available. The background instability caused by the conflict was beginning to affect Roman economic interests in the region, particularly those related to the grain trade, and the settled population would have been increasingly frustrated by the apparent inability of the state to protect them from Tacfarinas. It was not yet a full-blown crisis, but the implication in Tacitus is of a situation gradually slipping out of Rome's control. The Romans were able to win every battle against Tacfarinas, yet somehow could not find a way to win the war. Every time he suffered a defeat, Tacfarinas would just withdraw to the desert or mountains, regroup his men and wait for the right moment to return. He still attracted significant numbers of recruits despite his losses in the field, and there is no indication that the wider indigenous population turned against him in this period. It was another incursion of Tacfarinas into Roman territory that had prompted the search for a new proconsul, as his return once more indicated that the problem would not go away by itself.

Adding to the regional instability was the prospect of political disruption associated with regime change in Mauretania. Since 25 BC, Juba II had been the most reliable Roman ally in the this part of the world, the best since Masinissa in the second century BC. Juba was in his 60s when the conflict broke out, however, and had already started considering the succession of his son Ptolemy, probably since about AD 11. Juba had not been popular with some of the Mauretanian population when he was given the kingship, particularly among the Mauri who lived in the western part of the realm. They felt that living under Juba's rule was akin to living under Rome's, a prospect they did not welcome, and their involvement with Tacfarinas' conflict in AD 17 probably amounted to a full-blown act of rebellion on their part. It was clear that Ptolemy would be no more popular as ruler and that Juba's death might be used by some, the Mauri in particular, as an opportunity for further rebellion – indeed it eventually was, accompanied by mass defections of Mauri from Juba's army to that of Tacfarinas.[14] Juba would have been aware that if a more localized rebellion were to break out against the accession of his son, Rome might well just step in and annex the kingdom. To try to make the succession as smooth as possible, Juba had introduced Ptolemy to co-rule fairly early on, progressing to joint rule by *c.*AD 17, and he had probably also started campaigning with the Romans, although Tacitus suggests that this only happened in the final year of the war.[15] Juba may also have been aware that Rome did not regard Ptolemy particularly highly,[16] and wanted to ensure that his son had a good working relationship with them so they would be less likely to take over his kingdom.

From a Roman perspective too, it would be better if the war against Tacfarinas could be concluded before anything happened to Juba. If there were uprisings after his death, these rebels could easily join forces with Tacfarinas to create what would be a very daunting army for Rome to face, and the situation would risk opening up additional fronts in the war. It was not the first time that the potential death of a longstanding ally in the region had prompted military action (the imminent demise of Masinissa in the mid-second century BC likely being one of the reasons that Rome had initiated the Third Punic War). When Blaesus was sent to Africa, he was no doubt charged with ending the war as rapidly as possible, but before he could fully open operations against Tacfarinas, a diplomatic incident would dramatically increase the urgency of his task.

An Embassy to Rome

As discussed previously, it is questionable whether or not Tacfarinas intended to lead a rebellion against Rome right from the start, or whether he was a local bandit thug who became particularly powerful. Rome never recognized him as a rebel, ostensibly because they did not accept that he was fighting for legitimate grievances, or that his aim was the liberation of his people rather than his own enrichment. Both types of individual were no doubt part of his army – bandits hoping to get rich, and rebels hoping to win their freedom from Rome – but the motivations of Tacfarinas himself are hard to discern. The most likely scenario seems to be that he did indeed start off as just a bandit, making a living the best way he could after deserting the Roman army, doing what many men in his situation did to get by. That his banditry escalated to the stage where it became a military problem for Rome is a testament to how well he conducted operations. But at some point he began to think about his future prospects, no doubt recognizing that the war would not last forever and that ultimately he was almost certainly not going to be the one who proved victorious. It was likely with this in mind that he attempted to open peace negotiations with Tiberius, through an extraordinary embassy sent direct to the emperor.

Tacfarinas asked for – or rather, demanded – a permanent territorial settlement for himself and his men, on which they could live free of Roman rule; in exchange for this, they would cease hostilities and the war would be at an end.[17] If Rome refused, Tacfarinas would continue his operations indefinitely, raiding settlements and attacking military installations and marching columns. Presumably, if the settlement of land was made Tacfarinas would have ruled it as a chieftain, defended by the personal army he already possessed – whether this really would have put their raiding days behind them is another matter (it seems unlikely, even just from an economic perspective). Tiberius, perhaps predictably, was not impressed by Tacfarinas' overture. In fact, Tacitus suggests that he took the suggestion as extremely insulting to both himself and Rome, among the worst of his entire life. Tacfarinas' status in Roman eyes as an auxiliary deserter and bandit (rather than a legitimate 'freedom fighter') only heightened the sting.[18] In a speech undoubtedly created by Tacitus but intended to sum up the emperor's feelings about the offer, he notes how other rebels of much higher status had not dared make such an insolent demand of Rome:

> Even Spartacus, after the annihilation of so many consular armies, when his fires were blazing through an Italy unavenged, while the commonwealth reeled in the gigantic conflicts with Sertorius and Mithridates – even Spartacus was not accorded a capitulation upon terms. And now, at the glorious zenith of the Roman nation, was this brigand Tacfarinas to be bought off by a peace and a cession of lands?

It was clear, then, that Tacfarinas would not achieve his territory and his peace. He had attempted to negotiate with Tiberius not as a rebel leader trying to bargain for his future safety, but as one legitimate leader to another, which particularly enraged the emperor. In some ways it was a surprising move on Tacfarinas' part, and suggests he was already trying to plan for a long-term future beyond the conflict.

Although Tacfarinas' motivation had clearly moved beyond just the proceeds of raiding by this point, he had still not quite assumed the mantle of rebel leader seeking the freedom of his people. The inherent biases which led to him being deemed solely a bandit by Tacitus have been discussed elsewhere, and as we have noted Tacfarinas' aims do seem to have been selfish in the earlier part of his campaign. The scale of the Roman response and its recognition of victories against him do suggest that they saw the war as more than just the suppression of banditry, and Tacfarinas' attacks on Roman military installations demonstrate that he was not exclusively attacking settlements for their wealth. But this does not mean he was rebelling on behalf of the entire population of northwest Africa, leading a popular resistance to drive Rome out of the region and restore the population to their own governance. The proposal that he put to Tiberius in AD 21 did not suggest that Rome should leave the region, or even attempt to negotiate better conditions for the majority of people. He was asking for a territorial settlement that would only be of advantage to himself and his men. No mention seems to have been made of anything that would benefit people more widely – such things as guarantees about freedom of pastoralist movement or ownership of land, not introducing taxation, or a reduction in conscription levels. If Tiberius had agreed to the settlement, nothing would have changed for the majority of people in the region; indeed, with Roman attention no longer on the conflict the administrative changes might be returned to with a vengeance, potentially making the inhabitants worse off than before.

So by AD 21, while Tacfarinas' ambitions may have grown, it is difficult to assume he had fully transformed into a rebel leader – he might still have been primarily working for his own interests. Nevertheless, the proposed settlement did not just benefit him: that the peace Tacfarinas offered would have resulted in his men being given land outside Roman control may reflect the fact that this was what many of his troops were actually fighting for.[19] He may have recognized that a land grant was an opportunity, however limited, to establish a small bastion of freedom, the only thing that might stand between northwest Africa and total Roman domination.[20]

Were there any grounds for Tacfarinas to believe Tiberius might agree to his suggestion, or was it a forlorn hope from the start? It is difficult to imagine with hindsight that the emperor would ever have agreed to these terms, but given the gruelling nature of the conflict, Tacfarinas may have hoped that the emperor would not find it too high a price for peace to be restored in the region, even temporarily. After all, Roman territorial holdings in northwest Africa were largely limited to the coastal regions and much of the territory Tacfarinas was operating in was of only peripheral interest to them. The continuing existence of the client kingdom of Mauretania demonstrated that Rome was still willing for parts of the region to be under indirect control, albeit in the hands of a trusted ally and client ruler (a role which it is certainly hard to imagine Tacfarinas carrying out). However, Tacfarinas had clearly underestimated the degree to which Tiberius hated him, and entirely misjudged the likely reception of his offer. Still, the refusal may not have disrupted his plans too much – and it is difficult to imagine that any peace established under these circumstances would have lasted very long. Thus the war would be renewed, now under the command of Blaesus, in the hopes of bringing it to a swift end.

A Change of Strategy

By the time that Blaesus arrived in Africa at some point in early AD 21, Rome had been directly at war with Tacfarinas for nearly five years, and he was active in the region for possibly double that. Although both Furius Camillus and Lucius Apronius had been well-rewarded for their efforts, with triumphal honours back in Rome, neither had made a significant contribution to ending the conflict. Things were at something of a stalemate. Both Camillus and Apronius appear to have assumed that Tacfarinas could be treated like any other rebellious provincial enemy. In their recent experience, the local chieftains would avoid meeting Roman troops in pitched battle for as long as possible in favour of an irregular guerrilla-type campaign, hoping to succeed in a war of attrition. In reality Rome would bear the losses until the rebels could be forced or persuaded into pitched battle, at which point the latter would sustain such substantial losses that they would have to surrender. This had worked in Illyricum during the revolt of AD 6–9 and more recently had proved effective against Arminius in Germany. It was costly to Rome in both manpower and resources, and obviously they would have preferred simply to meet and destroy the enemy on the battlefield right at the start of a campaign – but generally they knew, if they held on, such an engagement would eventually come. This was not proving to be the case with Tacfarinas, however. The tried-and-tested methods of provincial warfare were not working against him – or rather, they had limited successes which made absolutely no difference to his ability to continue the campaign. Both Camillus and Apronius had inflicted battlefield defeats on Tacfarinas' army, only for it to disappear into the desert or mountains and reappear, renewed, the following year. The Roman army was unable to make clear headway against the Numidians, who exploited every Roman weakness in the field, and when they found themselves in a new strategy that was not working for them, simply abandoned it and returned to their classic techniques.

One of Tacfarinas' strengths was that he knew this is what would happen. He had spent years learning exactly what the Roman army would do in specific combat situations, and given that he likely served in a cavalry unit based in Africa his knowledge would be specific to the region he now found himself fighting in. He could create a situation in which the Roman army would struggle to function effectively. The inherent dangers of auxiliaries later using their training and military skills *against* Rome were well understood and had been infamously illustrated in the case of Arminius in Germany in AD 9. But with Rome inextricably reliant on the auxiliary system for manpower, there was little alternative but to persist with the system and aim to minimize the number of times such a threat was realized. The only chance the Romans had of breaking the deadlock was to do something unexpected – and this was exactly what Blaesus did.

Tiberius handed the command of the war against Tacfarinas over to Blaesus, the implication in Tacitus being that he was given complete authority. From the start, Blaesus adopted an approach very different to that taken previously, no doubt recognizing that conventional methods of warfare used by the Romans thus far were not working. He made two major strategic changes. He took measures to reduce the size of the army available to Tacfarinas, and at the same time he changed the way that his own army was operating in the field to make them less predictable and better adapted to the unique conditions. Some of the methods he used to achieve these aims were quite dramatic. For example, he offered amnesties to any of Tacfarinas' allies who willingly surrendered to Rome.[21] Many took up the opportunity. This was a shrewd move on Blaesus' part, as it recognized the importance of a ready supply of manpower to Tacfarinas' cause – so no matter what losses the Roman army inflicted on him, he had been able to replenish his force and return with equal strength to the field. The amnesty threatened this constant renewal. It also played on the fact that perhaps not everyone who fought for Tacfarinas did so willingly – in the early stages, the Cinithii had been forced to fight for him, and others may have been as well. Deserting Tacfarinas would have proved difficult if there was no alternative, but Rome now offered the prospect of forgiveness and protection for anyone who chose to take advantage of their offer. Some may have fought willingly at first but later came to regret their position, particularly as Rome began to step up its counter-operations against Tacfarinas, and this may have seemed like an ideal time to defect (back) to Rome. The rebels in his force may also have slowly been losing hope, and were now ready to abandon a leader who had not delivered what they expected in terms of liberation from Rome.[22] Perhaps they even felt betrayed by Tacfarinas' attempt to negotiate with Tiberius, which had potentially offered them personal freedom from Roman rule, but would deliver nothing for the communities on whose behalf they were fighting. The Roman authorities may have guessed that some of Tacfarinas' men would see the negotiations as a betrayal, and the proferred amnesties consequently contributed to widen any divisions in his army.

Blaesus' policy appears to have had a significant impact on Tacfarinas' manpower resources. Tacitus notes that 'large numbers came in under the amnesty', although he does not attach any figure to that observation. It is impossible even to guess what proportion of Tacfarinas' force might have taken advantage of the Roman offer, although it certainly was enough to have had an effect on his support base.[23] But the fact that Tacfarinas was able to sustain operations for several more years suggests the amnesties may not have delivered the decisive blow that Rome had hoped for. He was still able to field a functional army, which demonstrates that the offer of clemency did not succeed in buying the surrender of his men wholesale. Either they still felt that the financial rewards of raiding with Tacfarinas were worth the risk, or a significant proportion of his army consisted of rebels against Rome by this point, who could not be bought at any price short of their liberation.

Blaesus' adoption of irregular strategy in the field is a particularly interesting development. Rome had realized by this stage of the war that Tacfarinas was not going to engage willingly in pitched battle, and there was seemingly no way to force him. He relied instead on what Tacitus called the 'petty knaveries of war'[24] – rapid, light-armed attacks from which they could retreat before facing any substantial opposition. The slow-moving legions, accompanied by large baggage-trains, were easy targets for surprise attacks, and by focusing much of his activity around the frontiers rather than the heavily settled coastal regions, Tacfarinas forced the Romans to operate in hostile terrain of which they probably had limited knowledge. The legions were unable to rapidly mobilize and respond to reports of Tacfarinas raiding settlements or attacking military installations. Because of such limitations, Roman troops had not been quick to provide back-up to their comrades caught in problematic situations elsewhere, and could not chase down Tacfarinas to put greater pressure on him. They could have tried to make him engage by carrying out their own attacks on the settlements of his supporters and thus erode his wider support, something which had proved effective in other provincial conflicts. Tacitus makes no mention of their trying this, but this is hardly surprising – given that he portrays Tacfarinas' support as coming primarily from the nomadic peoples of the region, he could hardly go on to describe Roman attacks on the settlements they allegedly did not have.

So if Tacfarinas was not going to change, then the Romans would have to. One of the strengths of the Roman army was its adaptability, with the training and discipline instilled in the troops facilitating almost any kind of operation. But what makes Blaesus' change in field strategy significant is that he seems to have adopted exactly the same guerrilla-type tactics that his adversary had been using so effectively. Tacfarinas would no longer be facing the slow-moving and pitched-battle-fixated Roman army that he knew how to handle so well, but a force which had identified its weaknesses and disadvantages in the campaign thus far, and made the effort to address them and level the field. Previously Tacfarinas had been able to use what he had learned as an auxiliary soldier against Rome – now Blaesus would use what he had learned from his predecessors against Tacfarinas. His new approach would transform the Roman army from a single lumbering force desperately trying (and failing) to catch Tacfarinas, to a number of dynamic, smaller and faster-moving units that could take the initiative in the field, rather than helplessly responding to the rebels' raids after the event. It would no longer matter that there was no pitched battle, because Blaesus would not be relying on a single decisive engagement. It was to be a war of attrition on both sides.

The New Roman Deployment

When Blaesus decided to adapt the Roman field strategy, Tacitus comments that it was the first time that 'the arts of Tacfarinas were met by a mode of warfare akin to his own.'[25] This shake-up of operations almost certainly took place in the summer of AD 21, soon after Blaesus had arrived in the region. He was assisted by the fact that he had far more manpower available to him than either Camillus or Apronius had done (at least for the majority of the latter's campaign). The 9th Legion Hispana had been sent to augment the 3rd Legion Augusta, giving Blaesus up to twice the number of legionaries his predecessors had commanded.[26] The men of the 9th were experienced in provincial conflict and irregular fighting, and would have been a valuable addition to the force. Presumably the 9th was accompanied by its associated auxiliary units, and the province was also host to at least one auxiliary cohort of Lusitanians who had been transferred during the proconsulship of Lucius Apronius. The Roman army in the region was likely to have been 20–30,000 men strong, potentially even more. Provinces had been conquered with fewer men. The sheer numbers involved at this stage clearly demonstrate, if there was any lingering doubt, that this was now all-out war between Rome and Tacfarinas.

The additional troops gave Blaesus far more flexibility in his deployment of men in the field. Although there had previously been detachments of the Roman army garrisoning different places across northwest Africa, the majority of the provincial army appears to have operated as a single large unit. Blaesus instead divided his army into three primary groups, each of which contained three distinct marching columns.[27] One of the groups was placed under the command of Blaesus' son, Lucius Junius Blaesus, who had previously served as a tribune under his father in Pannonia and was present during the problems with the legions in AD 14.[28] Junius Blaesus the Younger was sent to guard Cirta and its surrounding settlements. Cirta was only 80km (50 miles) inland from the Mediterranean Sea, and the fact that Cirta needed protection illustrates how far Tacfarinas' operations had advanced by this point. Another of the field groups was sent out under the command of Publius Cornelius Lentulus Scipio, the legate of the 9th Legion. Lentulus Scipio was a less experienced commander still in the early stages of his career, and had not yet even served as a consul in Rome. His appointment to such a level of seniority is therefore slightly unusual for the time,[29] although it made sense to keep him in charge of the legionaries he had been transferred to the region with, rather than putting them under someone new.

Lentulus Scipio and the 9th Legion were deployed in the area of Tripolitania (modern coastal Libya) and are described as being responsible for protecting the road to Leptis, a route which Tacfarinas had been using to raid settlements in this territory. It is not quite clear whether the settlement referred to in Tacitus is Leptis Magna (modern Labdah, Libya) or Leptis Minor (modern Lemta, Tunisia). Leptis Magna seems a bit too far east to have been so directly affected by Tacfarinas' raids, suggesting that Leptis Minor, a very wealthy trading city, was the intended reference. However, there is reason to think it was Leptis Magna, which would mean that Tacfarinas' campaign had impacted a far larger area than is generally believed. An inscription found on a statue base on the *cardo* (main road) in Leptis Magna records the public dedication of an honorary monument to Gaius Gavius Macer, a propraetorian legate of the 3rd Augusta.[30] Macer was probably involved in the final pacification and restoration of northern Africa after the war against Tacfarinas, and may have taken part in the conflict at an earlier stage if his previous career had also been with the 3rd Augusta. It was a substantial monument, probably once topped with an equestrian statue, likely of Macer himself. Although this clue alone does not prove that Tacfarinas reached as far east as Leptis Magna, there seems little point in the location of such a monument in the city if the war had had no effect there, especially as the statue would have been at public expense. Further possible evidence lies in a fragment of another monumental inscription from the *cardo* of Leptis Magna, dedicated by one 'Scipio' around the time of the war against Tacfarinas (late 10s/early 20s AD).[31] Again, on its own this fragment proves nothing, but does give another indication that Tacfarinas' raiding may have extended as far as Leptis Magna. Whichever Leptis it was, the deployment of the troops under Lentulus Scipio limited Tacfarinas' movements further east, offering more protection to the wealthiest and most vulnerable parts of the northern African coast.

The final field unit was under Blaesus himself, who probably took command of the 3rd Legion Augusta, augmented by particularly capable troops. He is likely to have remained in the core territory of Africa Proconsularis, using the pre-existing bases of the legion (at Ammaedara, and likely also Tacape and Capsa). This would place him in the heart of the territory occupied by the Musulamii, who had been supporters of Tacfarinas from early on and who had made him a chieftain prior to the outbreak of war. Blaesus' primary objective was to secure key strategic locations in the region, either with military installations or entrenchments, leaving small garrisons of men as needed in each location. This tactic severely limited Tacfarinas' freedom of movement in the area, because wherever he tried to turn he found himself confronted with Roman troops, in front of him, flanking him or, most problematically, behind him. Tacfarinas' men could no longer quickly escape the Roman forces after surprise attacks, and found themselves restricted just in moving around – suffering in much the same way that their enemy had done over the previous years. The deployment of the three Roman forces prevented Tacfarinas moving to the north, east, or west without challenge, and sub-units could detach from the main armies as required to chase down his forces when they appeared nearby. Slowly but surely, the Romans were tightening their grip on the rebels, inflicting casualties whenever they trapped parts of his army in the field. The new Roman tactics were not yet sufficient to completely destroy Tacfarinas, but they were beginning to have a significant impact on his operations. He was slowly driven back towards the desert fringes, away from the vulnerable settlements on the coast.

Encouraged by the success of this new approach, Blaesus continued to deploy his forces in an irregular manner. His tripartite army was split into numerous even smaller detachments, each under the command of an experienced centurion who could be trusted to lead. How large the detachments were is difficult to say. A centurion was typically used to commanding 80 men (or 160 in the case of a first centurion (*primus pilus*)), but these African detachments may have been larger – without knowing how many were created (Tacitus just says there were many) it is impossible to give even a rough estimate. The further (sub-)division of the army allowed for an intensification of the landscape control which was already proving effective against Tacfarinas. Smaller units were able to move even more rapidly through the landscape, allowing them to take the initiative against their enemy rather than always being on the back foot and just reacting to his attacks.

These changes to the Romans' field strategy must have come as a nasty surprise to Tacfarinas and he evidently struggled to come up with effective counter-measures. He had fewer troops than before, while the Romans had more than in the first stages of the campaign. Having advanced almost to the Mediterranean sea, Tacfarinas had been forced back into the borderlands of the province, taking shelter in the desert not just after a major defeat, but because that was now the only place he could find safety. Even then, he was forced to move every time Rome discovered where he was. The Romans' adoption of irregular field tactics nullified the effectiveness of his own and he no longer had the edge in speed or flexibility. The situation looked bleak. Tacfarinas may have hoped to hold on until the end of the campaign season, in early autumn. In previous years the Romans had withdrawn from the field at that point, to winter in the heartlands of Africa Proconsularis, probably in the territory of the earliest province.[32] Tacfarinas had no reason to expect anything different at the end of summer AD 21, which would give him a few months of respite to recuperate and plan his strategy for the following year.

However, Blaesus had no intention of leaving the field for the winter. Over the last months of AD 21 and into 22 the garrisons stayed in position in the newly-established forts, deployed as though it was the beginning of the campaign season rather than the end. Men who were familiar with desert conditions, many no doubt recruited locally, were deployed in flying columns to continue harassing Tacfarinas even in the desert. Blaesus established a chain of forts in the manner the Romans would usually do in advance of a major campaign, which provided vital logistic support for the troops in the field. Tacfarinas was forced to encamp his own men in the desert, and whenever the Romans received intelligence of their whereabouts they would send in troops to harry them from the position. By specifically using soldiers either recruited from or familiar with desert areas, Blaesus undermined Tacfarinas' advantages with superior knowledge of the landscape, and the rebel leader was evidently unable to outpace his enemy at any point. For the first time since AD 17 the Romans indisputably had the upper hand in the conflict and it must have seemed just a matter of time before the war was ended.

A Premature Exit

Towards the later stage of the campaign, at some point in AD 22, Blaesus' men captured Tacfarinas' brother, a personal loss to add to the many men who had also been killed (or captured) from his army. However, Blaesus does not appear to have been as determined to force Tacfarinas into pitched battle as his predecessors had been. The decision makes sense in the context of his campaign, as gathering his two legions and associated auxiliaries together would have been a logistical nightmare and would have required the abandonment of the many military installations which had proved so effective in limiting Tacfarinas' movement and effectiveness. Perhaps he did not feel that a pitched battle was any longer necessary, given that Tacfarinas had sustained large manpower losses (including that of a close relative), which he would struggle to replenish given lower levels of support in the region, inspired in part by the Roman amnesty and in part by his own failures. Tacfarinas had been forced to withdraw into the desert without a battle needing to be fought, and it doubtless made little sense for Blaesus to force one now, when his strategy was already proving a success – and when abandoning it might undermine its effectiveness and allow Tacfarinas to return to the field. The Roman use of irregular warfare against their irregular enemy had proved effective where its conventional counterpart had not; to abandon the former for the latter at this stage was at best unnecessary and at worst dangerous.

Evidently at this point Blaesus believed Tacfarinas to be defeated. Despite Tacfarinas still being alive, which the Romans really should have learned by this stage was a problem, Blaesus withdrew his troops from the desert. Tacitus recognizes with hindsight that it was a mistake, observing that the action was taken prematurely and was not in the interests of the province, as those who were capable of restarting the war, including Tacfarinas himself, were left alive.

Tiberius does not appear to have disapproved of Blaesus' decision, however, agreeing that the war could be considered over. For the rest of AD 22 and until the end of Blaesus' proconsulship in 23, northwest Africa was evidently considered free of the threat Tacfarinas had posed. Blaesus was hailed as 'Imperator' by his men, a traditional spontaneous honour given by soldiers to their commander in recognition of their success in the field; multiple commanders could hold the honour at once. Tiberius then officially ratified the honour (the last time the title was ever given to someone who was not a member of the Imperial family).[33]

Blaesus was also awarded triumphal honours in Rome for his efforts in Africa, although Tacitus suggests that these were only given as a result of his relationship to Sejanus.[34] This is not entirely fair. It was true that Blaesus' campaign had not been pretty and may even have seemed 'un-Roman' at times, adopting many of the unorthodox tactics Tacfarinas had previously used against Rome. Nor had Blaesus won a major victory on the battlefield as both his predecessors had, however limited those victories had turned out to be in the long run. His army in northwest Africa had effectively become a guerrilla force, with the heavy-armed legionary infantry sidelined in favour of the light-armed *auxilia*. These changes, necessary as they were, may not have been popular in Rome. But his campaign had been effective, and it seemed – certainly at the time his honours were awarded – that they were sufficient to end the war. Whatever methods and strategies he had been forced to employ, they had been what was necessary for the situation. It would have been strange for him to be denied triumphal honours for ending the war when two of his predecessors had received them for mere interim victories. It was not a perfect victory, but it seemed enough.

Tacfarinas was now still alive and at liberty, but with his freedom to operate limited by the Roman garrisons established by Blaesus and the depletion of his army, he was in some ways a shadow of the threat he had posed before. Rome had good cause to hope that he had finally had enough of conflict with them and would take the opportunity of peace. However, they would soon discover that Tacfarinas was not done with Rome yet. Left alive in the desert, despite his diminished army and wealth, Tacfarinas still had the will and determination to challenge Rome in Africa – and in this final stage, his last throw of the dice, he would call for outright rebellion from everyone discontented with Roman rule.

Chapter 9

Publius Cornelius Dolabella and the End of the War (AD 23–24)

When Quintius Junius Blaesus returned to Rome in AD 23, it must have been with the satisfaction that he had finally managed to secure victory over Tacfarinas. This would mean he had put an end to the threat that had plagued Africa Proconsularis and beyond for years and had done it without fighting a single pitched battle. Tacfarinas had been left alive, but Rome obviously believed there was little prospect of him returning to operations once more, suggesting that the defeat inflicted on him had been fairly comprehensive. Even better, Blaesus had gained his success before Juba II of Mauretania died. The campaign appeared to have achieved everything that Rome could have hoped for and plans were made for a return to normality in Africa Proconsularis. The 9th Legion Hispana was to be relocated back out of the region, taking its auxiliary units with it, although it remained in place while the proconsulship was transferred from Blaesus to his successor, Publius Cornelius Dolabella. For probably the first time in Tiberius' reign Rome was not facing the prospect of Tacfarinas and his army raiding along the extreme southern borders of the Empire.

But in reality, the war was far from over. Tacfarinas was not permanently defeated and he had no intention of dropping his campaign against Rome. The final phase of the conflict would in many ways be its most dangerous, and was indisputably now a situation of regional rebellion. Peoples who had not supported Tacfarinas since the early part of the war in AD 17, such as the Mauri, rejoined him in AD 23/24, for what may have seemed like their last and best opportunity to win a measure of liberation from Roman rule. In this period Tacfarinas presented himself as a freedom fighter whose primary aim was to drive the Romans from Africa – the first time this was made explicit, although many of his men may have been fighting for this since they joined him. It turned out that Blaesus, like his predecessors, had left the war against Tacfarinas unfinished – and just like them, had claimed triumphal honours after doing so. As Tacitus dismissively noted, 'once they [the proconsuls] considered their exploits sufficient for a grant of triumphal decorations [they] usually left the enemy in peace; and already three laurelled statues adorned the capital, while Tacfarinas was still harrying Africa.'[1]

Future operations would now be taken over by Publius Cornelius Dolabella, who had perhaps not expected to have to face Tacfarinas. Fortunately for Rome, he would prove to be exactly the right man for the job, and by the summer of AD 24, the long and costly struggle would finally come to an end. The war against Tacfarinas under Dolabella is by far the best documented period of the conflict.

Publius Cornelius Dolabella

After Blaesus was recalled to Rome, probably in mid-to-late AD 23, he was replaced by Publius Cornelius Dolabella, another experienced provincial commander. Likely born in the last two decades of the first century BC, he was a member of the Roman aristocracy, the son of Publius Cornelius Dolabella[2] and his wife Quinctilia, a younger sister of the later infamous Publius Quinctilius Varus.[3] In his early life, being the nephew of Varus must have been a significant advantage, given his uncle's position of trust at the heart of the Imperial circle prior to AD 9.[4] Dolabella's career does not seem to have suffered in the aftermath of the Teutoburg disaster. He was appointed consul in AD 10, serving alongside Gaius Junius Silanus, who later became proconsul of Asia in AD 21 (and was accused of misconduct there on his return to Rome the following year). Silanus was replaced in office halfway through the year by Quintus Junius Blaesus, Dolabella's predecessor in Africa. Dolabella became consul of Dalmatia towards the end of Augustus' reign, and was still in position there when Tiberius took the throne. Probably through inertia on the part of the new emperor, Dolabella remained in Dalmatia for several years, as we see from an inscription from Zadar (Croatia) dating to AD 18/19 which names him as proconsul;[5] he probably remained there until AD 19/20.[6]

After his return to Rome, Dolabella attempted to ingratiate himself with the new Imperial regime, but misjudged his actions on two notable occasions. In AD 21, he attempted to persuade Tiberius to hold a personal triumph following a small rebellion in Gaul, suggesting that the emperor should travel from Campania to Rome and be received in the city with an ovation, a proposal which Tacitus thought 'carried sycophancy to the absurd point'.[7] Tiberius' response was blunt, turning down the suggestion on the basis that 'after subduing some of the fiercest of nations, and receiving or rejecting so many triumphs in his youth, he was not so bankrupt in fame as to court in his age a futile honour conferred for an excursion in the suburbs.' No doubt chastened, Dolabella made a further effort to gain Tiberius' favour the following year through his public response to the scandal relating to his co-consul Gaius Junius Silanus' governorship of Syria, the latter being accused of extortion and misconduct in office, and of treason and sacrilege after his return to Rome.[8] Dolabella spoke out publicly against Silanus, proposing that in the future no individual of 'scandalous life and bankrupt reputation' should be considered for governor of a province, to protect the populations of these areas – the judge of suitability, he argued, should be the emperor himself.[9] Again, Tiberius rejected Dolabella's suggestion, this time on the basis that the suitability of an individual to run a province could not be ascertained before they arrived there, and to do otherwise would be to punish people before they had committed a crime.

Despite these two incidents of unsuccessful sycophancy, either of which could easily have backfired on Dolabella to the detriment of his career, he was appointed by the Senate as proconsul of Africa in AD 23/24, replacing Blaesus. It is hard to judge whether Dolabella was chosen for his military abilities as the level of conflict he had faced in Dalmatia, or earlier in his career, is unclear. Tiberius evidently believed that the war with Tacfarinas was over so the appointment of a capable military commander as proconsul might not have been considered a priority; and even if the Senate disagreed it might not have seemed wise for them to distrust Blaesus' victory by appointing a predominantly military individual, and risk incurring the wrath of his nephew Sejanus. Dolabella was not a terrible candidate for the proconsulship, but it looks as if he was far less experienced in irregular warfare than his two predecessors in office. His selection adds to the impression that Rome was convinced the war against Tacfarinas was pretty much over.

Instability in Northwest Africa

So certain was Tiberius that Tacfarinas was defeated he allowed the 9th Legion Hispana to be transferred out of Africa in AD 23. This took place soon after Dolabella's appointment, although the decision to remove it had probably been made under Blaesus. Tacitus suggests it was an error of judgement on Tiberius' part and that he acted 'as though no enemies were left in Africa',[10] despite growing evidence to the contrary. According to Tacitus, Dolabella was not happy about the decision, but was more concerned about obeying the emperor's orders than worrying about the chance of renewed conflict, so he did not protest his loss of troops.

Rome's position in Africa was further complicated in AD 23 by the death of Juba II of Mauretania and the accession of his son, Ptolemy. Juba had been an ally of Rome for decades, and had acted as a stabilizing influence on the region, despite being unpopular with some elements of the population. He had maintained acceptable levels of border security until Tacfarinas came along. Although the Mauretanian army proved unable to secure the region against Tacfarinas (something that Rome could surely sympathise with by this point), Juba's troops had provided valuable extra support to the Romans as they campaigned against the rebels. Juba's involvement throughout the war with Tacfarinas is attested by the victory coins he issued from about AD 15 onwards.

Juba II's heir was his son Ptolemy. He had been ruling alongside his father since *c.*AD 11, and became formal regent in 17, around the same time that the war with Tacfarinas broke out.[11] He had probably joined the Roman command on campaign during the conflict, although the scale of his involvement is not clear. He seems to have been viewed as young and relatively ineffectual by Rome; Tacitus refers to him as a 'heedless youth'.[12] Ptolemy's perceived relationship with Rome made him unpopular among elements of the Mauretanian population, particularly the Mauri who lived in the western coastal region of the kingdom. However, he would need Roman support to take the throne after his father's death and must have been concerned that the kingdom would simply be annexed by them instead. This did not happen in AD 23, but eventually did in 40 on Ptolemy's own death.

Ptolemy was related to the Roman aristocracy through his mother Cleopatra Selene, who was the daughter of Mark Antony and Cleopatra VII. Through his grandfather he was part of the Julio-Claudian dynasty, a cousin of Germanicus and the future emperor Claudius. He was sent to Rome as a child and joined the household of his aunt, Antonia the Younger, also the niece of Augustus and sister-in-law of Tiberius. Ptolemy was raised at the heart of the Imperial family. He remained in Rome until he was about 21 years old, at which point he returned to Mauretania and began learning the art of kingship from his father. Ptolemy became sole ruler of Mauretania in AD 23 when Juba II died, probably after Dolabella had taken office. Unfortunately for Ptolemy, the transition of power was not as smooth as he and his father had wished, no doubt due to the unpopularity among the indigenous population of his and his father's regime, and their links to Rome. An uprising broke out among the Moors, who hoped to take advantage of the 'heedless youth' in his inexperience to win their freedom from the 'royal freedmen and servile despotism' of their Mauretanian (and Roman) rulers.[13] But rather than campaign alone, they chose to ally themselves with someone opposing the same enemies, someone with experience in fighting against Mauretania and Rome in the region – Tacfarinas.

The Renewal of Hostilities

It should not really have been a surprise to Rome when Tacfarinas returned once more and resumed hostilities against them. Previous experience should have demonstrated that anything short of his death was unlikely to prove conclusive. Blaesus had forced Tacfarinas onto the back foot and undoubtedly had come closest to ending the conflict for good, but despite his declarations of victory in AD 23, the war was not over. Tacfarinas' army was augmented by alliance with several other peoples of the region, some potentially for the first time since the early stages of the war. The Mauri of Mauretania took the opportunity of regime change in the kingdom to join with Tacfarinas, hoping to establish a permanent freedom from royal (and subsequently Roman) rule. Some of them may previously have been serving in the Mauretanian army, but saw their chance to defect.[14] They obviously judged joining forces with Tacfarinas to offer their best odds for success.

Tacfarinas also made a new agreement with the Garamantes. Their king (whose name is unknown) agreed to hold Tacfarinas' booty for him, ensuring that it would not this time become a logistic burden (the army being obliged to stay close to it) that allowed them to be forced into pitched battle, as had happened during the proconsulship of Lucius Apronius. The Garamantean king also provided military support to Tacfarinas; although he did not take to the field himself, he despatched a large number of light-armed infantry. These new alliances helped to revive Tacfarinas' operations in the region, and helped to nullify the territorial disadvantages he had been put to during Blaesus' proconsulship. In that stage of the war Tacfarinas had found his movements restricted in every direction except south, forcing him back towards the mountains and desert. But the main territories of both the Mauri and the Garamantes (who were based in the Fazzān area of modern Libya) lay outside this area of Roman operation, meaning that Tacfarinas could open up new fronts in the conflict.

Neither the Mauri nor the Garamantes appear to have been constant allies of Tacfarinas throughout the conflict, although no doubt people from both groups had beern with his campaign on an irregular basis. Why they rejoined him in the late stages of the war is unclear, especially given how close he had come to absolute defeat at the hands of Blaesus. Perhaps they recognized that Tacfarinas still offered their best chance of winning (a level of) regional independence from Rome, and were thus willing to support him in a final round of hostilities. The changes to the region that were being introduced by Rome prior to the outbreak of conflict – land surveys, taxation and so on – may have been renewed following Tacfarinas' defeat, reminding the population of why they had wanted to fight in the first place. Tacfarinas no doubt leaned into their political motivations, and this may be the point at which he became more a true rebel leader than he ever had been before. He called for everyone who 'preferred liberty to bondage' to join him in a combined onslaught on the Romans, their aim being to cut off the remaining garrison.[15] This 'call' may be a standardized literary device, differing little from the same term used in accounts of other provincial rebellions.[16] However, Tacitus' use of it here is interesting, as it implies a recognition that the conflict now had transformed into a rebellion, whatever it had been at the start. It is in this final stage that Tacitus describes Tacfarinas as other than a bandit and deserter for the first time, referring to him as *dux* (usually rendered as 'arch-rebel').[17] The change in the language used, and the documented reinvolvement of peoples like the Mauri and the Garamantes, suggest that this phase of the war was regarded as different in kind to what had come before.

From Tacfarinas' perspective, this was an excellent time to resume hostilities. The transfer of the 9th Legion Hispana out of Africa had diminished Rome's military power in the region; the auxiliary units that had been transferred in may have departed around the same time. Dolabella evidently did not agree with the removal of the legion but did not dare to protest it to the emperor. Tacitus may have used the premature withdrawal of the 9th Legion to make his veiled criticism of Tiberius, emphasized by the fact that Tacfarinas' cause began to revive soon after.[18] The Roman authorities – if not Dolabella himself – appear to have viewed northwest Africa as pacified and were acting accordingly. They did not expect to be attacked again by Tacfarinas: Mauretania was under the rule of a new king and dealing with its own domestic problems, and the new proconsul of Africa Proconsularis was relatively inexperienced in provincial warfare, certainly less than Blaesus had been. But from Tacfarinas' perspective Roman interests in Africa were weaker than they had been for years, possibly since the days of Marcus Furius Camillus – and he intended to take full advantage.

While Rome was more vulnerable, Tacfarinas was growing in both strength and confidence. News of his revival of fortunes spread quickly and even more recruits rallied to him, even from the Roman province itself, from which 'every man of broken fortunes or turbulent character' was drawn to the rebel force.[19] The reluctance to enlist with Tacfarinas which had developed under Blaesus, encouraged by the Roman's offer of amnesty to former rebels, appears to have dissipated by this point.

The transfer of the 9th Legion was a propaganda gift for Tacfarinas. He started a rumour that Rome was under attack from rebels on numerous frontiers, which would soon lead to the destruction of the Empire.[20] He claimed that

Rome was in the process of systematically abandoning northwestern Africa, with the transfer of the 9th merely the first step in the process. He proposed to his men, therefore, that they resume intensive hostilities against the Roman forces left in the region, namely the 3rd legion Augusta, and assured them that the combined onslaught of all those who wanted to free themselves from Roman (and Mauretanian) rule would be enough to overwhelm the garrison. Rather than sit and wait for freedom to come to them, as theoretically it should if Rome was indeed abandoning Africa (although this was not the case), Tacfarinas' men gained a renewed enthusiasm for attacking Rome and even more rebels were drawn to his cause. Arguably for the first time, Tacfarinas' campaign had become a war of liberation, with political aims rather than just the acquisition of booty through raiding. It was only a few years since Tacfarinas had incurred Tiberius' wrath by proposing he be given amnesty and a land settlement to rule, from which it seems he was hoping to gain something permanent from the war (and a peace) with Rome. Even if Rome still saw Tacfarinas and his men as common bandits, others in northwestern Africa now saw his campaign as a chance to free themselves from the Roman yoke, and joined him with that aim.

The Siege of Thubuscum

Tacfarinas entered the first stages of conflict with Dolabella by making a bold move: he laid siege to the Roman town of Thubuscum, whose exact location today is unknown. It has variously been identified as Thubursicum Numidarum (Khemissa, Algeria), Tubusuctu (Tiklat, Algeria), and Thubursicum Bure (modern day Teboursouk, Tunisia), but none of these proposals has a greater claim than the others.[21] Thubursicum Bure is the furthest east, and lies within the territory of Africa Proconsularis. Thubursicum Numidarum lies *c.*160km (99 miles) to its west, in the area that was formerly part of Numidia, probably within the territory of the Musulamii. Tubusuctu was the furthest west, *c.*300km (186 miles) from Thubursicum Numidarum, and was located within the kingdom of Mauretania. It was the site of a Roman colony established under Augustus to settle retired veterans from the 7th Legion Claudia. Modern consensus tends to favour Thubursicu Numidarum, which lay in the territory of the Musulamii, on the basis that Tacfarinas would not have had the inclination or manpower resources to make such a move further away. However, more recently Tubusuctu in Mauretania has been put forward as a more likely candidate.[22] Tacfarinas' army in AD 23/24 was larger than it had been at any point since AD 17, making it more than possible for him to undertake operations outside the territory of the Musulamii; it was also augmented by Mauri soldiers who had a particular interest in directing the conflict towards Mauretania. And Tubusuctu is significantly closer to the probable site of the final battle than Thubursicu Numidarum, so it makes more sense in the hurried narrative of the last stage of the war. If the siege did take place at Tubusuctu, it would mean that Tacfarinas' final actions were largely confined to Mauretania rather than within or near Africa Proconsularis.

Tacfarinas had tried a similar strategy at an earlier stage in the conflict, during the tenure of Lucius Apronius, laying siege to several Roman installations and towns. Back then, aside from the one victory at the fort near the Pagyda (where a Roman cohort fled, and was later decimated as punishment), it had brought him little success and was soon abandoned. Now he tried again, clearly expecting better results the second time around. No details are provided by Tacitus, but being under siege must have been a terrifying experience for the residents of Thubuscum, who had probably anyway been less inclined than the authorities in Rome to believe that Tacfarinas had been defeated once and for all. Dolabella's response was swift. Although he could no longer deploy the 9th Legion Hispana, the 3rd Legion Augusta were still present and ready for action, with their associated auxiliary units, a force of probably at least 10,000 soldiers. He mustered every available man and marched on Thubuscum, where he succeeded in raising the siege at the first attempt. While giving no description of the fighting, Tacitus suggests that Tacfarinas' men were afraid of the Romans by this point and unwilling to confront their infantry in pitched battle. They fled the scene, probably heading southwest into the pre-desert region of Mauretania.

Dolabella's Preparations for War

Dolabella understood very well that this single victory over Tacfarinas meant little. He may have driven his enemy away, but would have known how many times this had happened before during the war and that 'several expeditions against Tacfarinas had shown that a nomadic enemy was not to be brought to bay by a single incursion carried out by heavy-armed troops.'[23] He took steps accordingly and (re)fortified key strategic points, presumably including those which had been previously set up or garrisoned under Blaesus, attempting to re-establish Roman control of the conflict landscape. Concerns over the loyalty of the Musulamii also led to Dolabella ordering the execution of several of their chieftains who had been on the verge of joining Tacfarinas. The Mauri and Garamantes had already gone over to Tacfarinas, so Dolabella must have harboured serious concerns about the conflict escalating to an unmanageable level. Unlike Blaesus, however, he did not try to induce anyone to abandon the rebels with offers of amnesty, but rather sought to prevent others from joining them by threats and instilling fear. The entire region may have seemed poised on the edge of rebellion and Dolabella's actions could easily have backfired on him if the executions had been taken badly by the Musulamii – after all, they had not actually done anything and had only been thinking about joining Tacfarinas. Dolabella's pre-emptive punitive action to stop them entering the war against Rome could easily have brought about the very thing it was trying to prevent.

Recognizing that he needed more manpower, and that his priority was lightly-armed troops rather than heavy-armed infantry, Dolabella summoned Ptolemy of Mauretania to join him in the field with as many men as he could muster. Some have suggested that Ptolemy took primary command from this point onwards, with Dolabella relegated to the position of *consultor*.[24] Tacitus does use that term to describe Dolabella's command at this stage. When the army was deployed against Tacfarinas, Dolabella did not take command of a particular division, as Blaesus had, but made himself available as advisor to everyone as needed.[25] This might suggest that he was indeed operationally subordinate to Ptolemy and in some ways this would make sense, since at that time the war seems to have been mostly, or even entirely, fought in Mauretania rather than Africa Proconsularis. Also, Ptolemy almost certainly did have military experience from fighting in the earlier stages of the war, probably more than Dolabella, which may have put him in a better position to command the army in the field. Nevertheless, there is no indication in Tacitus beyond the use of the word *consultor* that Dolabella played a subordinate role to Ptolemy in any way, and it would be most unusual for a client king to be elevated above a proconsul.[26] Ptolemy no doubt commanded the Mauretanian troops, but almost certainly under the overall authority of Dolabella.

In the previous phase of the war, subdividing the Roman army had proved very effective against Tacfarinas, and Dolabella followed the same method. He split his available troops into four forces, putting each under the command of an experienced legionary legate or tribune. He also designated some units specifically for raiding, which he put under the command of hand-picked loyal Maurian auxiliaries, who knew the terrain and were veterans of irregular and desert warfare. As mentioned, Dolabella himself did not take command of a specific division of the army as Blaesus had, but acted as an advisor available to all as required. Dolabella strategized for his war with Tacfarinas in a way that closely resembled the approach taken earlier by Blaesus, who had been first to adapt conventional Roman field techniques to better suit the conflict. Dolabella had to work with half the troops that Blaesus had and did not benefit from a significant reduction in the enemy's manpower as the result of an amnesty – while if anything, Tacfarinas had more men than he had had before. But it is clear that Dolabella intended to continue with many of the tactics successfully used by Blaesus with one key difference: his campaign would not stop until Tacfarinas was dead. Dolabella knew that 'there would be no rest from war till the arch-rebel was slain',[27] and intended to achieve this by any means necessary.

A Retreat to Auzea

A short time after the confrontation at Thubuscum, word reached Dolabella that Tacfarinas had made camp at a half-ruined fort (almost certainly Roman or Mauretanian) in a place named Auzea (probably modern Sour El Ghozlane, Algeria).[28] The fort lay in a remote pre-desert area of Mauretania.[29] Tacfarinas had previously operated in the region and he knew about the fort because his army had attacked and set fire to it at an earlier stage in the war. The fort was in a strategically sound location, which is presumably why either Rome or Mauretania had fortified it in the first place. It was encircled by a large wood, which Tacfarinas believed would offer protection against a surprise attack, as the heavily armed Roman legions that fought against him at Thubuscum would have struggled in such terrain. Auzea was clearly a location he was familiar with and somewhere he believed he and his men could stay safely for a time without the Romans stumbling over them.

How Dolabella came to know that Tacfarinas and his army were holed up at Auzea is not mentioned by Tacitus. A scouting patrol may have happened across local gossip, or an informant keen for reward or Roman favour may have passed on the information. Once he had the information Dolabella determined to act quickly, to end the war for good by taking Tacfarinas unawares, perhaps for the first time in the entire conflict. He decided to despatch troops to Auzea in hopes they would arrive while Tacfarinas still occupied the position and could launch a surprise attack on the rebels. For the plan to work, speed was of the essence. So rather than marching his entire army to the fort, Dolabella sent only his light-armed infantry and cavalry to Auzea. These troops stood the best chance of covering the distance to the fort before Tacfarinas could move on and ruin Dolabella's plans. They also had to outpace any enemy intelligence that might warn the rebels that a Roman force was approaching – Dolabella was so concerned about his plan reaching Tacfarinas' ears that the soldiers were dispatched with only the commanders knowing their final destination. Dolabella may have suspected that there were spies in his camp,[30] or it may have been a precaution in case any soldiers were captured during the advance and interrogated.

Although the Roman troops were moving as quickly and lightly as possible, it would still have taken them several days to reach Auzea. The exact length of time partly depends on which site can be identified as Thubuscum, where it seems the Romans set off from after receiving the intelligence (although it is possible they had moved on in the interim). Thubursicu Numidarum is some 400km (248 miles) from Sour El Ghozlane, necessitating a much longer march than would be required from Tupusuctu, which was only around 100km (62 miles) away. The rapidity with which the Romans were able to reach Auzea provides further support for the previous siege having been located at Tupusuctu. The troops managed to arrive at Auzea before Tacfarinas had left his camp, which seems inconsistent with them taking a week or more to arrive. They approached the fort through the woods without raising any alarms, advancing by night to take up positions around the camp. That their presence was not detected suggests that Tacfarinas either did not set a watch, confident his position remained a secret, or that his sentries had been out in the woods and were neutralized before they could cry out.

The Final Battle

Dawn was just breaking when the Roman troops made their assault on Tacfarinas' camp. The attack had not been anticipated and many of his men were not even awake yet, let alone ready for battle. The Romans came into the attack shouting and accompanied by blaring trumpets, which must have been a sensory shock for Tacfarinas' men as they were rapidly woken from their sleep or their early morning routine. Tacitus' description of the battle gives some insight into the chaotic circumstances as the fighting began:

> Day was just breaking when with a fierce yell and a blast of trumpets they came on the half-awakened barbarians, while the Numidian horses were still shackled or straying through distant pasture-grounds. On the Roman side, the infantry were in massed formation, the cavalry disposed in troops, every provision made for battle: the enemy, in contrast, were aware of nothing, without weapons, without order, without a plan, dragged to slaughter or to captivity like cattle. The soldiers, embittered by the memory of hardships undergone and of battle so often hoped for against this elusive foe, took every man his fill of revenge and blood.[31]

The Romans approached in battle formation, both the infantry and cavalry, fully equipped and prepared for the fight despite their hurried march to Auzea. By contrast, Tacfarinas' men were literally caught napping. They could make no use of their cavalry, as the horses were still either tied up for the night or in pastures too far from the fort to retrieve once the battle had started. In the early stages they likely had little idea what was even happening; Tacitus says that they were 'aware of nothing, without weapons, without order, without a plan'.[32] They doubtless tried to put up some resistance once they realized they were under attack, but by then it was too late. Coming to the fight so unprepared, they were able to do little in their defence. Some were taken captive to be sold into slavery, many were killed, as the Roman soldiers took vengeance for seven long years of fighting and hardship, fear and humiliation. They had long waited for an opportunity to meet Tacfarinas' army in the sort of battle they were trained to fight, and now that they had it they would show no mercy.

While some of the rebels were taken captive, according to Tacitus, the emphasis in his brief account of the battle reflects on the amount of bloodshed, which he felt was justified based on the experiences the Roman soldiers had gone through at the hands of Tacfarinas up to this point. It is impossible to judge the scale of casualties in the encounter as it is not known how large Tacfarinas' army was at this stage, nor what proportion of his men were killed, but the death count must have been substantial, numbering in the high hundreds or even perhaps thousands of men. Dolabella was evidently eligible for triumphal honours after the war (despite not actually being awarded them), suggesting that at least 5,000 of Tacfarinas' men were killed in the campaign overall, and many of those deaths would have taken place in this battle. There were no doubt some Roman casualties, but they would have been minimal compared to those of the rebel army.

To be confident that this battle ended the war, the Romans had to ensure one thing: the capture or death of Tacfarinas. Dolabella may not have been present at the final battle, but he must have given orders that the rebel leader must not be allowed to escape. Word was passed around the Romans to head for Tacfarinas; after so many encounters with him over the years, enough of the soldiers knew what he looked like and were able to pick him out of the crowd. They captured his son as they advanced, taking him captive rather than killing him. In fact Tacfarinas' son appears to have been one of several notable captives, as Tacitus notes that the status of some of the prisoners taken in the battle was a credit to Dolabella in the aftermath of the war.[33] Finally they drew near to Tacfarinas, still on the field and surrounded by his personal guard, likely drawn from the most capable soldiers he had hand-picked and trained in the Roman manner. It was at this point of the battle that the Romans undoubtedly encountered the stiffest resistance, up against the best warriors Tacfarinas' army had to offer, all willing to die to protect their leader. They were cut down around him, defending him to the last, by an ever-increasing surge of Roman troops. Rather than risk being captured alive, only to be exposed to the humiliation and pain that would doubtless follow, Tacfarinas now threw himself on to the spears of the Roman soldiers and died on the battlefield, in what was suicide in all but name. There appears to have been no chance of his surrendering, as there was no chance that he would be offered mercy.

The Romans may have regretted that they were unable to capture Tacfarinas and take him back to Rome for appropriate punishment – probably a period of incarceration in the infamous Tullianum, followed by public display in a triumphal procession and finally execution. This had been the fate of the Gallic rebel leader Vercingetorix, after he surrendered at Alésia in 52 BC, hoping that Caesar would show mercy to him. He was instead imprisoned for almost six years, until Caesar's first Gallic triumph in 46 BC, and then ceremonially strangled at the temple of Jupiter Optimus Maximus in Rome.[34] Later rebels, such as Simon bar Giora, met a similar fate, demonstrating that this practice remained active into the later first century AD.[35] Boudica killed herself rather than fall into Roman captivity.[36] One British resistance leader, Caratacus, after being captured and taken to Rome presumably for execution, was actually pardoned by the emperor Claudius, saving himself by an appeal to Roman mercy,[37] but such an outcome was rare. In Caratacus' case, the fact that he was resisting conquest rather than rebelling against an existing occupation may have been in his favour.

Frustrating as it was to have Tacfarinas slip through their fingers, death on the battlefield, even by suicide, was not only accepted by Roman society but in many cases judged to be the most admirable option (although it is difficult to imagine Tacfarinas being admired by Rome for anything he did). Many Roman commanders had made the same choice when faced with captivity by the enemy, whether on the battlefield or after a defeat – particularly when their enemy was other Romans in a civil war. In living memory, Mark Antony and Cleopatra had done so after their defeat by Octavian, as had many of the defeated commanders during Caesar's civil war with Pompey, and the Liberators' War, between Mark Antony and Octavian on one side and the assassins of Caesar on the other. Generally, battlefield suicide to avoid capture did not bring any censure in Rome and when it did there were usually other issues at play; for example, when Velleius Paterculus condemned Publius Quinctilius Varus' suicide in the Teutoburg in AD 9 as a cowardly act, it was more likely due to his personal opinion of Varus than any moral judgement.[38] Roman battlefield suicides are not believed to have been done out of a desire to avoid shame and societal disgrace, but to avoid the pain and suffering which would result from captivity.[39] Tacfarinas' death robbed the Romans of an opportunity to avenge themselves on him more publicly, but it was not particularly surprising in context.

The battle at Auzea was more or less the last – as Rome had predicted, Tacfarinas' death largely ended hostilities, though some minor operations may have been required to finish off any outlying rebel activity. Ending the war had not required a large set-piece battle to bring him down, nor had the legionary troops of the province played any decisive role in the victory. Rome's success had instead come from adapting their strategy over several years to more closely resemble that of Tacfarinas, eminently more suited to both the terrain and the nature of irregular warfare. The rebels had drawn strength from being able to launch surprise attacks on the Roman army and disappear into the landscape afterwards; their defeat came when the Romans turned this strategy against them. Controlling the landscape had been key to Roman success, an approach initiated by Blaesus and continued by Dolabella. While Tacfarinas had the freedom to roam northwestern Africa unchecked his campaign had prospered; with the closing of his avenues of movement, one of his greatest strengths had been taken away. It is somehow fitting for such an irregular war that the end should come at an obscure half-ruined fort in the Mauretanian desert, with light-armed Roman soldiers and cavalry emerging through the dawn to bring devastation on a sleeping rebel camp – an unexpected event to end a very unusual conflict.

Victory Honours – for Some

If Dolabella had hoped that his success in Africa – the leader who had brought the war to a permanent end – would be recognized with honours similar to those of his predecessors, he was to be disappointed. He applied to Tiberius for triumphal honours like those awarded to his predecessors, but the request was turned down.[40] Tacitus suggests that the emperor's rejection was a concession to Sejanus, who did not want the honours awarded to his uncle Blaesus to be in any way diminished by being given to another so soon – especially someone who had completed the job that Blaesus had failed to do. But denying honours to Dolabella did little to preserve Blaesus' reputation. It was widely recognized in Rome that not only had Dolabella ended the war, unlike Blaesus, but had done so with half the troops, while also taking significant prisoners and, most importantly, ensuring the death of Tacfarinas – who once again is referred to as *dux*, rather than as a bandit. Tacitus does not dwell on the fact that Dolabella did not play an active role in the battle at Auzea – it was enough that his strategy and orders had led to the positive outcome, despite his not being personally present. Dolabella did enjoy some benefits of victory in Rome, albeit a few unusual ones. Most notable was the fact that the Garamantes sent a number of their tribesmen in tribute to Rome, hoping this would mitigate any Roman displeasure at their actions during the conflict, having seen what had ultimately happened to Tacfarinas.[41] Their appearance evidently caused quite a stir and they ended up serving as Dolabella's attendants.

While Dolabella may have been denied honours in Rome, there was at least one physical commemoration of his victory – not in Italy, but in Africa. An inscription on a statue base found in Leptis Magna (and since lost) openly commemorated Dolabella's victory over Tacfarinas, in a dedication made to Victoria Augusta:[42]

UICTORIAE
[.]U[..]..AE
P • CORNELIUS
DOLABELLA • COS •
5VIIUIREP[..] • SO
DA[..]S[..].[.....] • PRO
COS • ..CISOT[....-]
R...TEP.[....]

'For Victoria Augusta: Publius Cornelius Dolabella, consul, member of the committee of seven for sacred feasts, companion of the Titienses, proconsul, when Tacfarinas had been killed, placed [this monument]'

The inscription stone had been reused since antiquity in the fortification of the city's lighthouse and so it is impossible to suggest where the statue once stood. As it has subsequently been lost, further study on it has not been carried out. But it attests to the fact that Dolabella's victory was once publicly commemorated, in Africa if not in Rome, and perhaps more widely than the surviving archaeological record has yet revealed.

Ptolemy of Mauretania was also rewarded for his loyalty to Rome during the last part of the campaign. An old-fashioned honour given to client rulers was revived, in which a member of the Senate visited him and presented him with traditional victory gifts of an embroidered triumphal robe and an ivory sceptre, with the greeting 'king, ally, friend.'[43] Although Tacitus does not mention it, he was probably also given a curule chair, often part of the gift offering. These items closely resembled those worn or used by a Roman commander during a triumph, and were a way of signalling the important military contribution made by a foreign ally to a campaign, something which had become increasingly rare with the dawn of the Imperial period. Ptolemy was evidently proud of his honours, or perhaps just aware of their propaganda value as an ally of Rome hoping to keep his kingdom from annexation. He ordered statues in Mauretania to be updated to reflect the awards; the remains of one example from Sala (Morocco) bears Ptolemy in the traditional sculptural stance of a spear-carrier, but instead bearing a 30cm-long ivory sceptre.[44] From AD 25, images of the honours were also included on coin issues, showing the ivory sceptre propped against a curule chair, often alongside a victory wreath. He repeated these issues regularly, including on gold coins – a controversial decision, as gold coinage was only supposed to be issued either by the emperor or with his specific permission.[45] Finally, in AD 40 Ptolemy was invited to Rome by the emperor Caligula, where he was soon murdered, apparently by Imperial command. Ptolemy's pride in both his role in the war against Tacfarinas and the honours given to him afterwards, and the envy this evoked in Caligula (who had no actual military achievements of his own), have been suggested as reasons for his assassination.[46]

With the war against Tacfarinas over, Rome could continue to develop its administration in the region. The conflict had temporarily disrupted some of their planned actions, but had failed to drive Rome out of the region for good. The defeat at Auzea ended any hopes of permanently freeing northwest Africa from Roman rule and no one stepped into Tacfarinas' place to try to resume hostilities. The defeated rebels would have to go back to their communities and do the best they could to live under the Roman regime. Tacfarinas' war had created a tumultuous situation in Tiberius' early reign and had presented a significant military challenge to Rome. The conflict would not be well-commemorated by Roman historians, but even Tacitus' scant narrative gives an insight into a war that was likely much more damaging than it seems from the perspective of millennia. If nothing else, Tacfarinas should be better remembered today as a warleader who successfully took on the might of Rome for nearly eight years – whatever his reasons for doing so.

Chapter 10

Tacfarinas in Later History

In northwest Africa, the end of the conflict with Tacfarinas and all its associated disruption was no doubt welcomed by the Romans and other elements of the coast-based population. Previous victories, such as the Gaetulian War, had been publicly celebrated, and although there is more limited archaeological evidence in the case of Tacfarinas' war, it is difficult to imagine that those affected were apathetic about it.[1] How the wider African population felt, particularly the ones who were allied to Tacfarinas, is not addressed by the sources, but it is difficult to imagine that they were all pleased by the defeat. Although some of Tacfarinas' men were no doubt there for material rewards, others were rebels, fighting to try to improve their lives under Imperial rule or even to free themselves from it entirely. They had tried and failed and were evidently too disheartened to try to renew hostilities under another leader. But the aftermath may have been less harsh than they feared. Tacitus does not mention any reprisals against the communities that had provided soldiers for Tacfarinas' army. This may simply be an omission on his part, but may suggest Rome did not want to risk giving the population a genuine grievance that might spark off hostilities once more. Territory was probably not confiscated from them wholesale and, while measures like taxation were eventually introduced, the process appears to have moved much more slowly than it might have done if the war had never been fought.

Roman historians were not sympathetic to Tacfarinas. Subsequent history has been little better. During the French conquest and occupation of Algeria in the nineteenth and twentieth centuries, Tacfarinas represented a historical example of the danger posed by the regional population, used to justify a brutal campaign against them. There has been some reclamation of him as a national figure within modern northwest Africa, particularly in Algeria, but it has not been widespread. Although historical perspectives have become more nuanced in recent decades, Tacfarinas is still not a widely known individual – an obscurity which seems undeserved.

Northwestern Africa after Tacfarinas

There is no record of any major hostilities in the region relating to Tacfarinas after his death. Those who had joined him for banditry no doubt went back to their tribes or to the low-level activities they had been involved in before. Others who had rallied to his cause in the hope of securing greater freedom from Rome or Mauretania, particularly the Moors, seem to have been discouraged from further action by Tacfarinas' defeat. There probably were some lingering after-effects for Dolabella's successor(s) to deal with, judging by an inscription dedicated in Leptis Magna to Gaius Gavius Macer, legate of the 3rd Legion Augusta, who was probably in charge of overseeing the final pacification of the region. The inscription was on part of an impressive equestrian statue, the scale of which suggests that Macer's action had been of some substance, so events after the death of Tacfarinas may not have been as straightforward as the absence of comment in Tacitus' narrative might suggest.

For anyone fighting in Tacfarinas' army with the aim of forcing the Romans out of northwest Africa, the war was a failure. Rome did not give up any territorial claims in the aftermath of the conflict. Land surveys continued and taxation was introduced to the region, leading to a gradual shift from common pasture grounds to private property ownership among individuals in settlements located in more marginal areas of the province.[2] Some of the land in sparsely settled areas, particularly the pre-desert areas south of Cirta, may have ended up as Imperial estates that could later be given as land grants to veterans or others.

However, the expansion of Roman administration was gradual and Tacfarinas' war had potentially won a temporary reprieve in some areas from certain policies being introduced. Although there was another land survey during the reign of Tiberius, there was then not another until the time of Trajan, almost a century later.[3] The lands of the Musulamii, probably at the heart of Tacfarinas' campaign, were not fully surveyed until this later period and at the end of the process the people did not find themselves reallocated poor land in exchange for their productive territories.[4] Rather, large boundary stones demarcated a large area reserved for the Musulamii around Theveste, almost like a tribal reservation today, which would remain theirs in perpetuity.[5]

There were doubtless episodic outbreaks of violence both within the province and from outside, and the threat posed by raiding and banditry would have continued in the region throughout the Roman period.[6] The Roman troops based there may have been expected to protect the border communities from such threats; the Garamantes, in particular, appear to have remained fairly active in raiding.[7] In the reign of Caligula, command of the legionary garrison of Africa Proconsularis was transferred from the proconsul to a specially appointed *legatus augusti pro praetore*, so that an official ostensibly chosen by the Senate would not have a military command. Much of the resistance in the region that came after Tacfarinas was focused on Mauretania, particularly in modern northwestern Algeria and especially the Kabylie.[8] A number of forts have been found in this area, several of which appear to have been constructed as a response to ongoing unrest among the indigenous population – it was not somewhere that Rome could take its eye off, despite the difficulties of gathering intelligence in this type of terrain.

The last major revolt in northwest Africa came in AD 85 when the Nasamones, who lived in southern Libya near the Garamantes, rebelled against taxation being forced on them.[9] They killed all the tax collectors and defeated the Roman troops sent to quell the rebellion, even managing to capture and loot their camp. However, they then apparently overindulged massively on the wine and food that they found there and fell asleep, allowing the Romans to launch a counter attack on them, killing everyone indiscriminately. The emperor Domitian was said to have been thrilled by this outcome, noting to the Senate that he had 'forbidden the Nasamones to exist'. It was probably outrage at exactly this type of brutal treatment which had compelled many northwest Africans to rebel with Tacfarinas decades earlier.

By the AD 40s Roman territorial control had been established over the entire north African coastal region. Mauretania had been annexed in AD 40, after the assassination of King Ptolemy in Rome at the command of the emperor Caligula.[10] This was evidently not welcomed by the population, many of whom had rebelled both at the start of Ptolemy's reign and during that of his father Juba II, because they did not want to live under Roman rule – some, including the Mauri, had allied with Tacfarinas for this exact reason. During the reign of Claudius one of Ptolemy's loyal freedmen, a man named Aedemon, led a revolt in the hope of avenging his murdered master.[11] Some of the chieftains in the region joined the rebels, who evidently intended to try to stop Rome from taking direct control of Mauretania in the aftermath of Ptolemy's death.

In the early years of Claudius' reign the Roman army was sent in to quell the problems in Mauretania, under the command of Gaius Suetonius Paulinus (who would later suppress the Boudican revolt in Britain) and Gnaeus Hosidius Geta. The Romans struggled with the nature of desert warfare and could never provide themselves with as much water as they needed, as opposed to the enemy whose familiarity with local conditions meant they were always able to find supplies. The Romans were forced to pursue the rebels as far south as the

Atlas Mountains, the first time they had ever campaigned in that region, and eventually managed to inflict a severe defeat on them in AD 44. Just before the battle Geta had followed local incantations to bring on a rainstorm, which had immediately taken place, giving the rebels the feeling that the gods were not on their side. They voluntarily surrendered and Mauretania was divided into two Roman provinces, Mauretania Tingitana and Mauretania Caesariensis, evidently (at least in part) to split the Mauri population in two.

There was now nowhere in Africa north of the Sahara that was not part of a Roman province. However, Rome appears to have had to maintain a power balance with the peoples of these regions, who continued to hold some territories in their own right. A number of inscriptions found in Mauretania Tingitana record negotiations and agreements between Roman governors and some of the mountain tribes about land – the only example of this kind of agreement we have found carved in stone.[12] Dating from the AD 170s to 280, they evidence careful negotiations between Rome and the mountain peoples of northwestern Africa in this period – not peace talks after a war, but discussions attempting to prevent future conflict. The wider military archaeological record also suggests that these tribes did not serve in the Roman *auxilia*, as there are no units with any ethnic names linked to this area or any diplomas associated with people from it.[13] The potential threat from the indigenous population was evidently never quite forgotten.

During the rest of the first century AD, multiple expeditions were made to explore the regions lying to the south of Roman territory in northwest Africa, mainly through the Western Sahara and Central Sahara areas. During the reign of Claudius, a Roman army under the command of Gaius Suetonius Paulinus crossed the Atlas mountains and explored the territory beyond the range for 'many miles' beyond, possibly as far south as the borders of modern Senegal.[14] In AD 70, the *legatus* of the 3rd Legion Augusta, a man named Valerius Festus, led a campaign against the Garamantes after they had conducted a significant series of raids in the territory of Tripolitania (Libya), aiming to recover all the booty that had been taken.[15] Although the territory of the Garamantes was his main area of operation, it is possible that some of his men reached the river Niger and may have ventured as far south as Nigeria.[16] A few years later (*c.*AD 78–81), Septimius Flaccus led an expedition south beyond the territory of the Garamantes, potentially reaching as far south as Lake Chad.[17] Then again in *c.*AD 82–85, there was an expedition to the same area under the command of Julius Maternus, although this was probably an attempt to gather slaves rather than a military campaign.[18] Once the Romans had explored these regions, they seem to have lost interest in adding them to the territory of the Empire, perhaps recognizing that this would come at a significant cost.

The Severity of the Tacfarinas War

One of the lingering questions about the war between Rome and Tacfarinas is how significant a conflict it actually was. Some regard it as a minor banditry dispute on the far-flung borders of the Empire, a non-event elevated to something more significant by Tacitus for literary effect. For others, it was a significant regional rebellion, its severity underplayed by the wider Roman historical record. One of the issues is that Tacitus' narrative is the only surviving account of the conflict, lending credence to the idea that he over-egged the extent of the conflict to suit his own literary aims. There is some archaeological evidence however, almost exclusively in the form of inscriptions, that provide supporting evidence, mainly relating to the presence of particular military units in the region, or honours given to various individuals during the war. As yet, no battle sites associated with the war have been excavated and modern-day political events in the region have meant that less archaeological work has been conducted than one would wish.

Although many Roman military installations have been identified remotely in the area where Tacfarinas operated, most do not have any secure dating evidence, making it impossible to draw links between their establishment and the war. The lack of archaeology related to the conflict is increasingly problematic, as research in other provinces is illustrating how little military action ever made it into the historical record. Battlefield archaeology is identifying more and more sites of battles and sieges which were clearly part of a significant conflict but which has completely failed to be documented, particularly in the case of irregular campaigns on the margins of empire.[19] In the reign of Augustus, the Cantabrian Wars (29–19 BC) and Alpine Wars (15 BC) have little surviving historical documentation, though the archaeological record shows them to have been serious and of a significant scale, involving multiple battles, sieges, and ambushes that all went unremarked by Roman historians. Even major battles such as the AD 9 Battle in the Teutoburg (also known as the Varus Disaster) appear to have made relatively little documentary impact at the time, the only surviving extended narrative of it coming in Cassius Dio's account almost two centuries later (although a detailed account was probably contained in Pliny the Elder's lost history of the German Wars). Archaeological excavations on the Teutoburg battlefield and its surrounding area have been substantial, and have revolutionized the study of that battle.[20] It was likely not the scale or even intensity of a conflict that determined whether it would be historically documented or not, but rather what information was available to any individual historian, how interested he might have been and whether he thought his readers would find it enlightening. The severity of Tacfarinas' conflict can unfortunately only really be judged from a limited range of evidence, with Tacitus' account foremost among the available data – and he is not a writer whose words can always be taken at face value.

The possibility that Tacitus exaggerated the significance of the Tacfarinas conflict for his own literary intentions[21] is certainly not without precedent in ancient historical writing, with the importance of certain events often exaggerated because it suited wider purposes at the time. A perfect example of this is the Catiline Conspiracy of 63 BC, which Cicero seems to have deliberately elevated from a minor political discontent in Rome into a plot which threatened the very foundations of the Republic.[22]

Tacitus had a complex relationship with Tiberius, and the fact that the war took place during his reign may have resulted in it almost automatically receiving more attention than it would otherwise have been given.[23] There were a number of narrative points that he wanted to make about the early years of Tiberius' reign, some of which needed to be considered in the context of a foreign war, and Tacfarinas' conflict was the only one being fought at this time. The need for it to be seen as an important one is perhaps why Tacitus refers to it as a 'war' (*bellum*) rather than an 'uprising' (*tumultuatum*) or anti-bandit activity (*latrocinium*) – in contradiction of his dubbing Tacfarinas himself a bandit (*latro*), at least until the late stages of the war. The narrative allowed for a demonstration of Tiberius' errors of judgement, illustrated by his continual granting of triumphal honours to proconsuls who had not ended the war and his decision to prematurely withdraw the 9th Legion Hispana. The war thus became a narrative tool to make his readers draw particular conclusions about Tiberius, with certain elements exaggerated or underplayed as needed. The Tacfarinas war also made an excellent narrative contrast to the second-century BC Jugurthine War, allowing Tacitus to invite his readers to reflect on the difference between the glories of the Republic and the decadence of the Imperial period. The fact that the war dragged on for almost eight years demonstrated the incompetence of the Senate under the emperors,[24] as did the fact that they needed Tiberius to take over the proconsular selection in AD 21.

But really, the only way to judge the severity of the conflict is by measuring Rome's response to it and that does suggest it was something more than a mere case of banditry – or at least, that it became so over time.[25] Some even think that Tacitus actually underplayed the severity of the conflict, so not to undermine his underlying message that the Republican period was superior to the Imperial.[26] A large-scale rebellion or war which threatened Rome but was ultimately competently managed might not have suited his literary aims in attempting to show that Tiberius was an ineffective and poor emperor. Tacfarinas may have been defined as a bandit, not as a judgement on the severity or nature of his actions, but because rather than responding to a genuine grievance on the part of the provincial population he was acting under his own authority for what was at least partly personal gain. For the Romans, his identification as bandit would have carried enough negative associations to mean he would not find any sympathy for his actions.

However, this would not necessarily have been the case among the peoples of northwest Africa, who may have seen him more as a 'social bandit' – a figure considered by the state and elite to be a criminal, but with some support among his own people or class.[27] The concept of the outlaw who stands with a few men against the might of the king or state, on behalf of the powerless general population, is a seductive one. Figures such as Robin Hood and his mission to 'rob from the rich to give to the poor', fit into this model – a very sympathetic one in the modern day. At that time, it may have been no less appealing – even if Tacfarinas and his men were not really behaving like social bandits, if the general perception of them among the people was that they were, it would suggest he had fairly widespread support. For Tacitus to focus on this aspect of the conflict might have given the impression to Roman readers that Tacfarinas' cause was popular among parts of the provincial population, leading them to question whether there actually were more grievances than previously admitted. The more simplistic and negative the characterization of Tacfarinas, the less such awkward questions would arise.

The war was not confined to a small area of northwest Africa, but potentially encompassed most of the coastline and provincial interior as far as the Atlas mountains and edges of the Sahara, from Mauretania as far east as Tripolitania (modern Libya). This was a substantial amount of territory and suggests that Tacfarinas' operations were far larger than Tacitus' narrative might suggest. Although he avoided pitched battle against the Romans, Tacfarinas was not afraid to engage with the army under other circumstances. He probably won more victories than Tacitus suggests – this is evident from the fact that Auzea is mentioned as being somewhere that Tacfarinas had previously attacked and destroyed, without that phase of the campaign ever appearing in the preceding narrative. Unfortunately, unless it becomes possible to carry out some battlefield archaeology research in the region, it is unlikely that the true scale of operations and potential number of engagements will ever be known. The fact that additional troops were needed to deal with the conflict indicates that it expanded beyond what the provincial garrison could be expected to deal with. If it is the case that an emergency levy of Jews in Rome was connected to the war, as seems probable, it was evidently a pressing problem, as such actions were only undertaken in situations of dire military need.[28]

The severity of the conflict is also indicated by the fact that three of the four proconsuls involved in it were awarded triumphal honours for their efforts, with the fourth apparently only denied to avoid provoking jealousy. Such recognition would be unlikely merely for the suppression of standard bandit activity, not least as these honours came with the requirement that the campaign had inflicted more than 5,000 casualties on the enemy. The level of danger posed by the conflict may have varied over time, with the start (AD 17) and end (in 23/24) being the periods of greatest danger, when Tacfarinas seems to have had much wider regional support, as opposed to the middle years (18–22). The first and last years were when the conflict had the most potential to develop into a full-scale regional rebellion, with peoples such as the Mauri and Garamantes getting involved to try to liberate themselves from the prospect of Roman rule. The fact that the narrative and severity of the conflict shifted, particularly in its last stages, is indicated by Tacitus' changed terminology for Tacfarinas, shifting from calling him a 'bandit' (*latro*) to a rebel 'leader' or 'general' (*dux*).

Ultimately, however serious the conflict had become, it was never likely to lead to Rome's wholesale abandonment of northwest Africa or even just part of it. One of the fundamental weaknesses of Tacfarinas' campaign is that he was unlikely ever to be able to inflict a really substantial defeat on the Roman army. Although there are indications in Tacitus that Roman casualties were significant during the conflict – and the sufferings of the soldiers heavy, at least in their own eyes – there was no great defeat of the army on the battlefield, or even a near-miss. Rome does not seem to have faced the prospect of losing a legion in any of the attacks. Only in Germany, east of the Rhine, had Rome to-date willingly abandoned conquered territory following a heavy defeat (AD 9 in the Teutoburg, to Arminius). Even then, Tiberius chose to do so several years after the defeat and for political rather than military reasons – the army would doubtless have been able to recover these territories if it had tried. In his embassy to Tiberius, Tacfarinas had promised war without end if the emperor did not agree to negotiate and cede territory to the rebels, but it is hard to see how this conflict would ever have forced Rome to seriously reconsider its long-term future in northwest Africa. While the war was a problematic period for them and certainly had a negative impact on the region and beyond during the heaviest years of fighting, it was not a security threat to the Empire. Ultimately, Rome had the manpower and economic resources to keep up the war indefinitely – eventually Tacfarinas would die, one way or another, and the situation would be reassessed then.

Tacfarinas in Later History

Roman northwest Africa was poorly understood for most of subsequent history, right up to the nineteenth century. The relative inaccessibility of the region meant that it was not visited by antiquarians or travellers on the Grand Tour, despite the spectacular nature of many Roman sites there. The first organized documentation of Roman antiquities in the region was conducted under the auspices of the French military, who included them in topographic maps they prepared for campaigning.[29] As a result, most early (re)discovery of the Roman archaeology and history was carried out while the modern countries were under French and Italian colonial control, which had a significant impact on how their past was presented and understood.[30] The modern imperial powers viewed themselves as the successors to Rome in the region, an inheritance which was partly used to justify their presence.

During the French conquest of Algeria in the nineteenth century, links were drawn between the contemporary population and its later counterpart which were used to justify the use of extreme colonial violence in the conflict, which began in 1830 with the seizure of Algiers. There followed decades of resistance, in which the Kabyles of Algeria played a particularly prominent role. As the campaign struggled on, classically-educated French officers looked to the ancient sources for guidance on how to manage conflict in the region. Rome's war against Tacfarinas offered a particularly relevant example, not least as much of it had taken place in the same areas the French were now operating in and against the ancestors of the people occupying the region in their own day.

The French troops were commanded by Thomas Robert Bugeaud, a former soldier in the foot grenadiers who had significant exposure to banditry through his service in central Europe and Spain during the early decades of the nineteenth century. He was sent to Algeria in 1836 with the aim of establishing swift and total control of the territory. In planning their field strategy, Bugeaud and his officers compared the situation they faced in the region to the one Rome had experienced almost two millennia earlier, and aimed to use any lessons the ancient sources had to offer.[31] This reflects the fact that the type of warfare being taught in European military academies at the time was completely irrelevant to the Algerian situation, where the enemy did not occupy specific fortifications that could be attacked, did not rely on formal lines of communication, and would not engage in pitched battle. The resistance leader was Emir 'Abd el-Qader (also known as Abdelkader), who used a variety of irregular and guerrilla tactics against the French troops. He was seen as a latter-day Jugurtha or Tacfarinas, whose resistance could be dealt with in the same way Rome had handled their conflicts. In both the ancient and modern cases, these leaders were regarded as proof that the population of the region was predisposed to rebellion and could only be controlled with harshness and violence.[32]

The Algerian resistance avoided pitched battle wherever possible, leading to suggestions of cowardice – although when the French themselves adopted similar techniques, there was seemingly no such moral judgement. French operations in the region were shaped around what had proved effective in the past: highly mobile strike columns, using lighter-armed troops to reduce their vulnerability to attack, and roving patrols aiming to gather intelligence about the location and activity of the enemy. Such methods had proved very effective for both Blaesus and Dolabella in their respective periods in Africa. The French military used their own form of the *razzia*, an indigenous type of raiding practised among the peoples of the region since antiquity,[33] and comprising low-level attacks on native settlements with the aim of acquiring booty and captives. The raids conducted by Tacfarinas would have been recognizable as *razzias* and the French authorities identified the modern phenomenon with his activity.[34]

The French found the *razzias* had a logistical advantage in allowing soldiers to be maintained in the field without extensive supply lines, something Tacfarinas had taken advantage of. Their adoption of this unorthodox method was criticized in some of the European press, but the French officers saw it as a necessary adaptation of their field strategy to suit local conditions.[35] The French significantly increased the brutality of the practice however, and their raids became far more severe than typical *razzias* had historically been. They also made attacks on the civilian population, which are not documented in the Roman period conflict, though they may well have happened. Bugeaud used the war against Tacfarinas as a precedent and justification for employing a scorched earth policy in Algeria. The campaign was difficult for the French soldiers, who struggled with the constant but invisible threat of the enemy, the climate, the fast movements required, and the lack of food from a smaller supply line.[36] They also found it difficult to reconcile their expectations and previous experiences of warfare with the situation they faced in Algeria. The same could undoubtedly have been said of the Romans facing Tacfarinas, particularly in the earlier stages of the war; these may be exactly the factors that caused the soldiers to flee in the engagement at the Pagyda during the proconsulship of Lucius Apronius.

Italian and particularly French scholarship dominated the nineteenth and twentieth-century historical reception of Tacfarinas. As two imperial powers in the region, it is not surprising that their sympathies were entirely with Rome,

Tacfarinas' followers being equated with the hated and intransigent indigenous population of their own times. The enmity between the two sides in the later conflict meant the Berbers in particular had to be culturally marginalized, a process partly facilitated by making sure their historical equivalents were minimized in studies of the Roman era.[37] The focus of European scholars in this period was typically on the monumental Roman remains of northwest Africa, and the resistance to Roman culture was not an area of particular academic interest.[38] The indigenous population both in antiquity and their own day was portrayed as being largely without agency and in need of 'civilizing', and the antagonism between settled and nomadic populations was emphasized. Life under Roman rule, once the initial period of conquest was over, was depicted in an almost entirely positive light and all beneficial elements were identified as resulting from the Roman presence.[39] Inevitably, rebels such as Jugurtha, Juba I, and Tacfarinas were equated with their contemporary counterparts, particularly where there was fierce resistance to occupation.

After the Second World War, the countries in this region began to reclaim their independence, including Libya (1951) from Italy, and Morocco (1956), Tunisia (1957), and Algeria (1963) from France. This process allowed for new perspectives on their Roman period history. Tacfarinas was in some measure 'reclaimed' by the Algerians, particularly during and after their fight for independence from France. In 1968, the Algerian resistance figurehead/leader Ahmed Akkache published a short work on Tacfarinas through SNED, the state publishing house.[40] In it Akkache presents the rebel leader as a freedom fighter and liberator in a very dramatic way, with some episodes of fictional narrative presented as if they were fact. However, public conception of Tacfarinas was also complicated by his being identified with the Berbers – themselves marginalized in the post-independence movement compared to the Arab Islamic population.[41] He has since become part of the Berber 'Kabyle myth', which centres on the specifically Berber peoples of the region as opposed to the Arabic population, and culminated in the 'Berber Spring' uprisings of 1980/81.[42] Tacfarinas has been claimed by the movement as an historical Berber leader, a political inspiration alongside Jugurtha; it seems it was not just Tacitus who was struck by the similarities between the two figures.

Textbooks in post-colonial Algeria have sought to further distance the country from France by emphasizing the greatness of its pre-colonial history and glorifying the masculinity of ancestral heroes such as Masinissa, Jugurtha, Juba I, and Tacfarinas.[43] This was part of a wider attempt to establish a new historical narrative for a formerly colonial people that would emphasize their strengths, rather than their subjugation. Tacfarinas, though not a ruler on the level of Masinissa, Jugurtha, or Juba I, still represented the agency of the northwest Africans in antiquity, despite his eventual defeat. These figures could be celebrated as strong, courageous, and independent – characteristics that the Algerians had found themselves at a loss to identify with during the colonial period. The reclaiming of such qualities through textbook examples of pre-colonial national heroes gave students and motivated learners a sense of pride and belonging in their past, a counter to colonial-era French teaching which had characterized the Algerians as inferior, weak, and lacking in civilization.

Masinissa's reign was used to show that native northwestern Africans could rule themselves to near-universal societal benefit, bringing together a diverse range of peoples who had not previously lived under the same ruler. Jugurtha was praised for his courage and military skills and for his rebellion against undue Roman (i.e. colonial) influence. Tacfarinas was similarly recognized and praised as a precursor of the modern Algerian freedom fighters. In the textbooks of the post-colonial period, Tacfarinas' role as a liberator was highlighted, particularly episodes from later in the rebellion when Tacitus makes more references to this issue in his reported speeches. The writers of these books suggested (without any direct evidence) that the call to liberation was passed from Tacfarinas throughout northwestern Africa on wax tablets, papyrus letters, and in oral testimony, embellished by stories of his army's exploits and successes against Rome. Obviously, some word of these exploits must have spread in the region in order for new recruits to find their way to him, but there is no evidence for a vast network spreading the message of rebellion to all corners and peoples. The books scarcely touch on his activities as bandit and raider more than liberator, except to dismiss Tacitus' claims as groundless pejorative propaganda. Such distancing of Tacfarinas from banditry makes sense given the negative impact of the French use of the *razzia* against the indigenous population in the nineteenth century, only a few generations before – it would not do for Tacfarinas to be too closely associated with the activities of hated colonial powers. It no doubt also helped that Tacfarinas' campaign lasted around eight years, just as the Algerian independence movement against France had done. However Tacfarinas was never cited as an inspirational figure by Muammar Gaddafi in Libya, despite the fact that the war had partly taken place in his own country's territory; indeed, he showed little interest in the ancient past, and peoples such as the Garamantes were not much studied under his regime. Tacfarinas was a useful historical figure when inspiration for rebellion was needed, but there were problematic aspects of his characterization which the ruling parties were never quite sure how to handle.

Tacfarinas Today

European scholars in the later twentieth century typically focused on marginalizing or minimizing the occurrence and impact of resistance to Roman rule in northwesternAfrica, whereas African scholars have embraced it enthusiastically.[44] Even today many Algerian scholars have mixed feelings about the Roman period and it has been less well integrated into their nation's history, particularly in comparison with neighbouring Morocco and Tunisia, which have adopted a very different approach.[45] There is some cultural reclamation of the ancient past in northwest Africa's wider society. Today in Algeria and Tunisia 'Numidia' and 'Masinissa' are acceptable names for children and there is a singer whose stage name is 'Takfarinas', who celebrates his Kabyle background through music.[46] Some suggestion has been made that Tacfarinas should be referred to as 'Tiqfarin' as a more African spelling of his name,[47] although whether that would be any more familiar to the man himself than 'Tacfarinas' is debatable.

Tacfarinas has not been forgotten because he rebelled against Rome. There are a number of such rebels whose names were well-known in antiquity and whose conflicts against the Empire have been recognized as significant historical events. We can think of Viriathus in Lusitania (Spain/Portugal), Vercingetorix in Gaul (France), Arminius in Germania (Germany), Boudica in Britannia (England/Britain), Julius Civilis in Batavia (the Netherlands), and both Simon bar Giora and Simon ben Kokhba in Judaea (Israel/Palestine), to name just a few examples. Many of these figures were reinvented as symbols of national pride during the eighteenth and nineteenth centuries, particularly in states engaged in nation-building at the time. Large statues of Vercingetorix and Arminius (renamed 'Hermann') were constructed in the late nineteenth century at Alise-Sainte-Reine (France, 1865) and Detmold (Germany, 1838–75) respectively, while the early twentieth century saw the dedication of statues of Viriathus in Zamora (Spain, erected 1902) and Boudica in London (England, erected 1902). Julius Civilis was the subject of a statue made for Crown Prince Willem Frederik van Oranje (William of Orange), to stand in his hunting pavilion in Tervuren (Netherlands, 1821–2), while Simon bar Kokhba was depicted on the Knesset Menorah monument presented to Israel by Britain in 1956.

The modern memorialization of these rebels against Rome illustrates the emotional power of their actions some two millennia after they took place, as if they represent lasting elements of national character which can be a matter of pride even today. It does not matter that in almost all cases the rebellions were unsuccessful and the rebels themselves often came to unfortunate ends; their valiant attempts to re-establish their liberty from Rome was enough to secure their memory. Many continue to feature prominently not just in historical studies, but also in popular culture. In print, Arminius and his rebellion have featured in a significant number of novels in both English and German, as has Boudica; both have also been the subject of recent film and television adaptations.[48] There is clearly a strong contemporary interest in rebellions against Rome – though Tacfarinas has, as yet, not benefited.

Recognition and commemoration of the war against Tacfarinas is oddly lacking today – an oversight particularly notable given the timing of the conflict. This book was written in the first eight months of 2024 – the period marking the 2,000th anniversary of the preparations for, and execution of, the final Roman campaign against Tacfarinas. Yet despite the modern trend to celebrate notable dates of the ancient past, no public notice has been taken of the anniversary of Tacfarinas' defeat at any point from 2017 (marking the war's outbreak) to 2024 (when it ended). For comparison, the 2,000th anniversary of the Battle of the Teutoburg (or Varus Disaster) in 2009 was marked by a series of events across Germany, including dedicated museum exhibitions, books, public heritage events, and academic conferences, with much accompanying coverage in the popular press.[49] Meanwhile Tacfarinas has languished, with no popular recognition or commemoration of the recent anniversaries associated with his war against Rome. In many ways, the biases against him first established by Tacitus live on.

Today, Tacfarinas is relegated to a short paragraph in Roman histories of Africa and little more than a footnote in wider historical studies of the continent, if he is mentioned at all. Maybe people in the modern day are still influenced by the ancient views of him as a bandit, someone not worth celebrating, or remembering. Yet this 'bandit' managed to maintain a conflict against Rome for longer than almost anyone who attempted to fight against him and forced the Romans to make extraordinary changes in their field operations in order to win the war. He may not have been fighting for the freedom of his people but he was certainly fighting by choice. Tacfarinas had multiple opportunities to withdraw from the conflict, when Rome had driven him back to the mountains or desert and was seemingly willing to leave him alone after that – instead, he chose to keep returning to the field, in what eventually developed into a full-scale rebellion. The Romans made the mistake of underestimating Tacfarinas and his significance many times over: hopefully in the future, we will no longer repeat their error.

Notes

Introduction

1. See Woolf (2011): 33–43.
2. On revolts in this period more generally see Dyson (1971), or Woolf (2011).
3. Pliny the Elder *Natural History* 5.25.
4. Mattingly (2023): 227–8.
5. Garnsey (1983); Wilson (2017a).
6. Strabo *Geography* 17.3.15.
7. Pliny the Elder *Natural History* 5.29; *cf.* Mattingly (2023): 36–7. The exact location of the Ampsaga river is unknown, although it was clearly a politically important waterway (see España-Chamorro 2023); the Oued Rhumel in Algeria is the most likely candidate.
8. Strabo *Geography* 17.3.15; see Shaw (1982).
9. Numidian kings allied to Rome were credited by Greco-Roman writers with the introduction of formal agriculture to the region (e.g. Strabo *Geography* 17.3.151; Polybius *Roman History* 36.16.7–8), but there is archaeological evidence to suggest that farming was practised in some regions of Africa far earlier, particularly the cultivation of cereals (Cherry 1998: 15–16).
10. Mattingly (2022), (2023): 177. On trade conducted by the Saharan-based tribes see Wilson (2017a).
11. See Wilson (2005).
12. Particularly through the work of the UNESCO Libyan Valleys Archaeological Survey, and the comprehensive research of David Mattingly e.g. Mattingly (2003, 2022). See also Raven (1993): 44; Cherry (1998): 21.
13. Scheele (2017).
14. Tacitus *Annals* 3.20.
15. Velleius Paterculus 2.125.5 (honours), 2.129.4 (African war quote).
16. Jerary (2008): 184–5.
17. Aurelius Victor *De Caesaribus.* 2.3, *cf. Epitome* 2.8.
18. Woodman 2004.
19. Tacitus *Annals* 2.52; 3.20–1, 3.32, 3.73–4; 4.23–6.
20. Woolf (2011): 35.
21. Pomeroy (2012): 158.
22. On Tacitus' use of Tacfarinas to impugn Tiberius, see Devillers (1991).
23. Wolff (2014).
24. Vanacker (2015): 345.
25. Levene (2009): 228–9.
26. Wolff (2014).

27. Tacfarinas inscription, *IRT* 1021; Scipio inscription: *IRT* 739.
28. Tacitus *Annals* 4.25, 4.26.
29. Later in the narrative, Tacitus (*Annals* 4.25) makes reference to a fort in Mauretania which had been attacked by Tacfarinas' army, clearly indicating that their area of operations incorporated the kingdom's territory.
30. Cherry (2020): 1045.
31. Woolf (2011): 38–9.
32. Shaw (2004): 326–7; and see Shaw pp. 330–9 for general Roman attitudes towards bandits.
33. Kovács (2018).
34. Shaw (2004): 343–4.
35. Vanacker (2015): 345.
36. Grunewald (2004): 48–53.
37. Used by e.g. Florus (*Epitome* 2.31) to describe uprisings in Africa which had broken out during the reign of Augustus, although he does use this to cover conflicts which clearly escalated to become wars, such as the Gaetulian War (AD 3–6; see chapter three).
38. Shaw (2004); Wolff (2014).
39. Shaw (2004): 329.
40. Ulpian *Digest* 50.16.118.
41. Tacitus *Annals* 2.88.
42. On the modern reinterpretation of Tacfarinas as a freedom fighter see Gambash (2015): 70–1.
43. A practice known from elsewhere in northern Africa during the Imperial period. A letter sent home to his family by an Egyptian recruit in the second century AD notes that he has changed his name from Apion to Antonius Maximus, and asks his relatives to use this name in future correspondence with him (BGU II 423 (P. 7950)).
44. Mattingly (2023): 234, note 9.
45. On issues with the 'tribe' terminology and the inherent ethnic and cultural heterogeneity implications see e.g. Brett & Fentress (1996), Mattingly (2023).

Chapter 1

1. On the Punic Wars more generally, see Hoyos (2005), Goldsworthy (2006), Miles (2011), and the contributions in Hoyos' (2011) edited volume.
2. On Phoenician settlement in the region see Mattingly (2023): 78–85.
3. Strabo *Geography* 17.3.15, in Roman belief by Queen Dido.
4. On the rise of Carthage see Ameling (2011).
5. Polybius *Roman History* 3.39.1–6. For an overview of the development of the Carthaginian empire see Mattingly (2023): 85–91.
6. Mattingly (2023).
7. See Mattingly (2023: 133–54) for full details of the excavations at Althiburos.
8. On the settlements of the Garamantes see many of the works of David Mattingly, who conducted most of the archaeological work in the area, especially Mattingly (2016; 2022).
9. Mattingly (2016).
10. Particularly Mattingly (2023): 114–20, 209–16.

11. Brett & Fentress (1996): 24–5.
12. See Stone (2016).
13. On the rise of Rome in this period see Serrati (2011).
14. Plutarch *Life of Pyrrhus* 23.6.
15. See also Hoyos (2011) for the outbreak of the First Punic War, and Rankov (2011: 149–50) for a discussion of its causes.
16. Full discussions of the conflict can be found in e.g. J. F. Lazenby *The First Punic War: A Military History* (1996, UCL Press (London)).
17. Rankov (2011): 155–9.
18. Polybius *Roman History* 1.26.7.
19. Polybius *Roman History* 1.26.10– 28.14). Rankov (2011: 156–7) notes that the battle was probably fought nowhere near Cape Ecnomus.
20. Polybius *Roman History* 1.37.
21. Polybius *Roman History* 1.39.1–6.
22. See Rankov (2011: 159–63) for military operations in this period.
23. On Roman territorial expansion in this period, see Sampson (2016).
24. Polybius *Roman History* 2.22.1–6.
25. Polybius *Roman History* 2.31.1–7.
26. On the causes of the Second Punic War see Beck (2011). Zimmerman (2011: 282) notes that Rome did absolutely nothing to actually help Saguntum in the eight months it was under siege by Hannibal, further validating the idea that for them the attack was nothing more than a justification for war.
27. Livy 21.1.4 – 'to make himself an enemy of Roman people at the earliest possible opportunity'; a slight contrast to the version in Polybius (3.11.7), which says that Hannibal swore that he was 'never to think well of Romans'.
28. For the ancient accounts of the Second Punic War, see Polybius *Roman History* books 3–15 and Livy *The History of Rome* books 21–30; for modern narratives, see Goldsworthy (2006) and Miles (2011).
29. Polybius *Roman History* 3.33.7–16; including the Masyli, Masaesyli, Maccoei and Maurusi.
30. See Zimmerman (2011): 283–4.
31. On this period see Rawlings (2011).
32. Hoyos (2005: 95) agrees that there were few Roman survivors beyond the 10,000 who broke out of the Carthaginian attack, although Goldsworthy (2006: 180) suggests that there were probably more survivors who arrived as stragglers later. Others (Erdkamp 2011: 67) argue that about half the Roman force was killed, with those not accounted for in either group likely taken prisoner by the Carthaginians.
33. Fronda (2011): 246.
34. On the battle at Cannae, see Daly (2002). Cannae was a masterclass in battle tactics on the part of Hannibal and the Carthaginians, one which has been much studied by military historians. The German Schlieffen Plan, devised to achieve a swift victory at the outbreak of the First World War, was partly inspired by Hannibal's tactics at Cannae; its creator, General von Schlieffen, was a keen military historian who had composed a series of Cannae studies in the decades previous.
35. Polybius *Roman History* 3.66.2, 3.67.3, 3.116.5.
36. Livy *Roman History* 22.51.

37. Livy *Roman History* 24.48.
38. Livy *Roman History* 30.12.
39. Appian *Punic Wars* 10.
40. Livy *Roman History* 24.48.
41. Appian *Punic Wars* 10; Braund (1984): 11.
42. Livy *Roman History* 24.48.
43. Appian *Punic Wars* 10.
44. Livy *Roman History* 28.35. Masinissa was evidently bowled over by Scipio, a combined result of his reputation, generosity, and presentation in person. Masinissa had explained his movements to meet Scipio to Carthaginian authorities as travel for the purpose of raiding, and Scipio allowed him to plunder a small area before returning home so that suspicions would not be raised.
45. Appian *Punic Wars* 10–11.
46. Appian *Punic Wars* 11.
47. Appian *Punic Wars* 13–14.
48. Livy *Roman History* 30.13.
49. Livy *Roman History* 30.12.10–22.
50. Diodorus Siculus 27.1; Appian *Punic Wars* 27–8.
51. On the negotiations between Scipio and Masinissa over Sophonisba and subsequent events see Livy *Roman History* 30.13–15.
52. Livy (*Roman* History 30.15) and Appian (*Punic Wars* 28) have Sophonisba voluntarily taking the poison, with some admiration of her bravery; in Appian, she even asks her nurse not to cry because it was a glorious death. Diodorus Siculus (27.7.1) recounts that Masinissa forced her to drink the poison.
53. See Roller (2003): 147–9.
54. Livy *Roman History* 30.15; Appian *Punic Wars* 32.
55. Livy *Roman History* 30.16.
56. On the Battle of Zama see Carey *et al.* (2008).
57. Taylor (2019): 326–7.
58. See Kunze (2011) for a detailed account.
59. Including examples at Tugga, Sabratha, and on the island of Djerba.
60. On the relationship between state formation and monumental tombs in Numidia see Stone (2016).
61. Livy *Roman History* 42.23.
62. Livy *Roman History* 43.3.
63. See e.g. Grunewald (2004): 43–66.
64. Diodorus Siculus 32.1.
65. On the potential causes of the Third Punic War see also Le Bohec (2011): 431–6.
66. Pliny *Natural History* 15.20; Florus *Epitome* 1.31.
67. Goldsworthy (2006): 332; Kunze (2011): 405–8.
68. Baronowski (1995): 26–7.
69. Vogel-Weidemann (1989): 85.
70. Polybius 36.3.6–9.
71. Polybius 36.4.1–3.
72. Goldsworthy (2006): 338–9.
73. On the siege of Carthage see Le Bohec (2011).

74. Appian (*Punic Wars* 107).
75. Macrobius *Saturnalia* 3.9.7–8, although Appian makes no mention of it.
76. Appian (*Punic Wars* 128–30).
77. Appian (*Punic Wars* 131). The commander, Hasdrubal, had specifically asked for his wife and children to be kept safe as part of his terms of surrender.
78. Macrobius *Saturnalia* 3.9.9; Miles (2011): 353.

Chapter 2

1. Quinn (2004).
2. Mattingly (2011): 34–7.
3. On the dehumanizing of non-Roman populations see Shaw (2000).
4. Mattingly (2011): 34–5.
5. Sallust *Jugurthine War* 89.
6. On Roman attitudes to African nomadism see Shaw (1982).
7. Sallust *Jugurthine War* 18.1–2.
8. Strabo *Geography* 17.3.1.
9. Sallust *Jugurthine War* 101.
10. Morstein-Marx (2001).
11. The phrase is first attested in Sallust (*Jugurthine War* 108) in the context of Bocchus of Mauretania during the Jugurthine War late in the second century BC, decades after the end of the Punic Wars. It was later applied to figures from earlier Punic history, including Hannibal, who was described as being even less trustworthy than the average Carthaginian (Livy 21.4.9).
12. Starks 1999.
13. Polybius *Roman History* 14.1.4.
14. Sallust *Jugurthine War* 54.
15. Livy *Periochae* 50.7.
16. Appian *Punic Wars* 111.
17. Sallust *Jugurthine War* 5.6.
18. Strabo *Geography* 17.3.13.
19. The siege was conducted by Publius Cornelius Scipio Aemilianus (also known as Scipio Africanus the Younger), who had been a prominent commander in Africa during the Third Punic War and was entrusted by Masinissa with administrating his estate; it is unsurprising that Micipsa felt a degree of support should therefore be provided.
20. Sallust *Jugurthine War* 11.
21. Sallust *Jugurthine War* 5.7.
22. Sallust *Jugurthine War* 7.
23. Sallust *Jugurthine War* 101.
24. Sallust *Jugurthine War* 9.2.
25. Plutarch *Life of Marius* 10.2. Some texts imply the opposite, that Bocchus I married a daughter of Jugurtha (e.g. Sallust *Jugurthine War* 80.6), but this seems to be an error in textual transmission.
26. Sallust *Jugurthine War* 12.
27. Sallust *Jugurthine War* 15.
28. Sallust *Jugurthine War* 21–2.

29. Sallust *Jugurthine War* 35.
30. Sallust *Jugurthine War* 36.
31. The Romans forced their captives to pass 'under the yoke' (literally the bridle equipment of an ox or horse used to draw ploughs or carriages) to symbolize their loss of status and freedom. For a Roman army to submit to the process was the ultimate shame.
32. Sallust's *Jugurthine War* provides the main ancient account of the conflict. For a modern narrative, see Sampson (2010).
33. Sallust *Jugurthine War* 54.
34. Sallust *Jugurthine War* 91.
35. Sallust *Jugurthine War* 97–9.
36. Sallust *Jugurthine War* 108–13.
37. Plutarch *Marius* 12.3.
38. Appian *Civil Wars* 1.42.
39. Roller (2003: 25).
40. Plutarch *Marius* 40.
41. Plutarch *Life of Marius* 40; Hiarbas is referred to as 'Iampsas' by Plutarch.
42. On the civil war between Sulla and Marius see Sampson (2013).
43. See Roller (2023: 25–7) for a summary of events in this period.
44. Suetonius (*Caesar* 71) notes that Hiempsal II was still alive when Julius Caesar became praetor of Spain in 63/62 BC.
45. Suetonius *Julius Caesar* 71.
46. Sextus Quinctilius Varus was the father of Publius Quinctilius Varus, the Roman commander and politician who became notorious for the AD 9 defeat in the Teutoburg at the hands of the Cheruscan chief Arminius. Sextus followed the anti-Caesarian cause to the end, allying with Caesar's assassins (possibly he was one himself), joining them for the war against Octavian and Antony, and eventually committing suicide after the Battle of Philippi in 42 BC.
47. As documented by an inscription giving his rank (CIL I2.2.780).
48. Caesar *African War* 80–5. On the battle also see Sampson (2024).
49. Caesar *African War* 85. On Caesar's *clementia,* see Morstein-Marx (2021): 413–87.
50. Plutarch *Caesar* 53.5.
51. Appian *Civil Wars* 2.100.
52. Whittaker (1996): 587.
53. Sittius' death was mentioned in a letter by Cicero (*Ad Atticus*, 15.17), suggesting it was international news.
54. Appian *Civil War* 5.26; Dio *Roman History* 40.8.22–4.
55. Dio (49.43.7) claimed that Octavian made Mauretania into a client kingdom in 33 BC, but there is no other evidence of this, and it was not listed among the provinces when he became Augustus in 27 BC. Roller (2003: 95) points out that it would be highly improbable for an area to change from a kingdom to a province and back again in less than a decade, though not impossible. He also notes that at the time Octavian was heavily criticizing Mark Antony for making provinces on his own authority in the east and that it would look bad to do exactly the same thing himself in the west.
56. Whittaker (1996): 590–1; Roller (2003): 95. This scenario would later happen once Juba II had been installed in Mauretania, a friend and ally of Octavian but disliked by

much of the Mauretanian population; many tribes, particularly the Mauri, rebelled against Juba several times and later joined Tacfarinas in hope of freeing themselves from proxy-Roman rule.

57. Dio *Roman History* 49.43.7; *cf.* Roller (2003): 105.
58. Ampelius *Liber Memorialis* 38.1.4; Roller (2003): 1–3.

Chapter 3

1. See e.g. Whittaker (1996): 591–3.
2. Sallust *Jugurthine War* 111.
3. Whittaker (1996): 586–7.
4. On the date and creation of Africa Proconsularis see Fishwick (1993).
5. Dio 53.13.1-8; Strabo *Geography* 17.3.25; see Millar (1966).
6. Africa and Asia were the two major senatorial provinces, but they also included Achaea (Greece), Asia, Cyrenaica and Cyrene, Cyprus, Gallia Narbonensis, Hispania Baetica, Macedonia, Pontus and Bithynia, and Sicily.
7. See Brunt (1984): 432–5.
8. Duncan-Jones (2016): 37–8.
9. Le Bohec (1989): 336–7.
10. Dio 55.23.3; *cf.* Fentress (1979): 66.
11. For more on Varus' time in Africa, see Ball (2023).
12. On the client kingdom system see Braund (1984).
13. Roller (2003): 95.
14. See Jacobson (2001): 4–5.
15. Strabo (*Geography* 6.4.2, 17.3.7) and Dio (51.15.6) both claim that Juba II was given his 'ancestral lands' as part of the kingdom, presumably Numidia, although neither historian specifies. Roller (2003: 103) argues that Juba II was not given any of the Numidian territories, which (aside from his brief client kingship there) had been part of Roman Africa since 46 BC, and it would have made little sense to reverse the provincialization just to give the territory to Juba, especially given its importance in trade and agriculture. Perhaps, as Roller suggests, Juba was given a token portion of the least incorporated Numidian fringes, enough to allow Juba to say he had reclaimed ancestral territory with no negative impact on Rome.
16. Roller (2003): 3; *cf.* Mackie (1983).
17. Roller (2003): 102–3.
18. Florus *Epitome* 2.31; see also Whittaker (1996): 592–3.
19. Strabo *Geography* 17.1.53–4.
20. The head was found in 1910 by John Garstang, buried beneath what had been a temple staircase in Meroë. It was almost certainly from one of the statues taken in the Meroitic invasion of Egypt in 24 BC, evidently not returned as part of the peace settlement. It appears to have been deliberately placed beneath the staircase for symbolic reasons, so that every visitor to the temple would step on the head of Augustus on their way in and out of the building. For more on the Meroë head see Opper (2015).
21. On the life of Cleopatra Selene see Draycott (2022).
22. Roller (2003): 106.

23. Braund (1984): 91–103. When Herod the Great had angered Augustus by attacking the Nabataeans without permission, the emperor had written to him terminating their friendship and saying that from now on he would be treated as any other subject (Josephus *Jewish Antiquities* 16.9.1–4).
24. Roller (2003): 4–6, 106–8.
25. Cherry (1998): 35.
26. Gruen (1996): 166.
27. See Scheele (2017).
28. Dio 56.18.3, written in the context of the German population in the early C1st AD.
29. See Dyson (1971).
30. Whittaker (1996): 586–9.
31. Vanacker (2015): 350.
32. On the causes of provincial rebellions in the early Imperial period see Dyson (1971) and Woolf (2011).
33. On the military operations in the region under Augustus see Guédon (2018): 17–94.
34. Valerius Maximus *Memorable Deeds and Sayings* 2.8.1; see also Beard (2007): 206–11.
35. Roller (2003): 107–8.
36. On the origins of the Garamantes see Brett and Fentress (1996): 17–24.
37. See Mattingly (2003; 2016; 2017; 2022; 2023); also Liverani (2000).
38. Herodotus *Histories* 4.183. The Ethiopians are unflatteringly described as eating snakes and lizards, and speaking like squeaking bats.
39. Around 500 chariot cave-paintings have been found across the Sahara region, although it is not likely that all of them are associated with the Garamantes specifically.
40. Lucan *Pharsalia* 4.674.
41. Virgil *Aeneid* 6.691–7.
42. See Mattingly (2003): 76–9; (2011): 34–7.
43. Mattingly (2023): 174–5.
44. On Garamantean agriculture see Mattingly (2022).
45. Mattingly (2017: 14).
46. Wilson (2017a): 191–2.
47. Leitch *et al* (2017): 292–3.
48. On the Garamantean slave trade see Fentress (2011); *cf.* Wilson (2017a: 192–3). Rome also sent an expedition to Agisymba (Lake Chad) *c.*AD 90 which was potentially a direct slaving mission.
49. Nikita *et al.* (2011).
50. Pliny *Natural History* 5.36.
51. Pliny the Elder *Natural History* 5.5.
52. Pliny the Elder *Natural History* 5.5.
53. After Balbus, the only commanders offered triumphs were Augustus' potential successors (Hickson 1991).
54. Floris *Epitome* 2.31.
55. E.g. Strabo *Geography* 17.3.2; Pliny *Natural History* 5.17.
56. Sallust *Jugurthine War* 18.
57. Sallust *Jugurthine War* 80.
58. Dio *Roman History* 55.28.3.
59. Roller (2003): 102.

60. Sallust *Jugurthine War* 80, 88, 97, 99, 103. Although it has been suggested that some of the Gaetuli fought for Gaius Marius against Jugurtha, there is no clear evidence for this, and it is likely that the tribe remained allied with Jugurtha throughout the conflict (Fentress 1982: 326).
61. Fentress (1982).
62. Caesar *African War* 25, 32, 35, 55, 56, 61, 93.
63. Dio *Roman History* 55.28.3–4.
64. Florus *Epitome* 2.31.
65. Mackensen (2000).
66. Whittaker (1996): 595-3.
67. Velleius Paterculus 2.116.2; *ILS* 120, 8966.
68. Strabo *Geography* 17.3.23; Roller (2003): 109.
69. Dio *Roman History* 5.28.4.
70. Shaw (2004).
71. *Marti Augusto sacrum auspiciis Imp(eratoris) Caesaris Aug(usti) pontifi cis maxumi patris patriae ductu Cossi Lentuli co(n)s(ulis) XVuiri sacris faciundis proco(n)s(ulis) prouincia Africa bello Gaetulico liberata ciuitas Lepcitana*
'Sacred to Mars Augustus. Under the auspices of the emperor Caesar Augustus, chief priest, father of the country, and the leadership of Cossus Lentulus, consul, member of the committee of the fifteen for religious ceremonies (at Rome), proconsul, the province of Africa was freed from the war with the Gaetuli. The city of Leptis (set this up).'
72. Velleius Paterculus 2.116.2.
73. Florus *Epitome* 2.31.
74. Roller (2003): 110; Braund (1984: 35) notes that the honours were usually given by the Roman Senate, and may have been in Juba's case (it was not unknown for them to be granted to a client king), but that it is possible Juba awarded them to himself, imitating Roman practice (as he so often did).
75. Mazard (1955): 196–201, 282. See also Kenrick (2023): 245–6.
76. In the 40s AD, Caligula evidently decided that this was an unwise decision, and established a legionary legate position that would directly command the legion on behalf of the emperor (Hurlet 2006: 147–54).
77. Whittaker (1996): 593–4.
78. Mattingly (2023): 281.
79. Fentress (1979): 67.
80. Crook (1996): 126.
81. Tacitus *Annals* 1.53.
82. Dio *Roman History* 56.22.3–4.
83. The inscription AE (1940), 69 cites Lamia as a proconsul in the reign of Tiberius. See also Syme (1951): 122, note 33.
84. Velleius Paterculus 2.116.3.
85. AE (1913), 40.
86. Mattingly (2003: 249); *cf.* Mackensen (2000).
87. Bénabou (1976): 70; Lassère (1982): 13–22; Le Bohec (2014): 27; arguing against this are Shaw (1982): 42–3; Cherry (1998): 39, who suggest that the impact would have been minimal.

88. *IRT* 930: 'On the order of emperor Tiberius Caesar Augustus, Lucius Aurelius Lamia, proconsul, built (a road) from the town southwards for forty-four miles'. The inscription was found in Leptis Magna.
89. Lennox Manton (1988): 80–5, although some problems may have been avoided by using Punic routeways where possible, especially for non-military purposes.
90. Even fifty years later, the proposal to enforce taxation on tribes in this area during the reign of Domitian provoked a revolt (Dio 67.4.6).
91. Dyson (1971).
92. Mazard (1955): 283; Kenrick (2023): 252–3.

Chapter 4

1. Tacitus *Annals* 2.42.
2. Numidian: Lassère (1982): 23; Gaetulian: Wolff (2014).
3. Mattingly (2023): 235.
4. Brett & Fentress (1996): 24–5.
5. Gambash (2015): 71–2.
6. Tacitus *Annals* 2.88. He also detailed how many of those years had been spent in power.
7. Tacitus *Annals* 4.23.
8. Bénabou (1977): 298–302; Mattingly (2023): 236.
9. Saddington (1970): 103, notes that it is unwise to assume that Tacfarinas had a high rank or status in the *auxilia* just because of what happened to him later.
10. Sallust *Jugurthine War* 6.
11. A document from Hadrian's Wall (Tab. Vindol. 344) contains a complaint from a foreign merchant that he was beaten up by a Roman auxiliary officer and his goods (presumably wine or beer) poured away; the complaint noted that he had tried to obtain redress from some of his assailant's fellow-officers, to no avail.
12. Juvenal *Satires* 16.
13. Horsted (2021): 6.
14. Horsted (2021): 33–5.
15. Strabo *Geography* 17.3.7.
16. Appian *Civil Wars* 2.11.
17. E.g. Polybius 3.72.9, 3.116.5.
18. Sallust *Jugurthine War* 50.4–5.
19. See Horsted (2021): 8–9.
20. Livy 26.38.
21. During French operations in Algeria in the C19th, the toughness and hardiness of the indigenous mounted troops was observed and grudgingly admired, and their ability to do things the French cavalry could not was particularly noted (Rid 2009: 627); evidently this was a trait that had passed down the millennia.
22. Appian *Civil Wars* 2.11.
23. Livy 23.29.
24. Aelian 3.2.
25. Livy 35.11.
26. Dixon & Southern (1992): 164.
27. Horsted (2021): 6–7.

28. Horsted (2021): 11–3.
29. During the civil war between Caesar and Pompey, Numidians fighting for the Pompeian cause had once tricked Caesar by the use of a feint attack (Caesar *African War* 14), and had prevented him from reaching a water source at an important moment (Caesar *African War* 69).
30. Livy 24.48.
31. See also e.g. Appian (*Civil Wars* 4.54), when a Roman named Sittius allied with different African tribes and was apparently always able to command them to victory. Roman attitudes to Numidian troops under Numidian command were not often positive; in the Jugurthine War, Jugurtha was said to have held all the advantages over Rome except in the quality of his soldiers, who were not as courageous as their Roman counterparts (Sallust *Jugurthine War* 52.1–2).
32. Sallust *Jugurthine War* 54.4.
33. On allied cavalry in later Republican Rome see Sidnell (2006): 197–252.
34. Livy 32.27, 32.29; *cf.* Horsted (2021): 10.
35. On Numidians in the Imperial Roman Army see particularly Fentress (1979) and Shaw (1983). On the Roman *auxilia* more generally, see Haynes (2013).
36. For more on the organization of the Imperial cavalry see Sidnell (2006): 254–6.
37. Brent & Fentress (1996): 54–5.
38. Shaw (1982): 37–8.
39. Haynes (2013): 121–3.
40. Tacitus *Annals* 2.52.
41. Shaw (1982): 37–8.
42. On desertion from the Roman army see Coulston (2013): 26.
43. Haynes (2013): 3.
44. Shaw (1982): 37–8; Wolff (2014).
45. Shaw (2004): 350; *cf.* Haynes (2013): 364–5.
46. Wolff (2014).
47. For examples of these things see Tacitus *Annals* 1.17, 1.31, 1.35, 1.46.
48. Shaw (1982): 42–3; Cherry (1998): 39.

Chapter 5

1. Some suggest he probably took quite a lot of fellow soldiers with him, e.g. Wolff (2014).
2. Roller (2003): 6.
3. Tacitus *Annals* 2.52.
4. While Tacfarinas may have taken a significant number of his fellow Africans with him when he deserted, the overall number may still have been limited. Cherry (1998: 93–5) questions how many auxiliaries would have been recruited into the Roman army from northwestern Africa by this point, suggesting there were relatively few; thus there may not have been a significant number of indigenous ex-auxiliaries in Tacfarinas' army
5. Dio *Roman History* 52.27.4–5.
6. Gambash (2015: 71–2) argues that Tacfarinas cannot have been a member of the Musulamian royalty as that would have made his conflict with Rome an identifiably ethnic one, which would more likely have been referred to as the 'Musulamian War' rather than as a conflict against Tacfarinas specifically.

7. Tacitus *Annals* 2.52.
8. Cherry (1998): 39.
9. Vanacker (2013a).
10. Kenrick (2023): 252.
11. Dio *Roman History* 57.2.1–3.4.
12. Dio *Roman History* 56.33.5.
13. Levick (1999): 110–12.
14. Tacitus *Annals* 1.16–30 (Pannonia), 1.31–45 (Germany).
15. Ball (2023): 121–70.
16. Dyson (1975): 267.
17. Woolf (2011): 36–7.
18. Tacitus *Annals* 14.31.
19. Woolf (2011): 38–9.
20. Sallust *Jugurthine War* 91.5–7.
21. See Vanacker (2013a, 2013b).
22. See Shaw (1982); Vanacker (2014).
23. Vanacker (2013b): 202–11; Scheele 2017.
24. See Freeman (1997); Hingley (1996).
25. Fentress (2006): 28–9.
26. Mattingly (2023): 249.
27. Dio *Roman History* 62.3.2, 'Have we not been robbed entirely of most of our possessions, and those the greatest, while for those that remain we pay taxes?'; see also Dyson (1971).
28. Vanacker (2015).
29. Garnsey (1978): 239.
30. An exploration of the introduction of taxation in early Imperial Judaea, which is much better documented, provides some insight into the process as it might have taken place in northwest Africa – see Udoh (2020): 221–42.
31. See Cherry (1998): 143–4.
32. Fentress (1979): 125; although Cherry (1998: 148) notes that that amount of support may already have been required of the tribes under the earlier Numidian regime, so may not have been a major spark of discontent in the early C1st AD.
33. Dyson (1971); *cf.* Tacitus *Histories* 4.14.
34. Shaw (1982) – although at this point there were probably only a small number of auxiliaries from the region compared to its actual population (Cherry 1998: 93), and there may not have been enough to provoke a conflict on the scale that developed (Vanacker 2015: 345).
35. Bénabou (1976): 70; Mackendrick (1980): 49; Lassère (1982); Le Bohec (2014): 27.
36. Lassère (1982): 22.
37. Mattingly (2023): 249.
38. Shaw (1982): 42–3; Cherry (1998): 39; Vanacker (2015): 338–43.
39. Mattingly (2003), 2022.
40. Vanacker (2015): 342.
41. Mattingly (2023): 237.
42. Kath (2009): 155–7.
43. Whittaker (1978): 348.

44. Trousset (2002/2003).
45. See Mattingly (2017).
46. Wolff (2014).
47. See Shaw (2004).
48. Tacitus *Annals* 4.24.
49. Brett & Fentress (1996): 46.
50. Grunewald 2004: 34-5.; Dando-Collins (2023): 127–32; Mattingly (2023): 235–6.
51. Brett & Fentress (1996): 46.
52. Caesar *Gallic Wars* 7.77.14–16. Critognatus became notorious for the fact that in the same speech he purportedly suggested that the Gauls should use cannibalism to withstand a Roman siege, eating those whose age made them unsuitable for war.
53. Raaflaub (2018): 22–4; (2021): 66.
54. Tacitus *Agricola* 30–1.
55. See Dyson (1971).
56. On native revolts against Rome and their causes more widely see especially Dyson (1971), Woolf (2014), and Gambash (2015).
57. The abandonment of the German territories was not necessarily a military necessity prompted by the rebellion, however, but partly a political decision taken in AD 15 by Tiberius, who had no interest in reclaiming it. The rebellion was technically therefore successful, but only because it also suited Roman interests to withdraw.
58. Such as Tacfarinas, Boudica, Simon bar Giora. Boudica, in particular, received a lot of negative press, in no small part because she represented the antithesis of what a Roman woman 'should' be – she was dangerous to the social fabric of society as well as the military security of the empire. The same applied to the Romans' treatment of Cleopatra, who was viewed in much the same way by the historical record.
59. Increasingly revealed by battlefield archaeology; see Roymans & Fernandez-Götz (2018).

Chapter 6

1. Plutarch *Camillus* 1.1.
2. Mary Beard (2015: 138) suggests that 'Camillus is probably not much less fictional than the first Romulus', echoing the opinion of several other scholars of Early Republican Rome.
3. Augustus found it necessary to revise the consulship, introducing a system where four consuls were appointed every year, instead of the traditional two, with suffect consuls replacing each of the consuls halfway through the year; previously, suffects had only been appointed if the consul died during his year in office. This change was necessary to increase the number of men who had served as consul, a requirement for appointment to some of the most senior roles of the Roman career ladder, including consular legates (who would command legions), the proconsuls of Africa and Asia, and the urban prefects in Rome.
4. On the life and career of Varus see Ball (2023).
5. Syme (1951): 121–2; AE [1913], 40 names Habitus as a proconsul of Africa.
6. Tacitus *Annals* 2.52.
7. Cherry (1998): 39.

8. Unfortunately, there is little evidence for how the Senate communicated or instructed proconsuls during their time in office, aside from that embassies may have been sent from the provinces to speak to them on occasion; this is in contrast to the Imperial provinces ruled by the emperor, in which governors were instructed what to do by *mandata* sent to them directly from the emperor (for more information, see Millar 1966, and Burton 1976).
9. Tacitus *Annals* 2.41.
10. Garnsey (1983): 118–19.
11. Josephus *Jewish War* 2.16.4. On the supply of grain to Rome from Africa see Garnsey (1983).
12. Garnsey (1988): 228–9.
13. Mattingly (2023): 236.
14. Cherry (1998): 53.
15. Roller (2003): 205–6, as implied by some coins issued during the war, particularly Mazard (1955): 276.
16. Tacitus *Annals* 2.52.
17. Tacitus *Annals* 2.52; Horsted (2021).
18. For a full account of the revolt, see Abdale (2019).
19. Suetonius *Life of Tiberius* 16.
20. For a summary of Arminius' background see Ball (2023):115–17.
21. Wilbers-Rost (2017).
22. Dio *Roman History* 53.25.6–7.
23. Unzueta & Ocharán (2006).
24. Caesar *Gallic Wars* 5.26–37.
25. Tacitus *Annals* 2.14.
26. Dio *Roman History* 56.20.3.
27. Dio *Roman History* 57.3.1–2.
28. Tacitus *Annals* 1.16–30.
29. Tacitus *Annals* 1.31–45.
30. Tacitus *Annals* 1.31–45.
31. Roymans & Fernandez-Götz (2018).
32. Roman battle narratives by many historians, including Tacitus, were written with many literary conventions to the fore, shaped by a range of *topoi*, and with particular elements either emphasized or omitted depending on the impression the writer wanted to convey, or the connections he wanted the reader to make between one particular battle and another. As such, they are not necessarily to be read as accurate or neutral accounts of facts, but rather more as editorials or opinion pieces, conditioned by general and specific literary aims. For more on the creation and generic nature of Roman battle narratives, see Lendon (2017).
33. On the unreliability of Roman casualty figures, see Brunt (1971): 694–7.
34. Sabin (2000): 5–6.
35. Tacitus *Annals* 2.52.
36. Wolff (2014).
37. Gambash (2015): 64.
38. Mazard (1955): 284.
39. Gambash (2015): 70–1.

Chapter 7

1. Tacitus *Annals* 1.55, 1.72.
2. Velleius Paterculus *Roman History* 2.116.3. It is not clear when Apronius won triumphal honours, as Velleius notes only that he 'earned by the distinguished valour which he displayed in this campaign also, the honours which he actually won shortly afterwards.' However, it is unknown whether Velleius is referring to triumphal honours granted to Apronius in the aftermath of the Illyrian campaign and specifically for his conduct in that conflict, or to those he was later granted for his actions in Germany (AD 15–17; Tacitus *Annals* 1.72) and/or Africa.
3. The identification of Postumus as 'governor of Dalmatia' by Velleius is problematic, as the ancient evidence suggests that Dalmatia was part of the province of Illyricum rather than an independent province in its own right. It did eventually became a separate Roman province, but likely not until the second half of the first century AD. Prior to this, there may have been an 'Upper' and 'Lower' Illyricum administrated separately, but this is not certain, and would not explain why Postumus is identified as the governor of Dalmatia specifically. Although Velleius was a contemporary of these events and might therefore be expected to be an accurate source on the official titles of certain individuals, there is still scope for either compositional or transcriptional errors to have occurred in his work. Postumus may simply have been a commander in charge of any troops stationed in Dalmatia, rather than a specific governor.
4. Velleius Paterculus *Roman History* 2.116.1.
5. Tacitus *Annals* 1.63.
6. Tacitus *Annals* 1.72.
7. Tacitus *Annals* 1.60-62.
8. Tacitus *Annals* 1.64.
9. Tacitus *Annals* 1.65.
10. Tacitus *Annals* 1.72.
11. Tacitus *Annals* 2.88.
12. Tacitus *Annals* 3.20.
13. Tacitus *Annals* 3.11.
14. Gambash (2013): 73.
15. Tacitus *Annals* 3.20.
16. Scheele (2017): 68.
17. The word *razzia* is essentially a French transliteration of the Arabic *ghazya* (a surprise raid primarily for the purposes of plunder), developed after their exposure to the phenomenon during the conquest of Algeria.
    On the *razzia* see Rid (2009).
18. Tacitus (*Annals* 3.20) uses the term *castellum*, which suggests a small installation rather than a large camp; it is not clear whether it was a temporary position or one which was occupied by a garrisoning cohort on a longer-term basis.
19. Helmus & Glenn (2005): 31–7.
20. Rid (2009): 621–4.
21. *Virtus* particularly related to courage in battle, although over time it came to include other elements as well. On the development of *virtus* as a concept in the Republican period, see McDonnell (2009).
22. Plutarch *Caesar* 16.3–4; Caesar *Civil War* 3.53.4.

23. Tacitus *Annals* 3.21.
24. The practice is described by Polybius (*Histories* 6.38.1–4). Decimation was a scaled-up version of the punishment given to soldiers found guilty of individual transgressions against military discipline (falling asleep on sentry duty, running away in battle, theft from the camp). Although severe, the punishment aimed to address the 'crime' of negatively impacting the underlying moral discipline of a unit, and to dissuade others from taking similar actions in future.
25. Pearson (2019).
26. Appian *Civil War* 2.63, 2.94; Plutarch *Mark Antony* 44.3; Suetonius *Julius Caesar* 68.3. See also Taylor 2022: 116.
27. Pearson 2019: 665-6; see also Taylor (2022) for the suggestion that decimation during the C1st BC civil wars was an aberration resulting from individuals deliberately using an obsolete military punishment as a symbol of their power, rather than it being a customary practice on the military statue books throughout the Roman period.
28. Suetonius *Galba* 12.4.
29. Dio *Roman History* 48.38.4.
30. Tacitus *Annals* 3.21.
31. On the *vexilla veteranorum* see Keppie (1973).
32. CIL XIV, 3472. It is possible that this inscription refers to a different individual, but it dates to the reign of Tiberius and refers to an honorific title granted to Rufus for his actions at Thala – it is improbable that two men of the same name and title lived in exactly the same period, not least as the honours he was awarded were rare.
33. According to Pliny the Elder (*Natural History* 16.5), to be awarded the Civic Crown a soldier had to be a citizen, to have saved a fellow Roman citizen's life on the battlefield (a non-Roman ally was not enough), to have killed an enemy in doing so, and had not to have fallen back from the ground where it had taken place.
34. Apronius' failure to grant the crown is perhaps understandable given that it was an award which had become closely associated with the Imperial family during the reign of Augustus and into that of Tiberius, and in most cases, could only be bestowed by the emperor (Tacitus *Annals* 15.12). As a proconsul in command of a legion in his own right, Apronius technically had the power to issue the crown under his own authority – one of the only people in the Empire besides the emperor who could – but his hesitation to do so is unsurprising.
35. Tacitus *Annals* 3.21.
36. Garnsey (1988): 228–9.
37. Tacitus *Annals* 2.85–7, 3.9, 4.6.
38. Tacitus *Annals* 4.13.
39. This position was argued by Whittaker (1978: 348), who suggested that certain groups in Africa used this as a way to protest the reduction in their wealth and status due to Rome's direct intervention in the grain trade at this time. Others (e.g. Vanacker 2015: 343–4) disagree, suggesting it is difficult to identify a lowering of indigenous wealth with Roman activity during this period, and even harder to link it with an illicit grain trade which may not have actually been taking place.
40. Josephus *Jewish Antiquities* 18.3.5; Tacitus *Annals* 2.85; Suetonius *Tiberius* 36.
41. Wolff (2014): 54.
42. Woods (2008): 276.

43. Le Bohec (2012): 92); *ILAlg.* 2.6877. See also Jarrett (1969): 222, and Knight (1991).
44. Tacitus *Annals* 3.9.
45. *ILS* 939 = *CIL* 10.7257.
46. Tacitus *Annals* 3.21.
47. Traditional cavalry warfare and raiding in the region typically did not aim at inflicting high casualty rates as these would have been societally unsustainable – they were much more concerned with the acquisition of booty.
48. Tacitus *Annals* 4.23.
49. Osgood (2019): 161–2).
50. Tacitus *Annals* 3.73.
51. Tacitus *Annals* 3.32.

Chapter 8

1. Tacitus *Annals* 3.31. Although he remained emperor in name, Tiberius would later (AD 26) permanently withdraw to the island of Capri, governing as necessary from there; AD 21/22 appears to mark the start of this period of leaving Rome to rule itself in his absence. He had done a similar thing in 6 BC, retiring to Rhodes for some years before returning to Rome in AD 2, as a private citizen, upon the death of one of Augustus' heirs Lucius Caesar. Then in AD 4, when Gaius Caesar, the other heir, had also died, Tiberius had been fully restored to the Imperial family as adopted son and heir to Augustus.
2. Tacitus *Annals* 3.32.
3. Velleius Paterculus 2.114.5.
4. Through the probable marriage of Lepidus Vipsania Marcellina, a daughter of Marcus Agrippa by his second wife, Claudia Marcella Major, a niece of Augustus. One of Vipsania's sisters (Vipsania Agrippina) had been married to Tiberius before he was forced to divorce her to marry Augustus' daughter Julia the Elder; another sister, Vipsania Marcella, was the wife of Publius Quinctilius Varus, the high-flying politician and commander who was killed in the Teutoburg in AD 9. Lucius' Imperial connections were further strengthened by the marriage of his brother Lucius Aemilius Paullus to Julia the Younger (the granddaughter of Augustus by his daughter Julia the Elder and his long-time friend and companion, Marcus Agrippa). Several years later (*c.* AD 29), Lepidus' daughter Aemilia Lepida would marry Tiberius' adopted son and heir, Drusus Caesar.
5. 'capax imperii' Tacitus *Annals* 1.13; see also Syme (1983: 192). Tacitus goes on to note that Lepidus never ended up in trouble due to his ambition, contrary to several other ambitious individuals also mentioned by Augustus in the same speech, who all came to a bad end, mainly after plotting for power.
6. Velleius Paterculus 2.114.5.
7. Velleius Paterculus 2.125.5.
8. Tacitus *Annals* 3.11. On Germanicus' death and Piso's connections to it see Tacitus *Annals* 2.55–72.
9. Tacitus *Annals* 3.35.
10. Tacitus *Annals* 3.32. The date of Lepidus' appointment as proconsul of Asia has proved difficult to establish, as proconsuls of that name are known from both AD 21–22 and AD 26–28. The Lepidus considered to be proconsul of Africa is probably

the latter appointment, as illustrated by an inscription (AE 1934, 87), with the former a different politician of the same name, who had served as consul in AD 11, although it is unclear what had happened in his career to qualify him for the role. For further discussion see Sye (1983).

11. Velleius Paterculus 2.125.5; he is named as 'Bassus' by Velleius.
12. Tacitus *Annals* 4.2.
13. Blaesus would subsequently end up a casualty when Sejanus fell from power in AD 31, when he was executed for conspiring against Tiberius; Blaesus was charged with multiple crimes but committed suicide by falling on his sword in the presence of numerous witnesses, rather than face execution (Tacitus *Annals* 5.7).
14. Wolff (2014): 55.
15. Roller (2003): 252.
16. Tacitus *Annals* 4.23.
17. Tacitus *Annals*. 3.73.
18. He was also evidently not born into a Numidian ruling family, despite having become the chieftain of the Musulamii (Tacitus *Annals* 2.52), and his attempts to negotiate with the Imperial regime may therefore have been dismissed as illegitimate (Brett & Fentress 1996: 46).
19. Dyson (1975): 163–4; Shaw (1982): 37.
20. Lassère (1982): 25.
21. Tacitus *Annals* 3.73.
22. Lassère (1982): 25.
23. See Gambash (2015): 77.
24. Tacitus *Annals* 3.74.
25. Tacitus *Annals* 3.73.
26. Tacitus *Annals* 3.9. Their movement from the east coincided with the journey to Rome of Gnaeus Calpurnius Piso, widely suspected at the time to have poisoned Germanicus in Antioch (Syria) at Tiberius' (or Livia's) order; Piso met the 9th legion on the *Via Flaminia* as they travelled southwards to Africa.
27. Le Bohec (2014): 28.
28. Tacitus *Annals* 1.19; *cf.* Syme (1986): 163, 304. Lucius Junius Blaesus would end up committing suicide in AD 36 alongside his brother, Quintus Junius Blaesus the Younger, having fallen into disgrace with Tiberius several years after Sejanus' downfall and the suicide of their father (Tacitus *Annals* 6.40).
29. Syme (1986): 298.
30. *IRT* 531: Gaio GAVIO MACRO / LEGato PRO PRaetore III / LEPTICANI PVBLICE, 'To Gaius Gavius Macer for the third time legatus pro praetore, on behalf of all the Lepticanians'.
31. The possible connection between this inscription and the Scipio associated with Tacfarinas' war is also advanced by Livius.org (https://www.livius.org/articles/place/lepcis-magna/photos/lepcis-magna-cardo/#irt739).
32. Gambash (2015): 69; Vanacker (2015): 339.
33. Tacitus *Annals* 3.74.
34. Velleius Paterculus 2.125.5; Tacitus *Annals* 3.72.

Chapter 9

1. Tacitus *Annals* 4.23.
2. Due to the use of identical Roman names over successive generations, it can be difficult to establish which individuals were related by blood or what their exact relationship was. In this case, the father could be a Publius Cornelius Dolabella who served as consul in 44 BC, was the son-in-law of Cicero through a marriage to his daughter Tullia, and a commander under Julius Caesar (favoured by e.g. Syme 1986: 319). However, another possibility is a Publius Cornelius Dolabella who was suffect consul in 35 BC, a more obscure career politician and soldier known primarily from coins and inscriptions (see Tansey 2000). Either of these two could have been father to the Publius Cornelius Dolabella who ended up fighting Tacfarinas in Africa – but it is also possible that the consul of 44 BC was the father of the suffect consul of 35 BC, who in turn was the father of the African Dolabella.
3. Tacitus *Annals* 4.66; the relationship is implied in Dolabella being named by Tacitus as a relative of Publius Quinctilius Varus the Younger, whom he later prosecuted in court.
4. For the relationship between Varus and Augustus see Ball (2023): XX.
5. *CIL* III, 2908 = ILS 2280
6. This was a significant extension of the usual 3-year tenure of a provincial governor, although not that unusual during the reign of Tiberius. Dolabella's successor in Dalmatia, Lucius Volusius Saturninus (attested as governor in inscription *CIL* III, 9972), apparently remained in position throughout the entire remainder of Tiberius' reign, only being replaced after Caligula had taken the throne (Syme 1986: 192).
7. Tacitus *Annals* 3.47.
8. Tacitus *Annals* 3.66–8.
9. Tacitus *Annals* 3.69.
10. Tacitus *Annals* 4.23.
11. Roller (2003): 6.
12. Tacitus *Annals* 4.23.
13. Tacitus *Annals* 4.23.
14. Wolff (2014): 55.
15. Tacitus *Annals* 4.24.
16. Vanacker (2015): 337.
17. Tacitus *Annals* 4.25.
18. Wolff (2014).
19. Tacitus *Annals* 4.23.
20. Tacitus *Annals* 4.24.
21. Syme (1951); Whittaker (1996): 594; Vanacker (2015): 341–2.
22. Gambash (2015): 73–4.
23. Tacitus *Annals* 4.24.
24. Fishwick & Shaw (1976): 493.
25. Tacitus *Annals* 4.24.
26. Saddington (1978).
27. Tacitus *Annals* 4.25.
28. Tacitus *Annals* 4.25. Sour El Ghozlane was previously known as Aumale during the French colonial period.

29. The area would later be traversed by an important road running from the Mauretanian capital at Caesarea to the veteran colony of Sitifis (founded in AD 97 under Nerva), but was still relatively unsettled at the time of Tacfarinas.
30. Wolff (2014).
31. Tacitus *Annals* 4.25.
32. Tacitus *Annals* 4.25.
33. Tacitus *Annals* 4.26.
34. Dio *Roman History* 40.41.1–3., 43.19.4.
35. Dio *Roman History* 65.7.1; Josephus *Jewish War* 7.2.2, 7.5.3–6.
36. Tacitus *Annals* 14.37; although Dio (*Roman History* 62.12.6) says that she died of illness.
37. Tacitus *Annals* 12.37.
38. Velleius Paterculus 2.119.3.
39. Rauh (2015): 404–8. On Roman military suicide more generally, see van Hooff (1990): 87–110.
40. Tacitus *Annals* 4.26.
41. Tacitus *Annals* 4.26.
42. On this inscription see Bartoccini (1958).
43. Tacitus *Annals* 4.26. On the traditional gifts, see e.g. Livy 30.15.11–13, when such honours were presented to Masinissa of Numidia after the Second Punic War, and Livy 42.14.10, where King Eumenes II of Pergamon was granted the same.
44. Boude (1990): 349.
45. E.g. CNNM, #450.
46. Malloch (2004).

Chapter 10

1. Gambash (2015): 76–7.
2. Fentress (2006): 25–7.
3. Vanacker (2015): 350.
4. Mattingly (2023): 281; Brett and Fentress (1996); *cf.* Vanacker (2013b): 206.
5. Fentress (1979): 72–7; (2006): 29.
6. Faure (2022): 162–3.
7. Tacitus *Histories* 4.50; Dio *Roman History* 60.9.6.
8. Cherry (2020): 1050–3.
9. Dio *Roman History* 67.4.6.
10. On the assassination and its motivations see Malloch (2004).
11. Dio *Roman History* 60.9.1–6; Pliny *Natural History* 5.14.
12. Shaw (1986): 69–70.
13. Shaw (1986): 76.
14. Pliny *Natural History* 5.14–5.
15. Tacitus *Histories* 4.49–50.
16. Raven (1993).
17. Ptolemy *Geography* 1.8.5; see Wilson (2017b).
18. Fentress (2011); Wilson (2017a).
19. Roymans & Fernandez-Götz (2018).
20. See Ball (2023).

21. Roller (2003); Wolff (2014).
22. See Yavetz (1963).
23. Whittaker (1996): 594.
24. Le Bohec (1989): 343.
25. Gambash (2015): 70–4.
26. Levene (2009): 228–9.
27. See Shaw (2004: 327–8) for discussion of the social bandit in the Roman context.
28. Woods (2008).
29. Hitchner (2022): 4.
30. Mattingly (2011): 43–72.
31. Effros (2018): 103–10.
32. Rid (2009): 216.
33. Rid (2009): 618–20.
34. Effros (2018): 84. In some modern French translations of Tacitus, Tacfarinas' raids are referred to as *razzias*, although not in every case; earlier editions also tended to use different terminology.
35. Rid (2009): 618–20.
36. Rid (2009): 623–4.
37. Fenwick (2008): 77–8.
38. Fenwick (2008).
39. Mattingly (2011): 57–9.
40. Akkache (1968).
41. Fenwick (2008). This has led to further cultural problems which sometimes spiral off into violence, such as the 1980 'Berber Spring', where the Berber population demanded cultural and linguistic rights.
42. On the uprisings see Silverstein (1996).
43. Zeroukhi (2023).
44. Mattingly (1996); Fentress (2006): 3–4; Fenwick (2008).
45. Hitchner (2022).
46. Fenwick (2008); Vanacker (2014).
47. Mattingly (2023): 234.
48. Novels on Arminius (in English) include *Arminius: The Limits of Empire* by Robert Fabbri and *Ambush* by Geraint Jones, while Boudica featured in a series of books by Manda Scott, and *A Year of Ravens* by Kate Quinn. Arminius' rebellion and its aftermath were featured in the two series of the TV series *Barbaren* (2020–2), while Boudica was the subject of the 2023 film *Boudica: Queen of War*.
49. Including a multi-site exhibition 'Imperium – Konflikt – Mythos', held at Haltern am See, Kalkriese and Detmold respectively, which examined different aspects of the battle and its impact on German history, opened by the then-Federal Chancellor, Dr Angela Merkel. The Museum und Park Kalkriese alone, built (almost certainly) on the actual site of the battle, receives 100,000+ visitors a year, and even more in years where public interest has been raised.

Bibliography

Abdale, J. R. (2019). *The Great Illyrian Revolt: Rome's Forgotten War in the Balkans, AD 6–9*. Barnsley (Pen & Sword).

Akkache, A. (1968). *Tacfarinas*. Algiers (Société Nationale d'Edition et de Diffusion).

Ameling, W. (2011). 'The Rise of Carthage to 264'. In Hoyos, Dexter (ed.). *A Companion to the Punic Wars*. Malden & Oxford (Blackwell Publishing): 39–57.

Anders, A.O. (2015). 'The 'Face of Roman Skirmishing'. *Historia* 64 (3): 263–300.

Ball, J. (2023). *Publius Quinctilius Varus: The Man Who Lost Three Roman Legions in the Teutoburg Disaster*. Barnsley (Pen & Sword Military).

Baronowski, D. W. (1995). 'Polybius on the Causes of the Third Punic War.' *Classical Philology* 90 (1): 16–31.

Bartoccini, R. (1958). 'Dolabella e Tacfarinas in una iscrizione di Leptis Magna.' *Epigraphica (Rivista Italiana di Epigrafia)* 20: 3–13.

Beard, M. (2007). *The Roman Triumph*. Cambridge, MA (The Belknap Press).

Beard, M. (2015) *SPQR*. London (Profile Books).

Beck, H. (2011). 'The Reasons for the War'. In Hoyos, D. (ed.) *A Companion to the Punic Wars*. Malden & Oxford (Blackwell Publishing): 225–41.

Bénabou, M. (1976). *La Résistance africaine à la romanisation*. Paris (Maspero).

Bénabou, M. (1977). 'Tacfarinas, Insurgé Berbère Contre Rome'. *Les Africains* 7: 293–313.

Boude, J. (1990). 'Une Statue-portrait de Ptolémée de Maurétanie a Sala (Maroc).' *Revue Archéologique Nouvelle Série* Fasc. 2: 331–60.

Braund, D. (1984). *Rome and the Friendly King. The Character of the Client Kingship*. London (Croom Helm).

Brett, M. & Fentress, E. (1996). *The Berbers*. Malden & Oxford (Blackwell Publishing).

Brunt, P. A. (1971). *Italian Manpower, 225 B.C.–A.D. 14*. London (Oxford University Press).

Brunt P. A. (1984) The Role of the Senate in the Augustan Regime'. Classical Quarterly 34 (02): 423–44.

Burton, G. P. (1976). 'The Issuing of *Mandata* to Proconsuls and a New Inscription from Cos'. *Zeitschrift für Papyrologie und Epigraphik* 21: 63–8.

Carey, B. T., Allfree, J. B. & Cairns, J. (2008). *Hannibal's Last Battle: Zama and the Fall of Carthage*. Barnsley (Pen & Sword Military).

Cherry, D. (1998). *Frontier and Society in Roman North Africa*. Oxford (Clarendon).

Cherry, D. (2020). 'Armed Resistance to Roman Rule in North Africa, from the Time of Augustus to the Vandal Invasion'. *Small Wars and Insurgencies* 31 (5): 1044–57.

Coulston, J. (2013). 'Courage and Cowardice in the Roman Imperial Army'. *War in History* 20 (1): 7–31.

Crook, J. A. (1996). 'Augustus: Power, Authority, Achievement'. In Bowman, A. K., Champlin, E., & Lintott, A. (eds) *The Cambridge Ancient History. Volume 10: The Augustan Empire, 31 B.C.–A.D. 69*. Cambridge (Cambridge University Press): 113–46.

Daly, G. (2002). *Cannae: The Experience of Battle in the Second Punic War*. London (Routledge).

Dando-Collins, S. (2023). *Rebels Against Rome: 400 Years of Rebellions Against the Rule of Rome*. Nashville, TN (Turner Publishing Company).

Devillers, O. (1991). 'Le rôle des passages relatifs à Tacfarinas dans les Annales de Tacite'. *L'Africa Romana* 8 (1): 203–11.

Dixon, K. R. & Southern, P. (1992). *The Roman Cavalry: From the First to Third Century A.D.* London (Batsford).

Draycott, J. (2022). *Cleopatra's Daughter: Egyptian Princess, Roman Prisoner, African Queen*. New York (Apollo).

Duncan-Jones, R. (2016). *Power and Privilege in Roman Society*. Cambridge University Press.

Dyson, S. L. (1971). 'Native Revolts in the Roman Empire.' *Historia: Zeitschrift für Alte Geschichte* 20(2/3): 239–74.

Dyson, S. L. (1975). 'Native Revolt Patterns in the Roman Empire.' In Vogt, J., Temporini, H. & Haase, W. (eds) *Aufstieg und Niedergang der römischen Welt: Geschichte und Kultur Roms im Spiegel der neueren Forschung*. Volume 2 Part 3. Berlin (de Gruyter): 137–75.

Edwell, P. (2011). 'War Abroad: Spain, Sicily, Macedon, Africa'. In Hoyos, D. (ed.) *A Companion to the Punic Wars*. Malden & Oxford (Blackwell Publishing): 320–38.

Effros, B. (2018). *Incidental Archaeologists: French Officers and the Rediscovery of Roman North Africa*. Ithaca, NY & London (Cornell University Press).

Erdkamp, Paul (2011). 'Manpower and Food Supply in the First and Second Punic Wars'. In Hoyos, D. (ed.). *A Companion to the Punic Wars*. Oxford (Wiley-Blackwell): 58–76.

España-Chamorro, S. (2023). 'Between Mauretania and Numidia: Provincial Boundaries, Land Connections and Imperial Administration in North Africa (1st–4th Centuries AD)'. In Mataix

Fauer, P. (2022). 'The Army'. In Hitchner, R. B. (ed.) *A Companion to North Africa in Antiquity*. Hoboken, NJ (John Wiley): 152–72.

Fentress, E. W. B. (1979). *Numidia and the Roman Army: Social, Military and Economic Aspects of the Frontier Zone*. BAR International Series 53. Oxford (British Archaeological Reports).

Fentress, E. W. B. (1982). 'Tribe and Faction: The Case of the Gaetuli'. *Mélanges de l'École Française de Rome. Antiquité.* 94 (1): 325–34.

Fentress, E. (2006). 'Romanizing the Berbers'. *Past & Present* 190: 3–33.

Fentress, E. (2011). 'Slavers on Chariots'. In Dowler, A. & Galvin, E. R. (eds) *Money, Trade and Trade Routes in Pre-Islamic North Africa*. London (British Museum Press): 64–71.

Fenwick, C. (2008). 'Archaeology and the Search for Authenticity: Colonialist, Nationalist and Berberist Visions of an Algerian Past'. In Fenwick, C., Wiggins, M. & Wythe, D. (eds) *TRAC 2007: Proceedings of the Seventeenth Annual Theoretical Roman Archaeology Conference, London 2007*. Oxford (Oxbow Books): 75–88

Ferrándiz, E., Lopez Garcia, A., Alvarez Melero, A. & Romero Vera, D. (eds) *Law and Power: Agents of Social and Spatial Transformation in the Roman West*. Leiden (Brill): 191–217.

Fishwick, D. (1993). 'On the origins of Africa Proconsularis, I: The amalgamation of Africa Vetus and Africa Nova'. *Antiquités africaines* 29: 53–62.

Fishwick, D. & Shaw, B. D. (1976). 'Ptolemy of Mauretania and the Conspiracy of Gaetulicus'. *Historia: Zeitschrift für Alte Geschichte* 25 (4): 491–4.

Freeman, P. (1997). 'Romanization – Imperialism – What are we talking about?' In Meadows, K., Lemke, C. & Heron, J. (eds) *TRAC 96: Proceedings of the Sixth Annual Theoretical Roman Archaeology Conference. University of Sheffield, March 1996*. Oxford (Oxbow Books): 8–14.

Fronda, M. P. (2011). 'Hannibal: Tactics, Strategy, and Geostrategy'. In Hoyos, Dexter (ed.). *A Companion to the Punic Wars*. Oxford (Wiley-Blackwell): 242–59.

Gambash, G. (2015). *Rome and Provincial Resistance*. Routledge (New York & Abingdon).

Garnsey, P. D. A. (1978). 'Rome's African Empire under the Principate'. In Garnsey, P. D. A. & Whittaker, C. R. (eds) *Imperialism in the Ancient World*. Cambridge (Cambridge University Press): 223–54.

Garnsey, P. (1983). 'Grain for Rome'. In Garnsey, P., Hopkins, K. & Whittaker, C. R. (eds) *Trade in the Ancient Economy*. London (Chatto & Windus): 118–30.

Garnsey, P. (1988). *Famine and Food Supply in the Graeco-Roman World: Reponses to Risk and Crisis*. Cambridge (Cambridge University Press).

Goldsworthy, A. (2006). *The Fall of Carthage: The Punic Wars 265–146 BC*. London (Phoenix).

Gonzalès, A. (1998). 'La révolte comme acte de brigandage: Tacite et la révolte de Tacfarinas'. In Khanoussi, M., Ruggeri, P. & Vismara, C. (eds) *L'Africa romana. Atti del XII convegno di studio, Tozeur, 11–15 dicembre 2002*. Rome (Carocci editore): 937–58.

Gruen, E. S. (1996). 'The Expansion of the Empire under Augustus'. In Bowman, A. K., Champlin, E., & Lintott, A. (eds.) *The Cambridge Ancient History. Volume 10: The Augustan Empire, 43 B.C.-A.D. 69*. Second Edition. Cambridge (Cambridge University Press): 147–97.

Grunewald, T. (2004). *Bandits in the Roman Empire: Myth and Reality*. London (Routledge).

Guédon, S. (2018). *La frontière romaine de l'Africa sous le Haut-Empire*. Madrid (Bibliothèque de la Casa de Velázquez).

Haynes, I. (2013). *Blood of the Provinces: The Roman* Auxilia *and the Making of Provincial Society from Augustus to the Severans*. Oxford (Oxford University Press).

Helmus, T. C. & Glenn, R. W. (2005). *Steeling the Mind: Combat Stress Reactions and Their Implications for Urban Warfare*. Santa Monica, CA: RAND.

Hickson, F. V. (1991). 'Augustus "Triumphator": Manipulation of the Triumphal Theme in the Political Program of Augustus'. *Latomus* 50 (1): 124–38.

Hingley, R. (1996). 'The 'legacy' of Rome: The Rise, Decline, and Fall of the Theory of Romanization'. In Webster, J. & Cooper, N. (eds) *Roman Imperialism: post-colonial perspectives*. Leicester Archaeology Monographs No. 3. Leicester (School of Archaeological Studies): 35–48.

Hitchner, R. B. (2022). 'The Historiography of North Africa in Antiquity: An Overview'. In Hitchner, R. B. (ed.) *A Companion to North Africa in Antiquity*. Hoboken, NJ (John Wiley): 3–8.

Hobson, M. S. (2016). 'Roman Imperialism in Africa from the Third Punic War to the Battle of Thapsus (146–46 BC)'. In Mugnai, N., Nikolaus, J. & Ray, N. (eds) *De Africa Romaque: Merging cultures across North Africa*. London (Society for Libyan Studies): 103–20.

Van Hooff, A. J. L. (1990). *From Autothanasia to Suicide: Self-Killing in Classical Antiquity*. London (Routledge).

Horsted, W. (2021). *The Numidians 300 BC–AD 300*. Oxford (Osprey).

Hoyos, D. (2005). *Hannibal's Dynasty: Power and Politics in the Western Mediterranean, 247–183 BC*. New York (Routledge).

Hoyos, D. (2011). 'The Outbreak of War'. In Hoyos, D. (ed.) *A Companion to the Punic Wars*. Malden & Oxford (Blackwell Publishing): 131–48.

Hurlet, F. (2006). *Le proconsul et le prince d'Auguste à Dioclétien*. Pessac (Ausonius).

Jacobson, D. M. (2001). 'Three Roman Client Kings: Herod of Judaea, Archelaus of Cappadocia and Juba of Mauretania'. *Palestine Exploration Quarterly* 133: 22–38.

Jarrett, M. (1969). 'Thracian Units in the Roman Army'. *Israel Exploration Journal* 19 (4): 215–24.

Jerary, M.T. (2008). 'Septimius Severus the Roman Emperor, AD 193–211'. *Africa: Rivista trimestrale di studi e documentazione dell'Istituto italiano per l'Africa e l'Oriente* 63 (2): 173–85.

Kath, R. (2009). 'Die Straße als provincia: die römische Raumerfassung und der Konflikt mit den Musulamii (1. Jh. n. Chr.). In Kath, R. & Rieger, A.-K. (eds) *Raum – Landschaft – Territorium. Zur Konstruktion physischer Ràume als nomadischer und sesshafter Lebensraum*. Wiesbaden (Reichert): 149–72.

Kenrick, A. (2023). *African Kings, Roman Rule: The Life of Juba II and Cleopatra Selene of Mauretania*. Unpublished PhD thesis submitted to the University of East Anglia.

Keppie, L. J. F. (1973). 'Vexilla Veteranorum'. *Papers of the British School at Rome* 41: 8–17.

Knight, D. J. (1991). 'The Movements of the Auxilia from Augustus to Hadrian'. *Zeitschrift für Papyrologie und Epigraphik* 85: 189–208.

Kovács, P. (2018). 'Interfectus a latronibus intrusis: Beiträge zum Tod eines Freigelassenen aus Scarbantia'. In Nemeth, E. (ed.) *Violence in Prehistory and Antiquity*. Kaiserslautern (Parthenon Verlag): 301–17.

Kunze, C. (2011). 'Carthage and Numidia, 201–149'. In Hoyos, Dexter (ed.). *A Companion to the Punic Wars*. Malden & Oxford (Blackwell Publishing): 395–411.

Lassère, J.-M. (1982). 'Un Conflit 'routier': Observations sur les causes de la guerre de Tacfarinas', *Antiquités africaines* 18, 11–25.

Le Bohec, Y. (1989). *La Troisieme legion Auguste*. Paris (CNRS).

Le Bohec, Y. (2011). 'The "Third Punic War": The Siege of Carthage (148–146 BC)'. In Hoyos, Dexter (ed.). *A Companion to the Punic Wars*. Malden & Oxford (Blackwell Publishing): 430–45.

Le Bohec, Y. (2012). 'Décurions et centurions auxiliaires sous le principat en Afrique-Numidie'. *Acta Classica* 55: 83–98.

Le Bohec, Y. (2014). 'La guerre en Afrique sous le Haut-Empire: Chronologie'. In Coltelloni-Trannoy, M. & Le Bohec, Y. (eds), *La guerre dans l'Afrique romaine sous le Haut-Empire*. Paris (CTHS Histoire): 23–34.

Leitch, V., Duckworth, C., Viénod, A., Mattingly, D., Sterry, M., & Cole, F. (2017). 'Early Saharan Trade: The Inorganic Evidence'. In Mattingly, D. J., Leitch, V., Duckworth, C. N., Cuénod, A., Sterry, M., & Cole, F. (eds) *Trade in the Ancient Sahara and Beyond*. Cambridge (Cambridge University Press): 55–79.

Lendon, J. E. (2017). 'Battle Description in the Ancient Historians, Part I: Structure, Array, And Fighting.' *Greece & Rome* 64 (1): 39–64.

Lennox Manton, E. (1988). *Roman North Africa*. London (Seaby).

Levene, D. S. (2009). 'Warfare in the Annals'. In Woodman, A. J. (ed.) *The Cambridge Companion to Tacitus*. Cambridge (Cambridge University Press): 225–40.

Levick, B. (1999). *Tiberius the Politician*. Revised edn. London (Routledge).

Liverani, M. (2000). 'The Garamantes: A Fresh Approach'. *Libyan Studies* 31: 17–28.

Mackendrick, P. (1980). *The North African Stones Speak.* London (Croom Hill).

Mackensen, M. (2000). 'Les castra hiberna de la legio III Augusta à Ammaedara/Haïdra'. In Khanoussi, M., Ruggeri, P., & Vismara, C. (eds.) *L'Africa Romana. Atti del XIII convegno di studio, Djerba, 10–13 dicembre 1998.* Rome (Carocci): 1739–60.

Mackie, N. K. (1983). 'Augustan Colonies in Mauretania'. Historia*: Zeitschrift für Alte Geschichte* 32 (3): 332–58.

Malloch, S. J. V. (2004). 'The Death of Ptolemy of Mauretania.' *Historia: Zeitschrift für Alte Geschichte* 53 (1): 38–45.

Marasco, G. (1990). 'Tiberio e l'esilio degli Ebrei in Sardegna nel 19 d.C.'. *L'Africa Romana* 8: 649–59.

Mattingly, D. J. (1996). 'From one Colonialism to Another: Imperialism and the Maghreb'. In Webster, J. & Cooper, N. (eds) *Roman Imperialism: Post-colonial Perspectives.* Leicester Archaeology Monographs No. 3. Leicester (School of Archaeological Studies): 49–70.

Mattingly, D. J. (2003). *The Archaeology of Fazzān. Volume 1, Synthesis.* London (The Society for Libyan Studies).

Mattingly, D. J. (2011). *Imperialism, Power, and Identity: Experiencing the Roman Empire.* Princeton (Princeton University Press).

Mattingly, D. J. (2016). 'Who Shaped Africa? The Origins of Urbanism and Agriculture in Maghreb and Sahara'. In Mugnai, N., Nikolaus, J., & Ray, N. (eds.) *De Africa Romaque: Merging cultures across North Africa.* London (Society for Libyan Studies): 11–26.

Mattingly, D. J. (2017). 'The Garamantes and the Origins of Saharan Trade: State of the Field and Future Agendas'. In Mattingly, D. J., Leitch, V., Duckworth, C. N., Cuénod, A., Sterry, M. & Cole, F. (eds) *Trade in the Ancient Sahara and Beyond.* Cambridge (Cambridge University Press): 1–52.

Mattingly, D. J. (2022). 'Beyond Barbarians: The Garamantes of the Libyan Sahara'. In Hitchner, R. B. (ed.) *A Companion to North Africa in Antiquity.* Hoboken, NJ (John Wiley): 64–80.

Mattingly, D. J. (2023). *Between Sahara and Sea: Africa in the Roman Empire.* Ann Arbor (University of Michigan Press).

Mazard, J. (1955). *Corpus Nummorus Numidiae Mauretaniaeque.* Paris (Arts et Métiers Graphiques).

McDonnell, M. (2009). *Roman Manliness:* Virtus *and the Roman Republic.* Cambridge (Cambridge University Press).

Mellor, R. (1993). *Tacitus.* New York (Routledge).

Miles, R. (2011). *Carthage Must be Destroyed.* London (Penguin).

Millar, F. (1966). 'The Emperor, the Senate and the Provinces.' *Journal of Roman Studies* 56 (1 & 2): 156–66.

Morstein-Marx, R. (2001). 'The Myth of Numidian Origins in Sallust's African Excursus (Iugurtha 17.7–18.12)'. *American Journal of Philology* 122 (2): 179–200.

Morstein-Marx, R. (2021). *Julius Caesar and the Roman People.* Cambridge (Cambridge University Press).

Nikita, E., Siew, Y. Y., Stock, J., Mattingly, D., & Lahr, M. M. (2011). 'Activity patterns in the Sahara Desert: An interpretation based on cross-sectional geometric properties'. *American Journal of Physical Anthropology* 146 (3): 423–34.

Opper, T. (2015). *The Meroë Head of Augustus.* London (British Museum Press).

Osgood, J. (2019). 'African Alternatives'. In Osgood, J., Morrell, K. & Welch, K. (eds) *The Alternative Augustan Age*. Oxford (Oxford University Press): 147–62.

Pearson, E. (2019). 'Decimation and Unit Cohesion: Why Were Roman Legionaries Willing to Perform Decimation?' *Journal of Military History* 83: 665–88.

Pomeroy, A. (2012). 'Tacitus and Historiography'. In Pagán, V. E. (ed.) *A Companion to Tacitus*. Oxford (Blackwell Publishing): 141–61.

Quinn, J. C. (2004). 'The Role of the 146 Settlement in the Provincialization of Africa'. *L'Africa Romana* 15: 1593–602.

Raaflaub, K. A. (2018). 'Caesar, Literature, and Politics at the End of the Republic.' In Grillo, L. & Krebs, C. B. (eds) *The Cambridge Companion to the Writings of Julius Caesar*. Cambridge (Cambridge University Press): 13–28.

Raaflaub, K. A. (2021). 'Caesar and Genocide: Confronting the Dark Side of Caesar's Gallic Wars.' *New England Classical Journal* 48 (1): 54–80.

Rankov, B. (2011). 'A War of Phases: Strategies and Stalemates 264–241'. In Hoyos, D. (ed.) *A Companion to the Punic Wars*. Malden & Oxford (Blackwell Publishing): 149–67.

Rauh, S. H. (2015). 'The Tradition of Suicide in Rome's Foreign Wars'. *TAPA* 145 (2): 383–410.

Raven, S. (1993). Rome in Africa. 3rd Edition. Oxford (Taylor & Francis).

Rawlings, L. (2011). 'The War in Italy, 218–203'. In Hoyos, Dexter (ed.). *A Companion to the Punic Wars*. Malden & Oxford (Blackwell Publishing): 299–319.

Rid, T. (2009). 'Razzia: A Turning Point in Modern Strategy'. *Terrorism and Political Violence* 21 (4): 617–35.

Roller, D. W. (2003). *The World of Juba II and Kleopatra Selene: Royal Scholarship on Rome's African Frontier*. New York (Routledge).

Roymans, N. & Fernandez-Götz, M. (2018). *Conflict Archaeology: Materialities of Collective Violence from Prehistory to Late Antiquity*. London & New York (Routledge).

Sabin, P. (2000). 'The Roman Face of Battle'. *Journal of Roman Studies* 90: 1–17.

Saddington, D. B. (1970). 'The Roman "Auxilia" in Tacitus, Josephus and Other Early Imperial Writers'. *Acta Classica* 13: 89–124.

Saddington, D. B. (1978). 'Notes on Two Passages in Tacitus (Ann. 4. 24. 3 And 15. 25. 3)'. *The Classical Quarterly* 28 (2): 330–2.

Sampson, G. C. (2010). *The Crisis of Rome: The Jugurthine and Northern Wars and the Rise of Marius*. Barnsley (Pen & Sword Military).

Sampson, G. C. (2013). *The Collapse of Rome: Marius, Sulla & the 1st Civil War (91–70 BC)*. Barnsley (Pen & Sword Military).

Sampson, G. C. (2016). *Rome Spreads her Wings: Territorial Expansion between the Punic Wars*. Barnsley (Pen & Sword).

Sampson, G. C. (2024). *The Battle of Thapsus (46 BC): Caesar, Metellus Scipio, and the Renewal of the Third Roman Civil War*. Barnsley (Pen & Sword Military).

Scheele, J. (2017). 'The Need for Nomads: Camel Herding, Raiding, and Saharan Trade and Settlement'. In Mattingly, D. J., Leitch, V., Duckworth, C. N., Cuénod, A., Sterry, M. & Cole, F. (eds) *Trade in the Ancient Sahara and Beyond*. Cambridge (Cambridge University Press): 55–79.

Serrati, J. (2011). 'The Rise of Rome to 264'. In Hoyos, Dexter (ed.). *A Companion to the Punic Wars*. Malden & Oxford (Blackwell Publishing): 9–27.

Shaw, B. D. (1982). 'Fear and Loathing: The Nomad Menace and Roman Africa'. In Wells, C. M. (ed.) *Roman Africa*. Ottawa (The University of Ottawa Press): 29–50.

Shaw, B. D. (1983). 'Soldiers and Society: The Army in Numidia'. *Opus: Rivista internazionale per la storia economica e sociale dell'antichità* 2(1): 133–59.

Shaw, B. D. (1986). 'Autonomy and Tribute: Mountain and Plain in Mauretania Tingitana'. In Baduel, P. R. (ed.) *Désert et montagne au Maghreb: Hommage à Jean Dresch*. Revue de l'Occident Musulman et de la Méditerranée (41–2): 66–89.

Shaw, B. D (2000). 'Rebels and Outsiders'. In Bowman, A. K., Garnsey, P. & Rathbone, D. (eds) *The Cambridge Ancient History XI: The High Empire, AD 70–192*. Cambridge (Cambridge University Press): 361–403.

Shaw, B. D. (2004). 'Bandits in the Roman Empire'. In Osborne, R. (ed.) *Studies in Ancient Greek and Roman Society*. Cambridge (Cambridge University Press): 326–74.

Sidnell, P. (2006). *Warhorse: Cavalry in the Ancient World*. London & New York (Hambledon Continuum).

Sigman, M.C. (1977). 'The Romans and the Indigenous Tribes of Mauretania Tingitana'. *Historia* 26 (4): 415–39.

Silverstein, P. (1996). 'Realizing Myth: Berbers in France and Algeria'. *Middle East Report* 200: 11–5.

Starks, J. H. (1999). '*Fides Aeneia*: The Transference of Punic Stereotypes in the Aeneid', *The Classical Journal* 94 (3): 255–83.

Stone, D. L. (2016). 'Burial Mounds and State Formation in North Africa: A Volumetric and Energetic Approach'. In Mugnai, N., Nikolaus, J. & Ray, N. (eds.) *De Africa Romaque: Merging cultures across North Africa*. London (Society for Libyan Studies): 39–54.

Stone, D. L. (2022). 'Archaeology'. In Hitchner, R. B. (ed.) *A Companion to North Africa in Antiquity*. Hoboken, NJ (John Wiley): 9–23.

Syme, R. (1951). 'Tacfarinas, the Musulamii and Thubursicu'. In Coleman-Norton, P. R. (ed.), *Studies in Roman Economic and Social History*. Princeton (Princeton University Press): 113–30.

Syme, R. (1983). 'Problems about Proconsuls of Asia'. *Zeitschrift für Papyrologie und Epigraphik* 53: 191–208.

Syme, R. (1986). *The Augustan Aristocracy*. Oxford (Clarendon Press).

Tansey, P. (2000). 'The Perils of Prosopography: The Case of the Cornelii Dolabellae'. *Zeitschrift für Papyrologie und Epigraphik* 130: 265–71.

Taylor, M.J. (2019). 'Reconstructing the Battle of Zama'. *Classical Journal* 114 (3): 310–29.

Taylor, M. J. (2022). '*Decimatio*: Myth, Discipline, and Death in the Roman Republic.' *Antichthon* 56: 105–20.

Trousset, P. (1982). 'L'Image du nomade saharien dans l'historiographie'. *Production pastorale et société* 10: 97–105.

Trousset, P. (2002/2003). 'Le Tarif de Zaraï: essai sur les circuits commerciaux dans la zone présaharienne'. *Antiquités africaines* 38–39: 355–73.

Udoh, F. E. (2020). *To Caesar What Is Caesar's: Tribute, Taxes, and Imperial Administration in Early Roman Palestine*. Providence, RI (Brown Judaic Studies).

Unzueta Portillo, M. & Ocharán Larrondo, J. A. (2006). 'El campo de batalla de Andagoste (Álava)'. In García-Bellido, M. P. (ed.) *Los campamentos romanos en Hispania (27 a.C.–192 d.C.). El abastecimiento de moneda, II*. Madrid (CSIC – Polifemo): 473–92.

Vanacker, W. (2013). 'Conflicts and Instability in Mauretania and Gaius' Realpolitik". *Latomus* 72 (3): 725–41.

Vanacker, W. (2013b). 'Many paths to walk. The Political and Economic Integration of Nomadic Communities in Roman North Africa (I–III cent. A.D.)'. In de Kleijn, G.

& Benoist, S. (eds) *Integration in Rome and in the Roman World: Proceedings of the Tenth Workshop of the International Network Impact of Empire (Lille, June 23–25, 2011)*. Leiden (Brill).

Vanacker, W. (2014). 'Many paths to walk. The political and economic integration of nomadic communities in Roman North Africa (I–III cent. A.D.)'. *Afrika Focus* 27 (2): 98–104.

Vanacker, W. (2015). '"Adhuc Tacfarinas" Causes of the Tiberian War in North Africa (AD Ca. 15–24) and the Impact of the Conflict on Roman Imperial Policy'. *Historia: Zeitschrift für Alte Geschichte* 64(3): 336–56.

Vogel-Weidemann, U. (1989). 'Carthago Delenda Est: "Aitia" and "Prophasis".' *Acta Classica* 32: 79–95.

Whittaker, C. R. (1978). 'Land and Labour in North Africa.' *Klio* 60: 331–62.

Whittaker, C. R. (1996). 'Roman Africa: Augustus to Vespasian'. In Bowman, A. K., Champlin, E., & Lintott, A. (eds) *The Cambridge Ancient History. Volume 10: The Augustan Empire, 43 B.C.–A.D. 69*. Second edn. Cambridge (Cambridge University Press): 586–618.

Wilbers-Rost, S. (2017). 'The Battlefield of Kalkriese: The Rampart at the Site "Oberesch" During and After the Battle'. In Hodgson, N., Bidwell, P. & Schachtmann, J. (eds) *Roman Frontier Studies 2009: Proceedings of the XXI International Congress of Roman Frontier Studies (Limes Congress) held at Newcastle upon Tyne in August 2009*. Oxford (Archaeopress): 571–6.

Wilson, A. (2005). 'Foggara Irrigation, Early State Formation and Saharan Trade: The Garamantes of Fazzan'. *Schriftenreihe der Frontinus-Gesellschaft* 26: 223–34.

Wilson, A. (2017a). 'Saharan Exports to the Roman World'. In Mattingly, D. J., Leitch, V., Duckworth, C. N., Cuénod, A., Sterry, M. & Cole, F. (eds) *Trade in the Ancient Sahara and Beyond*. Cambridge (Cambridge University Press): 189–208.

Wilson, A. (2017b). 'Trade across Rome's Southern Frontier: The Sahara and the Garamantes'. In Wilson, A. & Bowman, A. (eds) *Trade, Commerce, and State in the Roman World*. Oxford (Oxford University Press): 599–624.

Wolff, C. (2014). 'La Guerre de Tacfarinas (17–24)'. In Coltelloni-Trannoy, M. & Le Bohec, Y. (eds), *La Guerre dans l'Afrique romaine sous le haut-empire*. Paris (CTHS Histoire): 53–67.

Woodman, A. J. (2004). *The Annals. Tacitus, translated, with introduction and notes*. Indianapolis & Cambridge (Hackett Pub).

Woods, D. (2008). 'Tiberius, Tacfarinas, and the Jews'. *Arctos* 42: 267–84.

Woolf, G. (2005). 'Provincial Perspectives'. In Galinsky, K. (ed.) *The Cambridge Companion to the Age of Augustus*. Cambridge (Cambridge University Press): 106–29.

Woolf, G. (2011). 'Provincial Revolts in the Early Roman Empire'. In Popović, M. (ed.) *The Jewish Revolt against Rome: Interdisciplinary Perspectives*. Leiden (Brill): 27–44.

Woolf, G. (2014). *Tales of the Barbarians: Ethnography and Empire in the Roman West*. Malden, MA (Wiley-Blackwell).

Yavetz, Z. (1963). 'The Failure of Catiline's Conspiracy'. *Historia: Zeitschrift für Alte Geschichte* 12 (4): 485–99.

Zeroukhi, L. (2023). 'Gender in Algerian French textbooks'. *Tensões Mundiais, Fortaleza* 19 (39): 209–30.

Zimmerman, K. (2011). 'Roman Strategy and Aims in the Second Punic War'. In Hoyos, Dexter (ed.). *A Companion to the Punic Wars*. Malden & Oxford (Blackwell Publishing): 280–98.

Index